Answers to Questions Catholics Are Asking

Tony Coffey

HARVEST HOUSE PUBLISHERS

EUGENE, OREGON

Cover by Koechel Peterson & Associates, Inc., Minneapolis, Minnesota

Cover photo © Photos.com/Jupiterimages

ANSWERS TO QUESTIONS CATHOLICS ARE ASKING
A revised and updated edition of *Once a Catholic*
Copyright © 2006 by Harvest House Publishers
Published by Harvest House Publishers
Eugene, Oregon 97402
www.harvesthousepublishers.com

Library of Congress Cataloging-in-Publication Data

Coffey, Tony, 1943-
    Answers to questions Catholics are asking / Tony Coffey.
        p. cm.
    ISBN-13: 978-0-7369-1786-5 (pbk.)
    ISBN-10: 0-7369-1786-1 (pbk.)
    Product # 6917865
    1. Catholic Church—Doctrines. 2. Theology, Doctrinal—Popular works. I. Title.
    BX1754.C485 2006
    230'.2—dc22   2006001450

Contents

. . . .

For Leslie
Godliness marks your life

. . . .

A Journey from Rome

· · · · · · · · · · · · · ·

It is amazing how one event can change the course of your life forever. What started out, for me, as just another ordinary day turned out to be the most extraordinary day of my life.

A police announcement on the radio, after the morning and midday news, asked for two young women driving a foreign-registered car to contact the police immediately for an urgent message. The car was first spotted in west Ireland, and the message given. The father of one of the young women had died suddenly in the United States. She flew from Shannon Airport while the other young woman made her way to Dublin, where she was stopped by two men who had also heard the police bulletin on the radio. And that is how I met Leslie, who led me to the Lord and later became my wife.

My upbringing in Ireland was during a period when the Roman Catholic Church exercised power in every area of a person's life: family, society, education, and politics. The Church's power was never questioned, and everyone submitted to its authority. During this period the Church enjoyed unprecedented growth—the seminaries and convents were full, and foreign missions enjoyed a high profile. The Church took full advantage of this by placing a great emphasis on mission work, particularly in Africa. Looking back now, I marvel at the ingenuity of the

Church. They organized for every school in Ireland to be involved in missions: Each week, every child brought "a penny for the black babies." Each student had a card with a decade of the rosary printed on it, and each time we gave a penny, we marked the card. When we completed the card, we wrote our name on it, and this was sent to the foreign mission. We were told that, as a result, African children were being christened with our names. This would not be politically correct in today's culture, but at that time no offense was intended, and this system was an ingenious way of both raising money and making all the Catholic children aware of the mission work of the Church. Today there are many Africans living in Dublin, and when I am invited to speak at their churches, I tell them about "the penny for the black babies." For all I know, one of them might very well be named after me!

While growing up, I never questioned the power exercised by the Roman Catholic Church and was content to observe the rules and regulations enjoined on me. Church was important to me, and I practiced my religious duties faithfully. For some years I served Mass as an altar boy, and at age 11 I went to boarding school for five years to be educated by the Dominican priests. Mass, evening devotions, and the rosary were part of daily life. During those formative years it was instilled in me that the Roman Catholic Church held the keys to the kingdom of heaven and was the custodian of the sacraments, which were essential for my salvation. I counted myself fortunate to have been born a Roman Catholic.

What, then, caused me to leave the Roman Catholic Church and embrace a faith based on the teaching of the Bible alone? Among the reasons were major changes that came from Vatican II (which convened from 1962–1965) and the influence of Pope John XXIII. Some of the beliefs and practices I had been taught were changing. For example, eating meat on Friday was no longer considered a sin, and some "saints" to whom I had prayed were removed from the Church's list of saints on the grounds that they probably never existed. So when I was introduced to the Bible as the sole authority for a person's life, I was greatly impressed with the idea of placing my trust in something that never changes.

I began attending a Bible study and felt drawn to what the Bible said. Though a spiritual awakening was taking place, I wasn't entirely comfortable. I missed the "bells and smells," the statues, and pomp of the Roman Catholic Church. Like most Roman Catholics I had a religious vocabulary, but the reality of the concepts the words expressed never registered with me. To a great extent my faith was in the Church, not in a personal God. I thought I was right with God because I was in the right Church. Loyalty to the Church was equated with being loyal to God. And I certainly was not alone in that line of thinking.

There was never a time in my life when I did not believe in God, or that Jesus died and rose again. But I still sensed something was missing. I possessed religious information, but it didn't translate into anything personal for me. Then "the light went on." From the Bible I began to see that God really did love me and that Jesus died personally for me, securing a full pardon of all my sins. Rather than simply viewing Good Friday merely as a historical fact, I now began to see that what happened on Calvary directly involved me. Jesus had died for me. What I had always believed was beginning to become real for me. While I rejoiced over my spiritual progress, I was also aware that the inevitable decision facing me would be devastating to my family. And it was. For about two months before I committed my life to the Lord, I knew what I needed to do. I delayed because I was counting the cost of following Jesus. There could be no turning back. I had to give my life to Jesus irrespective of the cost. To this day I cannot be certain if someone said this to me or if the Lord put the thought in my heart, but it came to my mind that if I followed Jesus I would never go wrong; I could never be lost if I put my full trust in Jesus. And so, in June 1967 I committed my life to the Lord Jesus Christ and was baptized, trusting the Lamb of God to take away my sin (John 1:29).

Shortly after my conversion I felt God's call for me to enter fulltime ministry. This was something I had given serious thought to while a Roman Catholic. I entered Bible school and quickly learned that I was biblically illiterate. The Bible was not studied in Catholic boarding school. The next few years of study brought me into new territory that was both enlightening and challenging, and I began finding answers to my questions. One scripture in particular opened a panoramic view of God's will: "There is salvation in no one else, for there is no other name given under heaven whereby we must be saved" (Acts 4:12). I saw in those words that Jesus is the answer to all my questions. He and he alone is the one I must always follow. There is no one else.

My walk with the Lord has not been problem free; a relationship with God does not immunize us against the difficulties that life sometimes brings. Yet never once have I doubted the faithfulness of God or the blessed assurance of his redemptive work in my life. Never have I wavered in my faith in the Lord Jesus Christ. I have seen God come to my rescue again and again, sustaining and strengthening me by his grace. Even in the midst of some difficult times, God has always been there for me. In fact, it has been during those times that I have grown closer to him. Trials have a wonderful way of refining our character and making us more dependent upon him. I look back on my life without regret for the decision I made, in spite of the personal hardships that came my way. Truthfully, there is never a day that passes that I do not love the work God has called me to do. I am constantly filled with gratitude for what the Lord has done for me and through me. I continue to be amazed at the truth of the gospel: Jesus died to pay the penalty for my sin, and he did this because he loves me with an unconditional love. The daily reading of God's Word is woven into my life, and I never tire of hearing what God has to say. His Word is inspired by the Holy Spirit and through his Word his voice is heard (2 Timothy 3:16-17; Hebrews 4:12). His promises, faithfulness, unfailing love, and holy sovereignty continue to impact my life. The further along the road I travel with the Lord, the more I grow to love him who has been exceedingly gracious to me, a sinner. The good that is in my life has all come from God, who, through the Holy Spirit, works to transform me more and more into the image of Jesus. And when I fail him—and I do—he is always gracious to me.

I always point people to that which touched my heart years ago: "Trust Jesus and follow him; then you will never be lost." I have not had any reason ever to doubt the veracity of that statement and have staked my life on it.

Speaking the
Truth in Love

. . . .

I came away from the discussion realizing I had received my first "biblical mugging." Young and inexperienced, I was no match for someone who was well-versed in Scripture and seasoned by an unkind attitude. My attempts to defend my belief were met with a torrent of scriptures that I failed to explain adequately. I was the opponent, and no mercy was shown. No hand of kindness was extended to help clarify my belief, and no consideration was given for the fact that I was a sincere person trying to please God. No attempt was made to come alongside me and treat me gently. A lopsided conviction that he was right and I was wrong prevented him from exhibiting the love of God. Not for a moment did I feel I was loved or valued. I remember the event as if it was only yesterday, though it occurred over 30 years ago. For three days afterwards I was still shaken and upset. I relate this incident so that the reader will know that I do know what it is like to be on the receiving end of unkind, disrespectful treatment. Therefore, I am going to discuss the major differences that exist between the Roman Catholic Church and the Bible in a manner that does not humiliate, degrade, or needlessly offend any Roman Catholic.

I have never understood why anyone would think that in defending the truth (or their version of the truth) somehow they are justified in being unkind to others with whom they disagree. Where did this dreadful thinking come from? That truth must be defended is not in dispute, but a bad attitude is never acceptable. In fact, the Bible clearly says we are to speak the truth in love (Ephesians 4:15).

The only one who taught perfect theology was Jesus, the Son of the living God. There is not a text of Scripture which he did not understand perfectly. There is not a topic, a moral judgment, or point of doctrine for which he does not have the correct answer. He is right on everything. Yet look at how he dealt with people— he was always kind, loving, respectful, patient; never did he raise his voice, nor was he rude or inconsiderate. He was always gentle. He worked to move people from unbelief to faith in a most compassionate way, yet never compromising the truth. He didn't tone down his claim that without him no one will go to heaven, or that without his atoning death we would all die in our sins and go to hell, or that he was God in human flesh. Some never believed his claims, yet he dealt kindly with them. The only people for which Jesus reserved strong criticism was for those whom he knew to be hypocrites. By contrast, to Thomas, an honest doubter, he made a special appearance after his resurrection to give Thomas the opportunity to replace doubt with faith.

There is a saying that truth is like light to sore eyes. I think that is a good way of putting it. We all know how unpleasant it is for someone to turn on the light when we are sleeping. Many live in a spiritual slumber, some never having had a spiritual thought for years. For some the light of the glorious gospel must be revealed slowly, allowing them to wake up and adjust to the shaft of light that has penetrated their darkness.

This book is written with a Roman Catholic audience in mind; therefore, I am conscious how easy it would be to give needless offense. When I was a Roman Catholic, all my beliefs were held sincerely and honestly, and I assume the same of those who read this book. I have tried to put myself in the place of the reader and ask, "What does this book need in order for me to keep reading it?" It was not hard to come up with the right answer. To keep my attention, a book needs to be grounded in Scripture, not opinion. And the writer needs to display a kind and respectful spirit while dealing with doctrines that are sincerely believed by many, yet at the same time, the writer should not fail to say what needs to be said. I would want the writer to show a loyalty to the Lord Jesus Christ and a holy jealousy in defending the will of God. Finally, I would want to feel myself being drawn closer to God because of what I am reading. I have endeavored to do all these things in the course of writing this book.

I realize not everyone who reads this book will feel I have been true to these intentions. Some may be offended by what I say. Others will read this book with their minds already made up, so nothing I say will change them. Then there are others whose lives will be blessed. Their eyes will be opened to the wonderful truths of the Scriptures and they will find that their every need can be met in Jesus Christ alone. That pleases me greatly. And still others will see this book as being out of touch with the ecumenical spirit of the age, a relic of the distant past.

When it comes to a book such as this, there are huge issues that need to be confronted. Is the Bible our sole authority for all that we believe and practice? Is the gospel the only way of salvation? With the inevitability of death facing each one of us, these are questions for which we need answers—urgently.

There has always been a need to defend truth. Jesus repeatedly defended truth against the error that existed in his day. And the watchful eyes of the apostles kept fatal error from gaining a foothold in the church. When the gospel was being undermined by legalistic teaching the apostle Paul (who wrote so eloquently that love is patient, kind, not easily angered, etc.) spared no words in his condemnation of such false teaching. Here is a flavor of what he said: "If we or an angel from heaven should preach a gospel other than the one we preached to you, let him be eternally condemned! As we have already said, so now I say again: If anybody is preaching to you a gospel other than what you accepted, let him be eternally condemned!" (Galatians 1:8-9). Paul believed that the gospel must not only be proclaimed, it must also be defended against error. And today, taking a stand for truth is simply not the popular thing to do. So-called "tolerance" is fast becoming the acceptable norm. Dogmatic statements are unfashionable. This is a dangerous road for Christians to be on. Truth is not determined by how many believe it or how popular it is; something is true if God says it is true. And all of us, without exception, must adjust our beliefs to conform to what God has said.

I am concerned about an unhealthy type of tolerance that is growing in popularity and being embraced by many. This type of tolerance leads some to feel that there are no absolutes to defend, and you can believe whatever happens to be right for you. We can see the logical conclusion of such a perspective on matters such as abortion, homosexuality, and gay marriages. Are we to remain silent about what the Bible teaches lest we give offense or be viewed as a bigot? I think not. There are times when we dare not be silent. And this applies to the purpose for which this book was written. Between Roman Catholic teaching and Bible teaching are several fundamental differences that need to be addressed. In a short letter, Jude exhorted some believers with these words: "I felt I had to write and urge you to contend for the faith that was once for all entrusted to the saints" (verse 3). The faith of which Jude spoke is the truth that Jesus died for our sins, was buried, and rose from the dead. He is the only way of salvation. That's the faith for which we must contend. The word *contend*, according to *The Oxford English Dictionary*, means: "[to] engage in a struggle or campaign to achieve, assert as a position in an argument." This definition leaves no room for passive resistance where the faith is concerned.

Today there are theologians as well as lay people who are à la carte Catholics. My intention is to present to Catholics exactly what their Church teaches. There are areas of theology under constant review, and the Catholic Church is in dialogue with Christians in other traditions, resulting in the publication of a number of agreed-upon statements on various doctrines. However, the official doctrines of the Roman Catholic Church have remained unchanged. The teachings of the Council of Trent are as binding on Catholics today as they were when first issued. Some readers regard them as outdated, but they are still the official teachings of the Roman Catholic Church and have never been rescinded.

I feel comfortable knowing that throughout this book I point people to Jesus and encourage them to build their faith on the solid foundation of his teachings. Surely that cannot be wrong! In fact, it is exactly what the Lord wants us to do:

> Everyone who hears these words of mine and puts them into practice is like a wise man who built his house on the rock. The rain came down, the streams rose, the winds blew and beat against that house; yet it did not fall, because it had its foundation on the rock. But everyone who hears these words of mine and does not put them into practice is like a foolish man who built his house on sand. The rain came down, the streams rose, and the winds blew

and beat against that house, and it fell with a great crash
(Matthew 7:24-27).

The written word doesn't always reveal the tone intended, as the
apostle Paul knew only too well. He said some hard but necessary
words to the Christians in Galatia, but then hastened to ask them,
"Have I now become your enemy by telling you the truth?" (Galatians 4:16). He didn't stop there. He wanted them to know that the
truth he shared came from someone who cared deeply about them,
so he continued, "How I wish I could be with you now and change
my tone" (verse 20). Tone is so important; it reveals what is really
in the heart. I too have had that apostolic feeling while writing this
book. I want the tone of what I say to be right. I want to exalt the
atoning sacrifice of the Lord Jesus Christ above every error that
would detract from it. I want my words to come from a heart filled
with the conviction that if we follow Jesus Christ, we will never be
lost. In our walk with the Lord we will be neither Catholics nor
Protestants; we will simply be Christians just as they were in the
early church. Traditions that have detracted from truth must be
discarded. If your heart beats a little faster at the prospect of simply
being a Christian—a member of the body of Christ, the church—
then this book is written for you.

My prayer is that the quest of the Bereans will become the quest
of all of us: "The Bereans" we are told, "were of more noble character than the Thessalonians, for they received the message with
great eagerness and examined the Scriptures every day to see if what
Paul said was true" (Acts 17:11).

Finally, this book is not written to provide ammunition for the
overzealous who delight in scoring cheap points at the expense of
the beliefs of Roman Catholics. I distance myself from those who
engage in such unholy warfare.

1
The Catholic Church Today

· · · · · · · · · · · · · ·

Ever since Pope John XXIII called on the Roman Catholic Church to open the windows and let in the fresh air, a mighty wind has rushed through the Church and brought changes to what was perceived as a static institution. The time for the unchanging Church to change had arrived. The documents of the Second Vatican Council grew out of this environment and reflected the new face of Catholicism. The documents were received with enthusiasm by the Roman Catholic world, and nods of approval came from Christian traditions other than Roman Catholic. A new dawn was breaking.

The Catholic Charismatic Renewal also made its contribution to the changing face of Catholicism. Whatever misgivings one might have about some aspects of the movement, it must be credited with producing some positive results. For the first time, the Scriptures became a vital part of the lives of many Catholics.

The papacy also took on a new image. In its long history it never enjoyed as high a profile as it does today. No longer is the pope seen only within the confines of the Vatican; globe-trotting has become a papal duty. And the media have given the pope celebrity status.

The popularity of Pope John Paul II during his long reign was expressed in the outpouring of grief at his death in 2005. The Roman Catholic Church had lost a great leader. Throughout his reign, he faithfully held to the teachings of the Roman Catholic Church and did much to recover ground that had been lost to the liberal wing of the Church. His pontificate will not be forgotten in the dusty annals of history. Outside the Roman Catholic Church he had his admirers; his uncompromising stand on such moral issues as abortion, homosexual practice, gay marriage, materialism, and the importance of the family was refreshing in a morally lax world.

However, some of the teachings of John Paul II (and his predecessors) can never be accepted by those of us who hold the Bible to be the Word of God and our sole authority for what we believe and practice. For example, John Paul II tirelessly promoted devotion to the Blessed Virgin Mary and canonized over 400 saints, more than had been canonized by all the popes before him. On June 2, 1998, he issued a clarion call to all Catholics to pray for the souls in purgatory, assuring them that their prayers and the sacrifice of the Mass would secure the release of those souls suffering in purgatory.[1] These teachings are at variance with the gospel and demeaning to the perfect sacrifice of Jesus.

Conflicting voices are heard in the wider religious arena, each calling for our attention. Do we listen to the Roman Catholic Church, which purports to be speaking for God, or do we listen to Scripture, which is "the word of God.… [and] sharper than any doubled-edged sword, it penetrates even to dividing soul and spirit, joints and marrow; it judges the thoughts and attitudes of the heart" (Hebrews 4:12)? The Word of God, the apostle Paul tells us, is able to lead us to salvation through faith in Christ Jesus" (2 Timothy 3:15). Furthermore, he says, "All Scripture is God-breathed and is useful for teaching, rebuking, correcting and training in righteousness, so that the man of God may be thoroughly equipped for every good work" (verses 16-17). Whose voice do we listen to? God has revealed his will in Scripture; therefore, we cannot go outside of that. It is at this point that we must part company with the Roman Catholic Church, which holds that not all truth is contained in Scripture; the tradition of the Church must also be heard. In other words, all truth is derived from combining Scripture and the Tradition of the Roman Catholic Church.

THE WRONG MODEL

The model of the Roman Catholic Church is not one Jesus would endorse. For example, Jesus was approached by an overly ambitious mother who wanted her two sons to have places of prominence in the kingdom—one on the right side of Jesus' throne, and the other on the left. Such prominence would have reflected well on her for having raised such successful sons. In reply, Jesus looked to the Gentile world and referred to a model of what this mother (and the other disciples) wanted. "You know," he said, "that the rulers of the Gentiles lord it over them, and their high officials exercise authority over them." This they all recognized. Then Jesus said, "Not so among you" (Matthew 20:25-26). He was saying that this pyramid model with earthly rulers whose power is unquestioned was not what he came to build. My kingdom, he said, is not of this world. It bears no resemblance to anything you see in the world. It is entirely different. Positions of power and prestige, such as those that existed among the Pharisees, never impressed Jesus. He said, "They make their phylacteries wide and the tassels on their garments long; they love the place of honor at banquets and the most important seats in the synagogues; they love to be greeted in the marketplaces and to have men call them 'Rabbi'" (Matthew 23:5-7). What Jesus came to build bears no similarity to that which he found so repugnant.

Yet when we look throughout Europe in particular, what do we see? We see that the Roman Catholic Church has been a powerful political force to be reckoned with. The affairs of the state and the Church were interwoven. Kings, queens, and heads of government deferred to the Roman Catholic Church. Some powerful princes were also bishops. The magnificent cathedrals were also making a statement about the power of the Roman Catholic Church. Because of its alliance with the secular state, the Roman Catholic Church grew powerful and rich, owning vast tracts of land throughout Europe. And all of this was done in the name of him who said, "Foxes have holes and birds of the air have nests, but the Son of Man has no place to lay his head" (Matthew 8:20).

It's been said that power corrupts. There have been times throughout history when the Roman Catholic Church has used its power to ill effect. The Inquisition is a case in point. The sexual abuse of children by Roman Catholic priests—a problem that has come to light in recent years—was possible only because of the power and secrecy of the institution. Because of the magnitude of the problem and the extent to which Catholics have expressed concern over it, let's examine it a bit more closely.

SECRETS AND SCANDALS

The whole sordid scandal of children being sexually abused by Roman Catholic priests has been an embarrassment to the Church. The revelations of such evil behavior have shocked the faithful.

When these revelations first surfaced, many went into denial mode. The manner in which their Church handled the complaints, which go back at least half a century, has disillusioned many. I'm fully aware that Jesus said, "Let him who is without sin cast the first stone" (see John 8:7). I want to state that my purpose here is not to be needlessly critical of the Roman Catholic Church. But in discussing this issue, I want to provide an insight into how this could happen within the traditional structure of the Roman Catholic Church. I do not want to overlook the fact there are many priests and nuns who are good, decent people who have served their communities faithfully; their character should always be protected.

There can be a tendency to be silent about the bad things that have happened in life, saying, "It's in the past; forget about it." But that is a very dangerous position to take. Simon Wiesenthal died recently, at 96 years of age. Like many other Jews in Europe, Wiesenthal spent time in a Nazi concentration camp. He lost 89 members of his family to the Nazis and devoted his life to pursuing those responsible for these crimes. He brought over 1,100 criminals to justice. Through his efforts, he did not allow the world to forget the evil of the past. Was he right to do this? I believe he was. We need to understand and remember how one nation, rich in culture, could become responsible for the murder of six million people, lest it be repeated.

Similarly, the sexual abuse of children by members of a respected Church needs to be examined lest it be repeated. How the Roman Catholic Church handled the charges made by the victims tells us much about the Church and how she views herself.

We all make mistakes; we may later reflect upon a crisis and realize we could have handled it better. We can learn from our mistakes and respond more wisely the next time. Not so with the Roman Catholic Church: Its handling of sexual abuse charges made against priests has been a pathetic failure, not once, but over and over. In fact, a definite pattern has emerged. For example, consider Father Brendan Smyth. His name will not be forgotten in Ireland for a long time.

Smyth has the distinction of being one of the worst—if not *the* worst—serial abuser of children revealed to date; his evil trade stretched over 35 years and covered two continents. In 1968 he was sent from the United States back to Ireland when his bishop became aware that he was sexually abusing young boys and girls. Back in Ireland, Smyth continued abusing children until his conviction in an Irish court in June 1997. Smyth's evil conduct was known to the Norbertine Order of which he was a member and to Cardinal Daly, the Primate of Ireland. Yet nothing was done to stop him. This predator was allowed access to children without restraint. So great was the level of disgust for Smyth that when he died in 1997 he was buried at 4:15 AM in his order's cemetery in County Cavan. Four police remained in the background. The lights from the hearse were used to light the graveside. Concrete was poured over his grave.

Why was such an evil man allowed to continue in a ministry where he had access to children? Did the Roman Catholic Church not know that sexual abuse of children is wrong? Of course they knew that. But the image of the Church had to be protected. There could be no scandals, so allegations were either buried or ignored. Either way, nothing was done about the complaints. Is this excusable?

Let's look at an illustration from another discipline. A football coach is accused of sexually abusing young boys. He is dismissed but goes on to coach another team that is told nothing of his background. He abuses boys in that club and is again dismissed. He coaches yet another team and again abuses boys. It is outrageous to think that such would be allowed to happen—that a known pedophile would be allowed to move from club to club. Yet that is exactly how the Roman Catholic Church handled priests charged with sexually abusing children. When charges were made against a priest, he would be moved by his bishop to another parish, where he was free to continue his evil. The good people of the parish would not be told that a sex abuser has been sent among them and they had better protect their children at all times. No such warning would be given by the bishop to the flock. And so "Father" would endear himself to trusting parents, who were flattered that "Father" visits so frequently and shows such special interest in their children. When the horror was revealed, "Father," the family friend and confidant, would be reported to the bishop and reassigned to a new parish where the evil cycle would be repeated.

Unfortunately, this is not fiction but fact. It has happened again and again and again, not with one or two priests, but with hundreds. Who then is responsible for providing protection from the law and a safe haven for these pedophiles? The Roman Catholic bishops, those claiming to be successors to the apostles. Can you believe it? The mind boggles at such outrageous behavior.

What has deeply offended Catholics is the sense of having been betrayed by those in privileged positions. A priest holds a position of power in the community. He is an authority figure. During the fifties and sixties in Ireland, the clergy held extraordinary power. What the priest said was final. No one dared contradict him. To accuse him of sexual abuse was unthinkable. And the pedophiles knew it. This provided them with unlimited scope to abuse children, and they did, with a vengeance, knowing that accusations would not be believed. They also knew that their bishops would not report them.

Unfortunately, charges against priests have come from all over the world. And the same pattern has emerged in every case: Ignore the accusation and move the priest. This is borne out by the investigation ordered by the Irish government into sexual abuse allegations in the diocese of Ferns in County Wexford, Ireland. The Ferns report (2005) reveals that the diocese not only knew about the allegations but did nothing about them. The inquiry reveals that one priest assaulted ten girls on the altar of the church where he ministered. The girls were examined by the Health Board, who then notified Bishop Brendan Comiskey. Nothing was done about the matter. The report also reveals the Church's lack of cooperation during the investigation. There is also evidence that the Vatican was aware of some allegations against priests yet failed to discipline the offenders. The notorious pedophile Father Sean Fortune, who was from Ferns, was a violent rapist and a repeat offender. Despite complaints to Bishop Comiskey, Fortune was never removed. In March 1999, Fortune was found dead from an overdose of drugs and alcohol.

Colm O'Gorman was abused by a priest in Ferns. He is now director of One in Four, a charity offering support and resources for people who have suffered sexual abuse. He has this to say about the Ferns report:

> The Ferns report demonstrates beyond any doubt that protestations that the church was unaware of the nature of child sexual abuse until it was alerted by the media in the 1990s are wholly false.
>
> It details how in 1962 the Vatican distributed a document entitled *Crimen Solicitanis* to every bishop in the world. The instructions from the Vatican, that this document was to be maintained in secret archives and was not to be published or publicly commented upon, are evocative of a Dan Brown novel.
>
> *Crimen Solicitanis* instructs the church officials and even witnesses and complainants are required to take an oath of secrecy in relation to any disclosed sexual abuse. The penalty for breach of that secrecy was automatic excommunication.
>
> While many commentators have suggested that this document

deals only with the ecclesiastical crime of solicitation—priests procuring sex in the confessional—the Ferns report and Mr. Justice Murphy are clear that it also relates explicitly to the cases of child sexual abuse.

This document may explain the abject failure of cardinals, bishops and priests to break silence and report these crimes to the State and civil authorities. The threat of excommunication was in effect a death sentence to men who saw their lives only within the context of their priestly vocations. It was an incredibly effective tool in preventing the disclosure of widespread sexual abuse in Roman Catholic dioceses across the world.

The Ferns report states that it found "no evidence of this document in the files of the Dioceses of Ferns that it had examined." Given the fact that bishops remain under an obligation, perhaps still under threat of excommunication, not to publish or comment upon the document, it is unsurprising that the diocese was unable to confirm its existence.

It seems unlikely that the diocese of Ferns, alone of all the Roman Catholic dioceses in the world, was left off the mailing list for such a sensitive and secretive document....[2]

Most shocking of all...Archbishop Alibrandi and his successors as Papal Nuncios knew of the scale of abuses, but they prevailed upon Irish church leaders like [Bishop] Comiskey to grapple with them under the code of canon law—church law—rather than hand over the errant clerics to the Gardai. Furthermore, Alibrandi and his successors invoked diplomatic immunity as the representatives of the Holy See to avoid giving evidence in court cases taken by victims.[3]

Even today there are those who deny that the Holocaust happened, even though a mountain of evidence confronts them. They just don't want to believe. The same is true with some Catholics; they just don't want to believe that their Church has been so corrupt. I saw this unwillingness to believe the evidence when the news broke that Bishop Eamon Casey was the father of a 17-year-old boy. Casey was a very popular bishop in Ireland, a larger-than-life character. So when it was revealed that he was the father of a son, everyone was shocked. Casey immediately left Ireland and went to Rome and resigned as bishop. Some time later Annie Murphy, the mother of the boy, was a guest on *The Late, Late Show*. A lady in the audience who had worked for Casey repeatedly denied that Casey was the father of the child. I thought her response was amazing because by this time, 1) Bishop Casey had said he believed he was the father; 2) Casey had told Pope John Paul II that he was the father, and the pope believed him and allowed him to resign; 3) Annie Murphy said Casey was the father; 4) and the boy looked like Casey. So why does this woman not believe when the evidence is so compelling? Because she does not want to believe that a priest broke his vow, and nothing will convince her otherwise. There are some Catholics who will never believe the level of corruption that exists in their Church even though the evidence is compelling.

It emerged from Annie Murphy that Casey had tried to persuade her to put the child up for adoption, but she refused. It was obvious Casey was attempting to protect himself and the image of the Church. The only reason the story came to light was because Casey had failed to support his son, and the media was notified. The same pattern has been evident in the sex abuse cases: the image of the Church was being protected through a web of secrets and lies. Is this what Jesus came to build? The suggestion is ludicrous.

My sympathy goes out to the victims and their families who have had to live through this nightmare and try to make sense of how a Church could have provided known pedophiles with free and open access to their lovely children. How could their Church have provided protection for sex abusers? Why were they not warned that the new priest who had come to their parish had abused children in a previous parish? Many lives have been ruined and emotional scars will be carried for life by these victims. Some never recover, and others have taken their own life. And the only reason some victims are finally getting their day in court is because they have had the courage to tackle the Church. It has not been the Church that has brought about this purging of evil; it has been the victims. And if the victims had not done so, the bishops would have continued taking refuge in *Crimen Solicitanis* and excusing themselves from any personal responsibility. It has to be daunting and confusing to the victims as they try and come to terms with how their bishops could have commited themselves to remaining silent when the most precious and vulnerable members of the Church—the children— were left unprotected to be preyed upon by known pedophiles in shepherd's clothing.

THE CHURCH JESUS CAME TO BUILD

Jesus looked at the institutional religion of his day and said that new wine cannot be put into old wineskins (Luke 5:37-38). New wine, as it ferments and ages, bursts old wineskins that have become hardened with age. The Roman Catholic Church is like a wineskin that cannot contain the new wine of grace and truth. It's an old wineskin that has been shown to be corrupt in that it concealed the evil of pedophile priests while also providing them with repeated opportunities to abuse the innocent and justifying its inaction by its oath of silence. It has grown rich, powerful, and, in the process, corrupt. This is not the church that Jesus came to build, and as the psalmist says, "Unless the LORD builds the house, its builders labor in vain" (Psalm 127:1). Jesus' church is his people, those whom he has redeemed. They are being transformed into his image by the indwelling Spirit. Holiness is their hallmark. His church is a universal body of believers in local congregations, communities of faith cared for by godly shepherds who feed the flock with the living Word of God. This is the new creation Jesus came to bring into existence.

The challenge to Catholics reading this book is to read through the book of Acts and see how the early church "did church." Note the simplicity yet effectiveness of its organization. See its evangelistic zeal, its care for the poor, and its commitment to prayer. See its ministry involving every member. So great was the impact of the work of the church on the pagan world that when Paul and his fellow workers arrived in Thessalonica, the people said, "These that have turned the world upside down are come hither also" (Acts 17:6 KJV). Today our sinful world needs to be turned "upside down" by a return to the saving message of the living Word of God.

2

The Formation
of the Bible

· · · · · · · · · · · · ·

How did the Bible come into existence? The Roman Catholic Church maintains she gave us the Bible and determined the number of books that would compose the canon of Scripture—in particular, the New Testament. The argument goes like this: The Church existed before a word of the New Testament was written. After it was written, the Church determined the canon. Therefore, the Church is the authoritative voice that must be obeyed, for without the Church we would not have the Bible.

THE CATHOLIC CLAIM

Q. 17 Who can determine what books make up the Bible? Just as Christ's infallible Church alone can assure us that the Bible is divinely inspired, so the Church alone possesses the authority to indicate what books are included in it.[1]

> The Church came into being before the New Testament and it is as a result of this that she claims to be the final arbiter in matters of interpretation. It was the Church which collected together the books and letters which make up the New Testament. She decided what was to be included and what was to be left out. Thus as the author of this collection the Church is in a better position than the reader to say what is meant by a particular passage.[2]

This argument sounds good and reasonable, but is it correct? Is the Bible a product of the Roman Catholic Church? Or did it come into existence in some other way? One could be forgiven for dismissing the question as being irrelevant; the important thing is that we have the Bible. But it is not as simple as that. The Roman Catholic claim that it is by their authority we have the Bible, and is therefore it alone is the official interpreter of the Scriptures. If we want to know the true meaning of Scripture, then we must listen to the Church that gave us the Bible.

Does the evidence support the Catholic claim, or does it point us in a different direction? We will take our first step toward answering this question by looking at how the Old Testament came into existence and the criteria that determined its canon.

THE OLD TESTAMENT CANON

Jesus endorsed the Old Testament Scriptures as being the authentic Word of God. After his resurrection, Jesus met with his disciples and told them everything that had been written about him in the Scriptures: "Beginning with Moses and all the Prophets, he explained to them what was said in all the Scriptures concerning himself" (Luke 24:27). What conclusion can we draw from Jesus' words? Since the Lord had come to fulfill all that was written about him in the Scriptures, there had to have existed a recognized canon of Scripture. We can see this to be the case by the Lord's frequent reference to Scripture. For example, in his discourse on his deity—that he is the Son of God, equal with the Father—he said, "the Scripture cannot be broken" (John 10:35). To what was he referring? It was to that body of Scripture we know as the Old Testament. While upbraiding the Jews for their refusal to accept him, Jesus said, "You diligently study the Scriptures because you think that by them you possess eternal life. These are the Scriptures that testify about me" (John 5:39). Note that Jesus did not say they were looking in the wrong place—at writing that did not constitute Scripture. They were looking in the right place, proving that there was a recognized body of work that was regarded as the Word of God.

On another occasion the Sadducees, a group of Jewish religious leaders, came to Jesus with a question about the resurrection. In reply Jesus said, "You are in error because you do not know the Scriptures or the power of God" (Matthew 22:29). The Sadducees could have resolved their error by referring to the Scriptures, which were a recognized source of authority.

In addition, Jesus was able to make a clear distinction between what Scripture teaches and what religious tradition teaches:

> "You have let go of the commands of God and are holding on to the traditions of men." And he said to them: "You have a fine way of setting aside the commands of God in order to observe your own traditions! For Moses said, 'Honor your father and your mother,' and, 'Anyone who curses his father or mother must be put to death.' But you say that if a man says to his father or mother: 'Whatever help you might otherwise have received from me is Corban' (that is, a gift devoted to God), then you no longer let him do anything for his father or mother. Thus you nullify the word of God by your tradition that you have

handed down. And you do many things like that" (Mark
7:8-13).

Jesus looked at the hypocritical behavior of the Pharisees and
saw that it was rooted in the traditions of men. How could Jesus say
that they had abandoned the commands of God, revealed in Scripture, unless a recognized body of Scripture already existed?

Finally, after a very rough reception in the city of Thessalonica,
Paul arrived in Berea, where he was pleasantly surprised by the attitude of the people. "Now the Bereans were of more noble character than the Thessalonians, for they received the message with
great eagerness and examined the Scriptures every day to see if
what Paul said was true" (Acts 17:11). Paul did not have to correct
them, saying that they were looking to the wrong source for verifi-
cation of his message. No; they were looking in the right place—the
39 books that comprise the Old Testament. These books had long
being recognized as the Word of God and subsequently canonized.
The people of God in the Old Testament were able, under the guidance of God, to compile the books we know as the Old Testament,
which Jesus endorsed. This occurred long before the Roman Catholic Church came into existence.

It is interesting to note how the books that compose the Old
Testament came into existence. The main criterion in determining
whether a book should be included in the canon pertained to its
author. Prophetic authorship was essential. If the author were
known to be a prophet of God, his works were preserved. This was
obviously at the direction of God. Moses was a prophet of God, used
by him in a mighty way. To ensure that we would have a permanent
record of God's revelation, Moses wrote down all that the Lord told
him. Furthermore, he placed his writings in a place of honor—next
to the Ark of the Covenant, where God was specially present among
his people (Deuteronomy 31:24-26).

Joshua succeeded Moses as Israel's leader and was a man "filled with the spirit of wisdom because Moses had laid his hands on him" (Deuteronomy 34:9). At the end of his life Joshua added another link to the chain—God directed Joshua and he "recorded these things in the Book of the Law of God" (Joshua 24:26). The Old Testament was beginning to take shape. Samuel is among the outstanding prophets in Israel's history, and he too contributed to the body of work that would become the Old Testament: "He wrote them [the regulations from God] down on a scroll and deposited it before the LORD" (1 Samuel 10:25). Note the special place of honor given to Scripture: "before the LORD." Furthermore, "as for the events of King David's reign, from beginning to end, they are written in the records of Samuel the seer" (1 Chronicles 29:29). The prophet Nathan also made his contribution to the formation of the Old Testament: "As for the other events of Solomon's reign, from beginning to end, are they not written in the records of Nathan the prophet...?" (2 Chronicles 9:29). And when Israel was faced with 70 years of captivity in Babylon, Daniel was able to refer to the writings of the prophet Jeremiah and see that God had foretold this captivity. Daniel "understood from the Scriptures, according to the word of the LORD given to Jeremiah the prophet, that the desolation of Jerusalem would last seventy years" (Daniel 9:2; see Jeremiah 29:10).

The prophets wrote on a wide variety of events in the history of God's chosen people, but there was one central theme to their writings: the coming of the Messiah. Jesus frequently claimed that he was the central figure in the Scriptures: "Beginning with Moses and all the Prophets, he explained to them what was said in all the Scriptures concerning himself" (Luke 24:27). Peter said the Old Testament prophecies fulfilled by Jesus provide ample proof that he is the Son of God and that the Scriptures provide all the assurance and guidance we need (2 Peter 1:12-21). Peter was saying we do not need to go outside of what Scripture says.

What have we said so far? The Old Testament was accepted by the people of God because it was written by the prophets of God. The writings of the prophets were preserved because of their divine origin. Though the people of God gathered these sacred writings, this never gave them a position of authority over (or even equal with) the Scriptures. By the time Jesus came, the canon (the recognized collection of books) in the Old Testament had been established, and had received the endorsement of Christ himself. These were the Scripture Jesus appealed to during his ministry, maintaining that the central message of the Old Testament spoke of his coming to save us from our sins and to bring us back to the Father.

Jesus taught definitely that God was the Originator of the Hebrew Old Testament. He quoted as authoritative or authentic most of the twenty-two books of the Hebrew canon. He considered every section, "Law and Prophets" and "Law, Prophets, and Psalms" (Luke 24:27,44), to be prophetic of Him. He believed that inspiration extended from Genesis through Chronicles (Matt. 23:35; tantamount to saying "Genesis to Malachi"). He asserted that the Old Testament as a whole was unbreakable Scripture (John 10:35); that it would never perish (Matt. 5:18); and that it must be fulfilled (Luke 24:44). He personally authenticated persons and events from Eden (Matt. 19:5) to Jonah in the "whale" (Matt. 12:40), including Daniel the prophet (Matt. 24;15), Noah and the flood (Luke 17:27), and the destruction of Sodom (Luke 17:29). Jesus not only defined the limits of the canon, that is, the twenty-two books of the Hebrew Old Testament, but he laid down the principle of canonicity, namely, the canon consists of that which is the "word of God." Illustrative of this point are Jesus' references to the Old Testament as the "word of God" (Mark 7:13), as that which "God said" (Matt. 19:5), or as that which was uttered "by the Spirit" (Matt. 22:43;

Mark 12:36). As for the New Testament, Jesus promised that the Holy Spirit would guide the apostles into "all the truth" (John 16:13) and bring all things that he had taught them to their remembrance (John 14:26). Thus, the principle that "canonicity is determined by inspiration" was pronounced by Jesus concerning the Old Testament, and promised in the New Testament.[3]

Author Edward J. Young also provides helpful insights on the relationship between the inspiration of the Scriptures and their place in the canon:

> When the Word of God was written it became Scripture and, inasmuch as it had been spoken by God, possessed absolute authority. Since it was the Word of God, it was canonical. That which determines canonicity of a book, therefore, is the fact that the book is inspired of God. Hence a distinction is properly made between the authority which the Old Testament possesses as divinely inspired, and the recognition of that authority on the part of Israel.[4]

THE NEW TESTAMENT CANON

By the close of the first century, the 27 books that compose the New Testament had been accepted by the early church as canonical. The evidence for this is verified by early church history. (In case you desire to read a more thorough treatment of this subject, I've listed several books for further reference at the end of this chapter.)

The Roman Catholic Church maintains that the collection of books that compose the New Testament canon was determined by them. This is incorrect. The purpose of this council was not to sort through dusty old scrolls that had been stored in some monastic attic and then announce to the Christian world which books were canonical and which were not. The council simply affirmed what the early church had long since affirmed—that the 27 books we know as the New Testament were canonical. We must not make the mistake of thinking that the Scriptures received their authority because some council made a public statement of their acceptance. The truth of the matter is that the early church accepted the Scriptures in much the same way as Israel accepted the Old Testament Scriptures—they believed the Scriptures to be inspired of God. The church rightly saw herself as subject to the authority of Scripture and not the other way around. Though the church existed before the New Testament was written, this did not give the church authority over Scripture or even authority equal to Scripture. The church must always be subject to the authority of God's written Word.

What enabled the early church to accept the canon of the New Testament so readily was the unique position of the apostles. They were the Lord's companions for most of his ministry, and he trained them for a special mission: world evangelism. Not only were they eyewitnesses to the resurrection of Jesus, but they were endowed with the necessary credentials to establish themselves as God's spokespersons. The miracles they performed testified to this role. We read that "the apostles performed many miraculous signs and wonders among the people" (Acts 5:12). This included raising the dead to life and restoring the sick to perfect health. Further confirmation was given to the apostolic ministry in that "God did extraordinary miracles through Paul" (Acts 19:11). Paul had no hesitation in pointing to the miracles performed by the apostles as proof of their divine calling (2 Corinthians 12:12).

For many years the apostles taught the church all that God was revealing to them, and the church accepted their teaching. The church had every confidence that what the apostles taught them was indeed the will of God. Like the prophets before them, they too would die, but God had taken steps to ensure that his message would always be available. The Holy Spirit guided the apostles to record God's will in the Scriptures, and the church accepted their writings.

Jesus gave the apostles the very words the Father had given him (John 17:8), and promised to send the Holy Spirit to teach them, guide them, and recall to their minds all that he had told them during his earthly ministry (John 14:26; 16:13). Part of the Spirit's guidance pertained to the writing of the 27 books that compose the New Testament. This should not be at all surprising, since the early church grew out of a Jewish heritage, which had accumulated the writings of God's former spokespersons. Under the Spirit's guidance, the early church followed the same practice.

Evidence shows that the canon of Scripture, the 66 books that compose the Bible, were canonized by the fact that they are inspired of God. The claim made by the Roman Catholic Church that they gave us the Bible cannot be sustained. God gave us the Bible. Louis Gaussen gives a wonderful summary on the subject. He says:

> In this affair, then, the Church is a servant and not a mistress; a depository and not a judge. She exercises the office of a minister, not of a magistrate.... She delivers a testimony, not a judicial sentence. She discerns the canon of the Scriptures, she does not make it; she has recognized their authority, she has not given it.... The authority of the Scriptures is not founded, then, on the authority of the Church: It is the Church that is founded on the authority of the Scriptures.[5]

It was inevitable that the writings of the apostles would be preserved, since they contained the fulfillment of all that the prophets had foretold about Jesus. Peter in his epistles gave a generous hint that this process was happening even while he was alive; he saw his writings being permanently available: "I will make every effort to see that after my departure you will always be able to remember these things" (2 Peter 1:15). The public reading of the apostles' writings alongside those of the Old Testament further indicates that God was bringing together (and the church was accepting) the New Testament Scriptures as the Word of God. By the close of the first century the complete will of God had been revealed and recorded in the Scriptures. We can dismiss the notion that the early church did not know the full extent of the New Testament canon until late into the fourth century, and that during this time they were waiting for the church to make an official pronouncement. This line of reasoning gives the Catholic Church an authority that is reserved for the Scriptures alone.

SCRIPTURE IS SUFFICIENT

To justify its position, the Roman Catholic Church often advances the argument that the Scriptures never claimed to be adequate to meet all our needs. They say this based upon the words of the apostle John: "Jesus did many other things as well. If every one of them were written down, I suppose that even the whole world would not have room for the books that would be written" (John 21:25). Read those words again and see if you think it was John's intention to state the written Word of God, the inspired Scriptures, were never intended to be the only source of authority for our beliefs and practices. Did John really say that? John never even hinted at such a thought. In fact, he said the direct opposite. In the previous chapter of his Gospel, John confirms that what he tells us about Jesus is sufficient to secure for us eternal life. When you have eternal life, you lack for nothing. And John tells us how to have eternal life from the Scriptures: "Jesus did many other miraculous signs in the presence of his disciples, which are not recorded in this book. But these are written that you may believe that Jesus is the Christ, the

Son of God, and that by believing you may have life in his name"
(John 20:30-31). John confidently affirms that the written Word of
God is sufficient to meet our needs. All we need to know about how
to live, and how to die in the Lord, is contained in Scripture.

Let me say this one more time: The Old Testament Scriptures
that Jesus came to fulfill were canonized centuries before the Roman
Catholic Church came into existence. And the procedure God used
to gather those books was the same procedure used for forming
the canon of the New Testament. I really do like how F.F. Bruce
puts it:

> What is particularly important to notice is that the
> New Testament canon was not demarcated by the arbi-
> trary decree of any Church Council. When at last a
> Church Council, the Synod of Carthage in A.D. 397,
> listed the twenty-seven books of the New Testament, it
> did not confer upon them any authority which they did
> not already possess, but simply recorded their previously
> established canonicity.[6]

God gave us the Scriptures as our final and only authority in all
matters of faith and morals. The church is subject to the authority
of the Scriptures. An excellent summary of what has been said is
given by Geisler and Nix:

> The most important distinction to be made at this point is
> between the determination and the discovery of canonicity. God
> is solely responsible for the first, and man is merely responsible for
> the last. That a book is canonical is due to divine inspiration. How
> this is known to be true is the process of human recognition. How
> men discovered what God had determined was by looking for the
> "earmarks of inspiration," which are the (1) authoritative, (2) pro-
> phetic, (3) authentic, (4) dynamic, and (5) accepted nature of the
> books. That is, it was asked whether the book (1) came with the

Authority of God, (2) was written by a man of God, (3) told the truth about God, man, etc., (4) came with the power of God, and (5) was accepted by the people of God. If a book clearly had the first earmark, the remainder were often assumed. The first three were used explicitly on most books, while the last two were usually applied implicitly only. It was by this procedure that the early Fathers sorted out the profusion of religious literature, discovered, and gave official recognition to the books that, by virtue of their divine inspiration, had been determined by God as canonical.[7]

QUESTIONS AND ANSWERS

Q. Didn't the Roman Catholic Church decide which books form the canon of Scripture?

No, this is not correct. The Roman Catholic Church claims that it determined which books were to be included in the canon of Scripture through the Magisterium. It is a fact of history that the canon had been determined long before any official pronouncement by the Church or any council.

Q. How was the Old Testament canon formed?

Long before the Roman Catholic Church came into existence the Old Testament canon had been determined. Jesus himself endorsed this canon, stating that he had come to fulfill all that the law and the prophets had said (Luke 24:25-27). He repeatedly taught from this recognized body of Scripture and referred to it as the Word of God. Throughout Israel's history the writings of Moses, Samuel, and others were given a place of honor "before the LORD" (Deuteronomy 31:24-26; 1 Samuel 10:25). Those who were known to be prophets of God, whose life and ministry testified to their calling, had their writing included in the canon.

Q. How was the New Testament canon formed?

The Roman Catholic Church claims that it was by its authority that the books composing the New Testament were canonized. In fact, the New Testament canon began emerging during the lifetime of the apostles. Prophetic and apostolic authorship was a primary consideration in determining the canon. Within the church these

writings enjoyed the same status afforded to the Old Testament
Scriptures. The church readily accepted as canonical the writings
of Paul, Peter, James, John, etc. The formation of the canon was a
relatively easy task because of the short time between the writing of
the earliest and the latest New Testament scriptures. The New Testament books had all been written by about A.D. 90. The last one
was written by the apostle John, an eyewitness of Jesus' ministry,
death, and resurrection.

**Q. What part did church councils have in the formation of the
canon?**

The simple answer is none. The councils of Hippo and Carthage in
the fourth century did not give us the canon of Scripture. Rather,
they simply confirmed what was already accepted as canonical.

For Further Reading

F.F. Bruce, *The Canon of Scripture* (Glasgow: Chapter
House, 1988).

Norman Geisler and William Nix, *From God to Us*
(Chicago: Moody Press, 1974).

J.I. Packer, *God Has Spoken* (London: Hodder and
Stoughton, 1966).

3
The Living
Word

. . . .

W hen Jesus declared his deity, he supported his claim by appealing to Scripture. "The Scripture" he says, "cannot be broken" (John 10:35). Whatever Scripture says must be obeyed. It is our compass that points the way to our heavenly destination. Such a clear statement should settle for all time that the Scriptures are indeed our only authority in all matters of belief and practice. Obedience to what Scripture says is not optional.

Yet many Roman Catholics accept the authority of their Church in addition to and sometimes over the Scriptures. The fullness of truth, they maintain, is contained not in Scripture alone, but in both Scripture and Tradition. By Tradition they mean the teachings of the Roman Catholic Church. These are teachings that do not have their roots in Scripture but have evolved over many centuries and have finally been defined as dogma by the Church.

The shift in my thinking began when I started reading the Scriptures. This was a new experience for me. I was both frightened and excited at what I was doing. I was frightened because I was wading in uncharted waters and going outside the boundaries of where I was told all truth resides: in the Church's official teaching. But I was excited to see how approachable the Scriptures are, and holding fast to that which never changes made a lot of sense to me. As I read the four Gospels I was continually impressed by how often Jesus referred to the Scriptures and never to tradition when he taught on matters of faith and morals. This was so unlike the practice of the Roman Catholic Church, which, in my experience, frequently appealed to the teachings of popes, papal encyclicals, and Tradition. I concluded that if Jesus accepted only the Scriptures, I would not be wrong if I followed his example.

Unlike evangelical Christians who accept the Bible as the only source of authority for what we believe and practice, the Roman Catholic Church embraces both the Bible and Tradition as their source for revealed truth. Their acceptance of Tradition as an additional source does not detract from their belief that the Bible is indeed the inspired Word of God. However, when truth is being sought from two different sources, conflict and contradictions are bound to manifest themselves. And they do.

The Roman Catholic position on authority states that the Church must have an infallible leader to guide the Church in the correct interpretation of Scripture, thereby keeping the Church on the straight and narrow path. Without infallibility, they argue, the Church is rudderless in a stormy sea. There is the perception that there is danger in allowing the Bible to be interpreted by those outside the Magisterium, as this could open the floodgates to every possible error and heresy.

This is how the official position is stated:

> The task of interpreting the Word of God authentically has been entrusted solely to the Magisterium of the Church, that is, the Pope and to the bishops in communion with him. [100]
>
> To the successors of the apostles, sacred tradition hands on in its full purity God's word, which was entrusted to the apostles by Christ the Lord and the Holy Spirit.... Consequently, it is not from the sacred Scriptures alone that the Church draws her certainty about everything which has been revealed. Therefore both sacred tradition and sacred Scripture are to be accepted and venerated with the same sense of devotion and reverence. Sacred tradition and the sacred Scripture form one sacred deposit of the word of God, which is committed to the Church.[1]

We must give credit where credit is due; the Roman Catholic Church makes it very plain where it stands—the Church does not draw on the Scriptures alone for what it believes and practices. Tradition, they say, has equal value with the Bible. Furthermore, interpreting the Scriptures is the exclusive right of the Magisterium.

This position presents some serious problems. For example, a Roman Catholic may begin to study the Bible and, through his study, begin to question what he has been taught: He sees that the death of Jesus paid in full the penalty of his sins. He begins to understand that the Lamb of God did in fact take away his sins and that through one perfect sacrifice offered on Calvary, reconciliation with God is made possible. He sees the theme of a full pardon in many of the epistles. He sees the certainty of forgiveness. All of what he has been reading conflicts with Roman Catholic teaching on purgatory, which states that he must suffer for his sins in purgatory before he can enter heaven. From what he has read in the Bible it is plain that when you are forgiven you are indeed forgiven. Now, what is he to do? If he goes to discuss the matter with his parish priest, who is well informed on Church teaching and holds firmly to the teaching of the Church, he will be told that he must accept the Church's official teaching on the matter. Even though he has marshalled impressive evidence from Scripture to support his case, he must accept the official interpretation of the Church irrespective of how convincing his arguments are from Scripture. To the Church it is obvious that he has arrived at an incorrect understanding of Scripture that must be rejected in favor of the Church's position. Do you see the dilemma? On the one hand our friend understands Scripture to say clearly that the death of Jesus cleanses us from all our sins; therefore, there is no condemnation awaiting us when we die. And yet the Church's position says there is condemnation, which will be experienced in purgatory. What is our Catholic friend to do?

I like James McCarthy's observation about this kind of dilemma:

> What is the result of surrendering teaching authority to one group of men and treating their interpretations as authentic and even infallible? The answer can be found by looking at how the Church handles Scriptures that present a challenge to the established Roman Roman Catholic beliefs or practices. Consider, for example, this portion of the Ten Commandments:
>
>> You shall not make for yourself an idol, or any likeness of what is in heaven above or on the earth beneath or in the water under the earth. You shall not worship or serve them... (Exodus 20:4-5).
>
> This command forbids the making of images for religious use. It also prohibits the worshiping of such objects. The primary

meaning of the Hebrew word translated "worship" (Exodus 20:5) is to bow down. Because of this commandment, both Jews and most non-Roman Catholic Christians shun the use of sacred objects such as statues in the practice of their faith. The Roman Catholic Church has its own interpretation of the commands of Exodus 20:4, 5 [2129-2132].

> They do not forbid images of Christ and the saints. But to make and honor the images of Christ our Lord, of His holy and virginal Mother, and of the Saints, all of whom were clothed with human nature and appeared in human form, is not only not forbidden by the Commandment, but has always been deemed a holy practice and a most sure indication of gratitude. This position is confirmed by the monuments of the Apostolic age, the General Councils of the Church, and the writings of so many among the Fathers, eminent alike for sanctity and learning, all of whom are one accord upon this subject. *The Roman Catechism.*

Note how in this explanation the practice of the Church is used to confirm the interpretation of Scripture. The same approach was used by the Second Vatican Council in its endorsement of the continued use of statues:

> From the very earliest days of the Church there has been a tradition whereby images of our Lord, his holy Mother, and of saints are displayed in churches for the veneration of the faithful. *Second Vatican Council.*

The Roman Catholic interpretation of Exodus 20:4,5 is the product of applying Roman Catholicism's supreme rule for Bible interpretation: The authentic meaning of any verse of Scripture is what the Magisterium of the Church has always said it means. [119] Or, to put it another way: What the Church believes and practices determines what the Scriptures teach or mean.... This approach to Scripture study is futile. It can only result in the

Church validating itself. Correction is impossible, because the norm of truth is not the plain meaning of Scripture as verified by comparison with other Scriptures.[2]

I think McCarthy has made a very valid point deserving of consideration. The Roman Catholic Church is saying, in essence, "This is what we have always practiced; therefore, Scripture must mean what we practice—even when the text of Scripture states the very opposite. Words that clearly say do not make any likeness of anything in heaven or on earth to bow down to it no longer mean what they say." With the Church's approval, Catholics can make any likeness they want of things in heaven or on earth. God says don't do it; the Roman Catholic Church says that's not what he meant. So the plain and obvious meaning of God's Word is no longer plain and obvious. Why? Because of Tradition.

In the same way, the Roman Catholic person I mentioned earlier who found the Bible to teach that the death of Jesus paid in full the penalty for our sins must now disregard this and believe the Tradition of the Church, which teaches that there is still a need for purification in purgatory. So the declaration that the Lamb of God "takes away the sin of the world" doesn't mean what it says. Why? Because the Roman Catholic Church has an established doctrine that must be defended. In this way, Church teaching takes precedence over Scripture.

THE TROUBLE WITH TRADITION

The Roman Catholic Church binds Scripture and Tradition together to defend its beliefs and practices and, again, speaks with clarity on its position:

> Hence there exist a close connection and communi-
> cation between sacred tradition and sacred Scripture....

Sacred tradition and sacred Scripture form one sacred deposit of the word of God, which is committed to the Church.... The test of authentically interpreting the word of God whether written or handed on has been entrusted exclusively to the living teaching office of the Church. It is clear, therefore, that sacred tradition and sacred Scripture, and the teaching authority of the Church, in accord with God's most wise design, are so linked and joined together that one cannot stand without the others, and that all together and each in its own way under the action of the one Holy Spirit contribute effectively to the salvation of souls.[3]

Q. 29. Does the Roman Catholic Church derive all her doctrines solely from the Bible?

No. While most of the Church's teachings are contained in the Bible, some others are not.[4]

Combining Tradition with the all-sufficiency of Scripture is a dangerous practice and one that repeatedly incurred the condemnation of Jesus throughout his ministry. The practice of the Roman Catholic Church is similar to that of the Jewish religious teachers of Jesus' day, who also put great importance on Tradition.

The tragedy of tradition is that it blinds people from seeing God. Tradition, because it is based on falsehood, ensures that people cannot have a relationship with God. Jesus deliberately violated the religious traditions of his day in order to expose them for the falsehoods that they were. One way he did this was to perform miracles on the Sabbath. To better understand the significance of this, let's look at what Scripture says about the Sabbath.

The Sabbath was given to the Jews to commemorate their deliverance from Egypt (Deuteronomy 5:15). They were charged with keeping that day holy by abstaining from work (Exodus 20:8-11). Over the centuries the teaching authorities had drawn up a long list of dos and don'ts regarding Sabbath observance. These rules were viewed as expressing the will of God and were enforced by the religious authorities. These traditions were put on an equal footing with Scripture. So when Jesus worked miracles on the Sabbath he was denounced as a sinner, a violator of God's law, because his miracles were viewed as work, and one wasn't supposed to work on the Sabbath. But did Jesus really break God's law, or did he violate the Jewish leaders' interpretation of the law, which constituted their tradition? What he broke was a man-made tradition that had produced a joyless, legalistic religion. Traditions, Jesus said, "load people down with burdens they can hardly carry" (Luke 11:46).

When Jesus restored a man to full health on the Sabbath, he was taken to task and accused of doing work on the Sabbath and being a lawbreaker. Jewish traditions, which the religious leaders considered to be on a par with the law of God, had been violated.

Yet Jesus not only defended his action by his miracles, but showed his accusers why they were unable to see who he was: God the Son, the One spoken of by all the prophets. They were the theologians of the day, the educated teachers who had studied the ancient Scriptures. They should have been the first ones to recognize him, but belief in their traditions had set their minds in concrete, leaving no room for the possibility of further light. "You diligently study the Scriptures," Jesus said to them. "These are the Scriptures that testify about me" (John 5:39).

Two points stand out here: First, these religious leaders did study the Scriptures, not casually but diligently. Second, the Scriptures they studied referred to Jesus. Yet they failed to believe in him! They had the Scriptures and they witnessed his miracles, but they remained in unbelief. Jesus then said, "If you believed Moses, you would believe me, for he wrote about me" (John 5:46). This is an astonishing statement because these leaders claimed to be disciples of Moses and avid readers of his writings, yet they couldn't see that Jesus was the central character in all of Moses' writings. The obstacle that caused their blindness was their religious traditions. Jesus was not what they had expected of the Messiah. Their disappointment had not been based on anything the Scriptures had said, but on the expectations their traditions had given them. Tradition became the standard by which they measured Jesus. Once Scripture was abandoned as the norm, these leaders were on the slippery slope to trouble.

Another example of Jesus in conflict with tradition is seen on the day that he restored the sight of a man born blind. The event was marked not with celebration, but with a public outcry. The miracle occurred on the Sabbath day. The authorities quickly proclaimed, "This man is not from God, for he does not keep the Sabbath" (John 9:16). They conducted an extensive inquiry of the blind man and his parents. "Is this your son?" they asked. "Is this the one you say was born blind? How is it that now he can see?" (verse 19). Frightened, the parents replied, "Ask him. He is of age; he will speak for himself" (verse 21). The parents replied in this sheepish fashion "because they were afraid of the Jews, for already the Jews had decided that anyone who acknowledged that Jesus was the Christ would be put out of the synagogue" (verse 22).

No one could deny that a miracle had indeed occurred, so what were the authorities to do about it? What official statement would they issue to put the minds of the masses at ease? They said, "We know this man [Jesus] is a sinner" (verse 24). To add a touch of respectability to their comments they declared, "We are disciples of Moses! We know that God spoke to Moses, but as for this fellow, we don't even know where he comes from" (verses 28-29).

When the blind man heard what they said, not only were his eyes wide open, but so was his mouth: "Now that is remarkable! You don't know where he comes from, yet he opened my eyes.... If this man were not from God, he could do nothing."

"You were steeped in sin at birth; how dare you lecture us!" they replied as they threw him out (verses 30-34). He was excommunicated!

Why did the religious leaders not see the divine evidence of God in the miracle? It was their traditions that blinded them. They viewed their traditions as the will of God and couldn't entertain the possibility that they just might be wrong. Yet the miracle that they could not deny should have caused them to reconsider that maybe, just maybe, they were wrong. When they were pressed to offer an explanation as to how Jesus performed his miracles, which they could not deny, they took refuge in the evil belief that he was in league with the devil (Matthew 12:22-32).

Another key point to observe is that the Bible never changes, but tradition does. For example, growing up as a Catholic, I remember when, before receiving Holy Communion on a Sunday, we had to fast from midnight Saturday onward. To break fast and receive Communion was a sin. The same applied to eating meat on a Friday. It was a sin to break your fast from meat. Today these laws are no longer in force. They were made by men and have been removed by men, proving that they did not come from God. Yet we were told that to break one of these laws was to sin against God. How could something be a sin yesterday but not a sin today?

I have seen how relevant Jesus' discussion is to our time. Over the years I have often discussed the Scriptures with Roman Catholic priests. I recall several times discussing with them the wonder of the cross of Christ and what that means to us: In his death, Jesus paid the full penalty of all our sins, and as a result we are now set free, never to face condemnation. Up to this point we would have agreement. Then I would ask, "Since the death of Jesus paid the full penalty for our sins, why is there a need for purgatory?" Without exception the reply would come, "But the Roman Catholic Church teaches...."

No matter how persuasive my arguments from Scripture, and no matter how clearly Scripture revealed that Jesus fully forgives us and that purgatory contradicts the sacrifice of Christ, the answer would always be the same: "But the Roman Catholic Church says...."

Do you see what is happening here? The evidence of Scripture, compelling though it is, is rejected in favor of Tradition that is based on the teachings of men. What Jesus said of the Jews of his day is applicable to much of Roman Catholic teaching as well: "Their teachings are but rules taught by men. You have let go of the commands of God and are holding on to the traditions of men" (Mark 7:7-8).

Apostolic Tradition

The Roman Catholic Church has attempted to justify its acceptance of Tradition by quoting Paul's words to the church at Thessalonica: " So then, brothers, stand firm and hold to the teachings we passed on to you, whether by word of mouth or by letter" (2 Thessalonians 2:15). The Roman Catholic Church says that the instruction given by "word of mouth" is equal to its practice of Tradition. But does it support the church? Let's see if this is so. Bible commentator John Stott's comments are most helpful:

> The apostle's exhortation is a double one: "Stand firm!" and "hold to!" He seems to picture a gale, in which they are in danger both of being swept off their feet and of being wrenched from their handhold. In face of this hurricane-force wind, he urges them to stand their grounds, planting their feet firmly on terra firma, and to cling onto something solid and secure, clutching hold of it for dear life.

> Both verbs are present imperatives. Since the storm may
> rage for a long time, they must keep on standing firm and
> keep on holding fast.[5]

The instruction given by Paul, whether by letter or word of
mouth, is authoritative and binding upon the believers. What Paul
made known to them by "word of mouth" was not his opinion or
well-intentioned views, but what God had revealed to him. When
Paul came to Thessalonica and spoke, he was making known to the
people what God had made known to him. He said, "When you
received the word of God, which you heard from us, you accepted it
not as the word of men, but as it actually is, the word of God, which
is at work in you who believe" (1 Thessalonians 2:13). This oral tradition was revealed truth made known to the apostles and bears no
resemblance to Roman Catholic Tradition.

JESUS' USE OF SCRIPTURE

Tradition as a growing body of belief has no support in the Word
of God. That God would make known his will through two sources
is foreign to Scripture. We can see how Jesus dealt with some of life's
most important questions by always pointing to Scripture alone. For
example, when someone asked the important question, "What must
I do to inherit eternal life?" Jesus supplied an authoritative answer:
"What is written in the law?…How do you read it?" (Luke 10:25-
26). He pointed his inquirer to the Scriptures.

It's worth considering how the Roman Catholic Church would
answer this question today. Would it direct the inquirer to the Scriptures, or would it say that to know the will of God one must listen
to the Church? We know that the appeal would not be to the Scriptures alone, since the Roman Catholic Church does not believe
that the entire will of God is contained in the Scriptures, but that

Scripture must be supplemented by the teaching of the Church. The picture, it says, is complete only when Scripture and Tradition are presented together. Yet if the same question were asked of Jesus today, surely he would not say, "You must listen to the Roman Catholic Church." Rather, he would point the inquirer to the Scriptures as he did during his earthly ministry.

On another occasion Jesus told a story of two men, one rich and the other a beggar. The day came when both men died and received their reward. The poor man went to heaven, and the rich man was lost in hell. From his place of torment he pleaded for someone to return to his family and tell them how to avoid ending up in the same place. However, his newfound zeal for mission work was really unnecessary. "They have Moses and the Prophets," the rich man was told, "let them listen to them" (Luke 16:29).

While the story has several important lessons, the one that is of greatest interest to us is that the Lord proclaimed the Scriptures (Moses and the Prophets) to be completely sufficient to show a person how to live for God. Jesus is teaching us that there is no need for anyone's family to be lost if they will but listen to what God is saying in the Scriptures. The problem is not that God is silent, but that we are poor listeners.

A long-standing disagreement existed between the Pharisees and the Sadducees, who taught that there is no resurrection. Jesus was called upon to give the definitive answer. He told the Sadducees, "You are in error because you do not know the Scriptures or the power of God" (Matthew 22:29). His point: If you knew what the Scriptures say, you would not be asking such a question. Note once again Jesus did not appeal to any authority apart from the Word.

A Pharisee who was an expert in the law came to Jesus and asked, "Teacher, which is the greatest commandment in the Law?" Jesus replied that loving God and your neighbor is the fulfillment of the law, and he said, "All the Law and the Prophets [referring to the Scriptures] hang on these two commandments" (Luke 22:39). There is nothing more important than to love God and your neighbor, and the instruction for that is found not in Tradition, but in Scripture.

There is yet another example of the Lord's use of Scripture alone, which occurred after he arose from the grave. On that Easter Sunday the Lord met two of his disciples on the road to the town of Emmaus. His death had emptied their hearts of all joy; their hopes were dashed. During the course of the evening Jesus revealed himself to them and, "Beginning with Moses and all the Prophets, he explained to them what was said in all the Scriptures concerning himself" (Luke 24:27). That must have been one fabulous Bible study! Jesus would have cited all the major Scripture texts that referred to his coming, his work of redemption, his resurrection, and his ascension to heaven. No wonder the two disciples said, "Were not our hearts burning within us while he talked with us on the road and opened the Scriptures to us?" (verse 32).

By the way, before his ascension Jesus told his disciples, "Everything must be fulfilled that is written about me in the Law of Moses, the Prophets, and the Psalms" (Luke 24:44). The point cannot be overstated that Jesus came not to fulfill tradition, but rather, the Scriptures.

THE APOSTLES' USE OF SCRIPTURE

The apostles continued in Jesus' footsteps, holding solely to the infallible Scriptures in their work of reaching the lost and nurturing the church.

With the coming of the Holy Spirit, the Lord's instructions to go into all the world and preach the gospel got under way. The first Pentecost Sunday after the resurrection marks the birth of the church of God. On that day the Spirit came and empowered the apostles to preach the gospel, resulting in the conversion of about 3,000 people (Acts 2:1-47). The apostles argued their case for Christ with an appeal to Scripture, and the church continued to instruct people in what Scripture had to say. From the beginning the church taught only what was found in God's Word, with no appeal to tradition.

Stephen, the first Christian martyr, was stoned to death by his fellow Jews after surveying the Scriptures in an attempt to show his persecutors that Jesus was the promised Messiah, the Savior of the world. Like the apostles, he taught only from the Scriptures (Acts 7:1-60). As the persecution against believers worsened, they continued to share the gospel: "Those who had been scattered preached the word wherever they went" (Acts 8:4). What do you think these people preached? It couldn't have had anything to do with Tradition, since such a body of belief didn't come into existence until much later. What these believers preached was the good news that Jesus Christ was the promised Messiah, as foretold in the Scriptures.

Evangelism went into overdrive with the conversion of Saul of Tarsus, later known as the apostle Paul. A gifted man with a zeal for God and a love for the lost, Paul succeeded in extending the boundaries of the kingdom of God. Through his tireless efforts many people came to Christ and the church was being established in cities throughout the world. Paul's starting place for his evangelism was often among his fellow Jews, and the source of his message was always the Scriptures. Surely any claim to being the true church founded by Christ must have the same practice as Paul: an unswerving fidelity to the authority of the Scriptures.

Listen to Luke's words as he records how Paul evangelized: "As his custom was, Paul went into the synagogue, and on three Sabbath days he reasoned with them from the Scriptures, explaining and proving that the Christ had to suffer and rise from the dead. 'This Jesus I am proclaiming to you is the Christ,' he said" (Acts 17:2-3). On another occasion Paul "vigorously refuted the Jews in public debate, proving from the Scriptures that Jesus was the Christ" (Acts 18:28). All Paul's evidence came from Scripture alone.

While Paul was under house arrest in Rome, many people came to him to inquire about the Christ he was preaching. How did Paul deal with their inquiries? "From morning till evening he explained and declared to them the kingdom of God and tried to convince them about Jesus from the Law of Moses and from the Prophets" (Acts 28:23). In his own defense Paul said, "I am saying nothing beyond what the prophets and Moses said would happen" (Acts 26:22). In other words, Paul never went outside Scripture. It was his only point of reference. Paul, who received his ministry by way of revelation from Jesus himself, knew of no source for his teaching that resembled Roman Catholic Tradition. The church is being faithful to the Lord when it points people to what is found in Scripture. That is why the Bereans were commended, "for they received the message with great eagerness and examined the Scriptures every day to see if what Paul said was true" (Acts 17:11).

It would be inconceivable to think that Jesus came and fulfilled all that the Scriptures had foretold, then ascended to heaven without leaving any means by which the gospel would be proclaimed to all the world. Jesus left his people, his church, to spread the good news God had already revealed and which became enshrined in Scripture. If ever a group of people knew exactly what the Lord intended his church to be, it was the apostles, since they were with Him from the beginning. How did they see the church fulfilling its teaching role in the world? Apostolic writings show that the church never held itself up as an authority to be obeyed, but always pointed to the ultimate authority—the infallible Scriptures.

WHO INTERPRETS SCRIPTURE?

The Roman Catholic Church teaches that to it alone Jesus gave the authority to interpret the Scriptures; therefore, what it teaches is always correct. "...interpreting Scripture is ultimately subject to the judgment of the Church which exercises the divinely conferred commission and ministry of watching over and interpreting the Word of God" [119]. An individual cannot interpret Scripture; that's the work of the Magisterium. After all, Peter said, "Above all, you must understand that no prophecy of Scripture came about by the prophet's own interpretation" (2 Peter 1:20). But does that verse support the Roman Catholic position that forbids private interpretation? Let's look at the context.

In Matthew 17 we read that Jesus led Peter, James, and John up a high mountain. There the three disciples saw the Lord with Moses and Elijah: "He was transfigured before them. His face shone like the sun, and his clothes became as white as the light" (verse 3). Later, Peter referred to this event to support his belief that Jesus is the Son of God. He was writing in response to some who were denying this truth: "We did not follow cleverly invented stories when we told you about the power and coming of our Lord Jesus Christ, but we were eyewitnesses of his majesty. For he received honor and glory from God the Father when the voice came to him from the Majestic Glory, saying, 'This is my Son, whom I love; with him I am well pleased.' We ourselves heard this voice that came from heaven when we were with him on the sacred mountain" (2 Peter 1:16-18).

Peter was offering eyewitness testimony to support his position that Jesus is the Son of God. He also called upon the testimony of the ancient prophets who foretold the coming of the Christ with minute accuracy. Centuries before Jesus came, the prophets said he would be born of a virgin in Bethlehem, betrayed for 30 pieces of silver, crucified between two thieves, and raised from the dead.

How could they write of events that had not yet occurred? Peter explained, "For prophecy never had its origin in the will of man, but men spoke from God as they were carried along by the Holy Spirit" (2 Peter 1:21). The source of the prophets' information was not themselves; it was not from "the prophet's own interpretation," but from the Holy Spirit.

The Roman Catholic claim that it is not the responsibility of anyone other than the Church to interpret Scripture finds no support in Peter's words. The Church claims that if there is no authority to interpret Scripture, then that leaves the gate wide open for people to introduce every possible heresy. Will this not lead to mass confusion and an assortment of competing beliefs? It would if there were not a proper way to interpret Scripture.

How to Interpret Scripture

The Roman Catholic Church teaches that only the Church can correctly interpret Scriptures. This places the Church as the authority that people must listen to and not Scripture. Yes, the Bible can be read for its devotional value, but interpreting it is the work of the Church. But is it valid for the Church to make such a claim?

I want to provide some standard guidelines for developing the necessary skills for looking at any Bible passage and extracting the correct meaning.

It hardly needs to be said that God gave us his Word with the expressed intention that it be understood. There is a correct procedure to follow to understand Scripture. If, for example, you are reading one of the epistles, you can ask yourself:

- To whom was the book written?
- What was the purpose for which the letter was written?

- What is the context surrounding a particular verse of Scripture?
- How would the recipient of the letter have understood the text?
- What is the obvious meaning of the text?
- Is my interpretation in harmony with the rest of Scripture?
- Was this text written with a particular culture in mind?
- What did the author intend the text to mean?

This is about examining a text in its context. It sounds so simple, but if we examine a text within its context we can arrive at a correct understanding. All sorts of strange teachings would be avoided if this was practiced. Furthermore, we must approach the text not with our minds made up, but with a heart open to the guidance of the Holy Spirit.

A TEACHING CHURCH

What provision did Jesus make to ensure that those who embraced the Christian faith would be brought to spiritual maturity? Just as the church has been charged with teaching the gospel to the lost, it is also responsible for being the vehicle through which Jesus ministers to the needs of his people. Christ has given the church gifts that are necessary for sustaining the church. These gifts are teaching gifts that are practiced by apostles, prophets, evangelists, pastors, and teachers. It is through their ministry that the people of God are brought to maturity in Christ Jesus (Ephesians 4:11-16).

The apostles and prophets had a unique ministry in the church; it was through them that the complete will of God was revealed. The early Christians "devoted themselves to the apostles' teaching" (Acts

2:42). The teachings revealed to the apostles by the Holy Spirit are the foundation upon which the church is built in every generation (Ephesians 2:20; 3:5).

Since the apostles would not live forever, God made provision to have their teachings permanently preserved in the New Testament. When the writings of the apostles and prophets emerged, the church held them as sacred, just as they had the writings of Moses, David, Isaiah, Jeremiah, and others. The same Holy Spirit who had revealed God's will to the apostles also guided them in the recording of the Scriptures: "All Scripture is God-breathed" (2 Timothy 3:16). Because the New Testament books were authoritative, having been produced by the Holy Spirit, they were accepted by the church and enjoyed the same status as the Old Testament books. They too were read in public when the church assembled (see Colossians 4:16; Revelation 1:11,19-20; cf. Luke 4:16-17; Acts 13:15).

Evangelists and pastors are gifted teachers whom the Lord continually gives to his church. Through them the Lord ministers to his people. Timothy was an evangelist used by God in a very fruitful ministry to the church. For example, when the church in the city of Corinth was faced with problems, it was Timothy whom Paul sent to instruct them in the things he had previously taught them (1 Corinthians 4:17). The work undertaken by Timothy was ordained of God, and Paul reminded the Corinthian church that Timothy was "carrying on the work of the Lord, just as I am" (1 Corinthians 16:10). The work of the Lord for his church today is still being carried out by those whom God has called to be evangelists.

Pastors are also gifted to teach the church and are charged with the responsibility of caring for the people whom God has placed in their care. Just as a shepherd cares for his sheep, pastors are to care for the flock of God, and will give account to God for their pastoral ministry (Hebrews 13:17; 1 Peter 5:1-4).

It is the work of evangelists and pastors to exercise their teaching gifts so that the people of God will "no longer be infants, tossed back and forth by the waves, and blown here and there by every wind of teaching and by the cunning craftiness of men in their deceitful scheming" (Ephesians 4:14).

DEPENDENCE OF GOD'S WORD ALONE

The role of the church has always been and continues to be to speak for God from his Word. This requires diligent study of the Scriptures and fervent prayer to God for guidance and wisdom. Only as the teaching of the church is gathered from within the boundaries of God's written Word is the church speaking with the authority of God.

The teachings of the Roman Catholic Church could never be reproduced from the Scriptures alone, for by its own admission much of Roman Catholic belief is drawn from both the Scriptures and the teachings of the Church. I intend no disrespect when I say this, but I must state clearly that no one could ever become a Roman Catholic by following only what the Bible teaches. One needs the extrabiblical teachings of the Roman Catholic Church to be a Roman Catholic. But when Tradition is introduced on an equal footing with the Word of God, the inevitable collision occurs. Only God's Word reveals God's will for his people. The church is faithful as a teaching church when it proclaims what the Scriptures say. The church must always heed the words of Jesus: "The Scripture cannot be broken" (John 10:35).

QUESTIONS AND ANSWERS

Q. **Can Church Tradition ever take precedence over Scripture?**

Never. Jesus said that Scripture cannot be broken; in other words, what God's Word says must be obeyed. All that we believe and practice is to be based upon what the Bible alone says.

Q. **If you allow "unauthorized" individuals to interpret the Scriptures, would that not leave the door wide open for all sorts of errors to exist?**

The Roman Catholic Church claims that she is the infallible interpreter of Scripture, thereby placing the Church above the Scriptures. Yet there are accepted disciplines that enable us to interpret Scripture correctly, and even the Bible itself encourages its readers to be "a workman...who correctly handles the word of truth" (2 Timothy 2:15).

Q. **Does not the Roman Catholic interpretation of Scripture provide us with the correct understanding?**

Unfortunately, the answer is no. The Roman Catholic Church comes to Scripture with the mind-set that not all truth is contained in Scripture, but some is also containted in Church Tradition. That's why, for example, it reads of the brothers and sisters of Jesus and says they are his cousins, even though the Scriptures plainly declare they are brothers and sisters. Since Roman Catholic Tradition says that Mary remained a virgin all her life, the Roman Catholic Church is forced to dismiss or "explain away" the fact Jesus had brothers and sisters.

Q. **Doesn't Peter, in his epistle, forbid the private interpretation of the Scriptures?**

Peter's words in 2 Peter 1:20-21 have been taken entirely out of context by the Roman Catholic Church in its attempt to establish the Church as the only authority who can interpret Scripture. Our discussion of Peter's words shows that Peter is teaching that Jesus is the Son of God and offering the fulfillment of prophecy as a proof. How else could the prophets have foretold with such accuracy events that were to occur centuries later if they had not been guided by the Holy Spirit? That's the point Peter was making. The prophecies owe their origin not to man's interpretations but to the Holy Spirit.

Q. **Did Jesus ever support the type of tradition practiced in the Roman Catholic Church?**

No. Throughout his ministry, Jesus was on a collision course with the religious authorities of his day because of their man-made traditions, which were keeping the people from seeing who Jesus was. Their body of religious tradition became the standard by which they measured everything, and since Jesus did not endorse their tradition, they rejected him. The Roman Catholic Tradition is similar to that which Jesus encountered and rejected.

Q. **Why should we listen only to what the Scriptures have to say?**

The Scriptures are the inspired Word of God (2 Timothy 3:16-17). They contain the will of God for mankind. Jesus came to fulfill the Scriptures, not Tradition. There is not a piece of oral tradition that Jesus came to fulfill. Furthermore, He always pointed people to the Scriptures when he answered their questions. And it was the apostolic practice to do the same.

Q. **Isn't it true that the Church is a teaching Church and therefore we must listen to what it has to say?**

The Roman Catholic Church presents itself as a teaching Church and what it teaches is binding upon its members. But the Bible presents a very different picture: that the church is a teaching church is true, but it teaches only what the Scriptures say. The church is not an authority on a par with or above the inspired Word of God.

Q. **Who teaches the church?**

God has given gifted people to the church in the form of evangelists, pastors, and teachers (Ephesians 4:11-16). Through their ministries, they teach the church with the goal of nurturing believers toward maturity in Christ Jesus. The source they draw upon for their teaching is the Word of God.

4

Upon
This Rock

. . . .

The Roman Catholic Church has long claimed that Jesus made Peter and his successors the head of the church on earth and that through the Magisterium, the voice of God is heard. But does this claim match with the evidence offered by Scripture and early church history? A look at the facts reveals that the papacy as it is known today has evolved over many centuries; its origin cannot be found in the Bible. Nor does early church history support such an early origin of the office of the papacy. A study of this subject is important because of what is being claimed.

Unlike evangelical Christians, who are very familiar with Scripture and quote it extensively, Roman Catholics, in general, are not trained in the Scriptures. But there is one Bible passage all Catholics can quote: "You are Peter, and on this rock I will build my church" (Matthew 16:18). The Catholic understanding of these words is that Jesus appointed Peter as the head of the church, the first bishop of Rome, with provision for a successor to be appointed. That succession has supposedly been passed to each bishop of Rome in an unbroken chain from the time of Peter, who is said to have been given universal jurisdiction over the whole church. In matters of faith and morals Peter and his successors speak infallibly; they are incapable of error when speaking *ex cathedra*.

Now, it's true Peter did have a high profile among the apostles. His name appears frequently in the New Testament. In fact, his name appears first in all the lists of the apostles. He was in that inner circle of individuals who worked the closest to Jesus. He, along with James and John, witnessed the Lord's transfiguration and heard the Father endorse Jesus as his Son. On a number of occasions Peter served as the apostolic spokesman. He was the first to preach the gospel to the Jews and later to the Gentiles, and he wrote two of the New Testament epistles. So the prominence of Peter cannot be denied. However, there is a difference between *prominence* and *primacy*. *Primacy* is what the Roman Catholic Church claims for Peter in its official teaching on that matter:

> The Lord made St. Peter the visible foundation of his Church. He entrusted the keys of the Church to him. The bishop of the Church of Rome, successor to St. Peter, is "head of the college of bishops, the Vicar of Christ and Pastor of the universal Church on earth." [936]

> In order that the mission entrusted to them might be continued after their death [the apostles] consigned, by will and testament, as it were, to their immediate collaborators the duty of completing and consolidating the work they had begun urging them to tend

to the whole flock, in which the Holy Spirit had appointed them to shepherd the Church of God. They accordingly designated such men and then made the ruling that likewise on their death other proven men should take over their ministry. [861]

Just as the office which the Lord confided to Peter alone, as the first of the apostles, destined to be transmitted to his successors, is a permanent one, so also endues the office, which the apostles received, of shepherding the Church, a charge destined to be exercised without interruption by the sacred order of bishops. Hence, the church teaches that "the bishops have by divine institution taken the place of the apostles as pastors of the Church, in such wise that whoever listens to them is listening to Christ and whoever despises them despises Christ and him who sent Christ." [862]

Has the Catholic Church correctly interpreted Jesus' words to Peter? Is all that they claim for the papacy to be found in Matthew 16:18? What does the context of the passage teach us? The golden rule when interpreting Scripture is to examine a text in its context. This ensures that the text is allowed to reveal its true meaning, and helps prevent us from importing into the text a meaning that is not there. Let us read the entire section of Scripture claimed by the Roman Catholic Church to support the papal office:

When Jesus came to the region of Caesarea Philippi, he asked his disciples, "Who do people say the Son of Man is?" They replied, "Some say John the Baptist; others say Elijah; and still others, Jeremiah or one of the prophets." "But what about you?" he asked. "Who do you say I am?" Simon Peter answered, "You are the Christ, the Son of the living God." Jesus replied, "Blessed are you, Simon son of Jonah, for this was not revealed to you by man, but by my Father in heaven. And I tell you that you are Peter, and on this rock I will build my church, and the gates of

Hades will not overcome it. I will give you the keys of the
kingdom of heaven; whatever you bind on earth will be
bound in heaven, and whatever you loose on earth will be
loosed in heaven" (Matthew 16:13-19).

Who Are You?

For context's sake, we need to keep in mind that Jesus' ministry
caused major controversy among the Jewish religious leaders. His
teachings and practices collided with their traditions, which they
considered an expression of God's will. Jesus was enjoying a mea-
sure of success among the common people, who were seeing the
distinct possibility that he could be the promised Messiah. While
the authorities were opposed to him and denounced him at every
opportunity, they could not be entirely dismissive of him. After all,
they could not deny his miracles, and his teachings did have a certain flavor of truth.

All this led to controversy surrounding Jesus' identity; opinions
as to who he was were in a constant state of flux. Jesus was aware of
this when he asked his apostles who people thought he was. Their
reply showed the extent of the speculation surrounding his identity. Is he John the Baptist, Elijah, Jeremiah, or some other prophet?
Who is he? Peter answered the Lord's question by proclaiming, "You
are the Christ, the Son of the living God."

This is an amazing statement. Peter had declared Jesus to be
the anointed One of God, the One who is indeed God. Jesus then
told Peter that his words were not the result of human speculation,
but that they came to him by way of revelation from the Father. In
response, Jesus declared, "You are Peter, and on this rock I will build
my church."

What is the rock upon which the church is built? Is it Peter, or
is it the revelation the Father had made known to Peter—namely,

that Jesus is the Son of God? Let's work this out. The purpose for which Jesus came into the world was to save sinners. He said so himself: "The Son of Man did not come to be served, but to serve, and give his life as a ransom for many" (Matthew 20:28). And, "The Son of Man came to seek and to save what was lost" (Luke 19:10). For the lost to be saved, they have to believe that Jesus is the Son of the living God. That is the foundation, the solid rock upon which the church is built.

We cannot divorce the Lord's comments about building his church from what the Father revealed to Peter; to do so ignores the context completely and distorts what Jesus was saying. The rock on which the church is built is not Peter but what the Father made known to Peter. References to God as a rock are common in Scripture, and Jesus was perfectly familiar with these texts: "For who is God besides the LORD? And who is the Rock except our God?" (Psalm 18:31). "Is there any God besides me? No, there is no other Rock; I know not one" (Isaiah 44:8). "There is no one holy like the LORD; there is no one besides you; there is no rock like our God" (1 Samuel 2:2). These texts portray a sovereign God who is rocklike: strong, stable, reliable, and a solid foundation for one's faith. Since Jesus is God the Son, the second person of the Trinity, we should not be surprised his use of the phrase "on this rock" is in reference to the truth that he is the Son of the living God. The apostle referred to Christ as a rock, saying "that rock was Christ" (1 Corinthians 10:4).

William Webster observed,

> Vatican I claims that the Roman Catholic interpretation of Matthew 16:18-19 has been held universally throughout the Church and that it can appeal to the unanimous consent of the Fathers. Yet the early Fathers are quite varied in their opinions and interpretations of Matthew 16:18-19. Some speak of the "rock" to

mean Christ, some to mean Peter and others to mean Peter's confession of Christ. No Fathers of the first two centuries can be cited as in support of the Roman Catholic interpretation of Matthew 16:18. They are silent on the interpretation of the "rock" and the overwhelming majority of the Fathers through the patristic age (Augustine, Tertullian, Cyprian, Chrysostom, Ambrose, Jerome, Basil the Great, Hilary of Poitiers, Cyril of Alexandria, Athanasius, Ambrosiaster, Pacian, Epiphanius, Aphraates, Ephrain, John Cassian, Theodoret, Eusebius, Gregory the Great, Isidore of Seville, John of Damascus, and many others) all disagree with the Roman Catholic's interpretation of Matthew 16:18. The vast majority of the Fathers do not recognize the personal prerogatives of Peter as being transferred in a personal way to the bishop of Rome, thereby making him the head of the church.[1]

Peter never believed that he was the rock upon which Jesus would build his church. In fact, his teachings, along with those of the other apostles, contradict the notion that Peter is the rock upon which the church is built. For example, when Peter proclaimed the good news about Jesus to the Jews, he said that their rejection of Jesus as the Messiah was foretold in Scripture. He said Jesus was like a stone rejected by the builders, and that the rejected stone is now the cornerstone of the building—in this case, the church. "He is 'the stone you builders rejected, which has become the capstone'" (Acts 4:10-11). And in his first epistle Peter said Jesus was "a rock":

> As you come to him, the living Stone—rejected by men but chosen by God and precious to him—you also, like living stones, are being built into a spiritual house to be a holy priesthood, offering spiritual sacrifices acceptable to God through Jesus Christ. For in Scripture it says: "See, I lay a stone in Zion, a chosen and precious cornerstone, and the one who trusts in him will never be put to shame." Now to you who believe, this stone is precious. But to those who do not believe, "The stone the builders

rejected has become the capstone," and, "A stone that causes men to stumble and a rock that makes them fall" (1 Peter 2:4-8).

The testimony of Scripture confirms that the rock upon which the church is built is not Peter, but Jesus. Paul expounded upon this in the book of Ephesians when he spoke about the church. He assured the Gentile converts that they were "no longer foreigners and aliens, but fellow citizens with God's people and members of God's household, built on the foundation of the apostles and prophets, with Christ Jesus himself as the chief cornerstone. In him the whole building is joined together and rises to become a holy temple in the Lord. And in him you too are being built together to become a dwelling in which God lives by his Spirit" (Ephesians 2:19-22). Elsewhere Paul wrote, "No one can lay any foundation other than the one already laid, which is Jesus Christ" (1 Corinthians 3:11).

So, the Roman Catholic Church's assertion that Peter is the rock upon which the church is built was not accepted by the apostles, nor by many of the early church fathers. Nor was there a consensus among the early church fathers about the interpretation of Matthew 16:18. Archbishop Kenrick of St. Louis, Missouri, prepared a speech to the First Vatican Council in 1870 which was never delivered but later published. In it he summarized the five patristic interpretations: 17 fathers understood the rock to be Peter, 8 the apostles, 44 (including Origen and Chrysostom) Peter's confession of faith in Christ, 16 (including Augustine, Jerome, and later Pope Gregory the Great) Jesus Christ himself, and a few the faithful in general. Kenrick concluded, "If we are bound to follow the majority of the fathers in this thing, then we are bound to hold for certain that by the 'rock' should be understood the faith professed by Peter, not Peter professing the faith."[2]

I WILL BUILD MY CHURCH

Having established that Jesus' divinity is the rock upon which the church is built, we need to ask, "How does Jesus build his church?" Let's start at the beginning. He builds his church by saving people from their sins, adopting them into his family, and making them members of his body, which is the church. The building of the church is the work of the Lord himself; as the apostles preached the gospel, "the Lord added to their number daily those who were being saved" (Acts 2:47). Jesus continues building his church today by saving the lost through the power of the gospel.

The Gates of Hades

After saying that he would build his church, Jesus said, "The gates of Hades will not overcome it." The Roman Catholic Church interprets this to mean that Jesus would be with Peter and his successors forever, and that everything the Roman Catholic Church teaches about the papal office would remain intact for all time. "Christ, the 'living stone,' thus assures his Church, built on Peter, of victory over the powers of death" [552]. Is that what Jesus meant? I don't believe so. Such an interpretation does injustice to the context of our Lord's words. Jesus was not referring to the church but his own imminent death. He was saying that not even death will prevail against his redemptive mission. He will triumph over death and accomplish what he set out to do. "I am the Living One," Jesus said. "I was dead, and behold I am alive for ever and ever! And I hold the keys of death and Hades" (Revelation 1:18). Jesus came "so that by his death he might destroy him who holds the power of death—that is, the devil—and free those who all their lives were held in slavery by their fear of death" (Hebrews 2:14-15). Because of Jesus' victory over death, it is now possible for people to be saved and for there to be a church. With Paul the church can say, "Thanks be to God! He gives us the victory through our Lord Jesus Christ" (1 Corinthians 15:57). The gates of Hades did not overpower Jesus when he died. And that's what Jesus was talking about in Matthew 16:18.

The Keys of the Kingdom

Not to any of the other apostles, but to Peter alone, Jesus said, "I will give you the keys of the kingdom of heaven" (verse 19). This is a singular, unique honor. Here is how the Roman Catholic Church interprets Jesus' words: "Jesus entrusted a specific authority to Peter: 'I will give you the keys of the kingdom of heaven....' The 'power of the keys' designates authority to govern the house of God, which is the church" [553].

Now I am not trying to create a caricature of Peter when I say this, but I cannot believe for one moment that upon hearing Jesus' words Peter concluded, "I've been appointed the head of the church on earth and all decisions of faith and morals will be decided by me, in consultation with the bishops and cardinals, and my pronouncements will be infallible. Furthermore, this appointment will be passed on to my successors until the end of time." There is nothing in Jesus' words, nor in the entire New Testament, nor the early church writings to support the Roman Catholic interpretation of Matthew 16:18. The Roman Catholic Church has created a problem by reading into the words of Jesus something that is not there.

Jesus' words are symbolic. He did not give Peter a literal set of keys. The Lord's comments to the religious leaders in Luke 11:52 show a similar use of symbolic language: "Woe to you experts in the law, because you have taken away the key to knowledge. You yourselves have not entered, and you have hindered those who were entering" (Luke 11:52). The "key to knowledge" was not a metal object, it was truth pertaining to entrance to the kingdom. The religious leaders were hindering those who wanted to enter. They were keeping from the common people "the key to knowledge"— the key to knowing the truth.

So what did Jesus mean when he said he would give to Peter the "keys of the kingdom"? To find out the answer, we must first ask other questions:

First, what do keys symbolize? Authority. Power. We see that in how Jesus speaks of keys. The apostle John received an amazing vision of the resurrected Christ which left him "as though dead" (Revelation 1:17). Jesus then said to John, "Do not be afraid. I am the First and the Last. I am the Living One; I was dead, and behold I am alive for ever and ever! And I hold the keys of death and Hades" (Revelation 1:18). The one who has the "keys" of death and Hades has power and authority over death. The grave can no longer hold its victims because of the resurrection. Jesus has stripped death of its power.

Second, what are keys used for? To allow us access to places that are closed. When Jesus gave Peter the keys of the kingdom of God, he gave him the truth—the message that opens the way into the kingdom of heaven.

Third, how did Peter use these keys? On the day of Pentecost, Peter was empowered by the Spirit and preached to a large crowd. "God has made this Jesus," Peter said, "whom you crucified, both Lord and Christ" (Acts 2:36). Convicted by the Holy Spirit of their terrible crime, the people cried out to Peter and the other apostles, "Brothers, what shall we do?" (verse 37). Peter told them to repent and be baptized—and thousands were added to the church that day. By preaching the gospel, Peter opened the way into the kingdom of heaven.

Fourth, Peter was the first to preach the gospel to the Gentiles, thereby opening for them the way into the kingdom of heaven (Acts

10–11). The same "keys" that let the Jews in also let the Gentiles in. Recalling this event Peter says, "God made a choice among you that the Gentiles might hear from my lips the message of the gospel and believe" (Acts 15:7). He had been given authority from Jesus to proclaim the gospel, thereby opening the kingdom of heaven.

Binding and Loosing

After giving Peter the keys to the kingdom of heaven, Jesus told him, "Whatever you bind on earth will be bound in heaven, and whatever you loose on earth will be loosed in heaven" (Matthew 16:19). On this subject the Catholic Catechism has this to say:

> In imparting to his apostles his power to forgive sins the Lord also gives them the authority to reconcile sinners with the Church. This ecclesial dimension of their task is expressed most notably in Christ's solemn words to Simon Peter: "I will give you the keys of the kingdom of heaven, and whatever you bind on earth shall be bound in heaven, and whatever you loose on earth shall be loosed in heaven." The office of binding and loosing which was given to Peter was also assigned to the college of the apostles united to its head. [1444]

> The words bind and loose mean: whomever you exclude from your communion will be excluded from communion with God; whomever you receive anew into your communion, God will welcome back into his. Reconciliation with the church is inseparable from reconciliation with God. [1445]

Injustice is done to Jesus' words by ignoring the context and concluding that Jesus gave Peter supreme authority over the entire church. Such a conclusion is incorrect. The authority to bind and loose must be considered in the light of what the rest of God's Word says. Therefore, we will proceed with that time-honored practice of comparing scripture with scripture.

What Jesus said to Peter about binding and loosing was also to the other disciples on another occasion. There, Jesus was giving instructions for dealing with sin that fractures the fellowship of believers. The person who sinned and caused the problem was to be confronted privately, and if he didn't repent, then witnesses were to be brought. If that failed, then the matter was to be brought before the church. If the offender still refused to repent, then the church was to exclude him from the fellowship. Jesus then concluded, "I tell you the truth, whatever you bind on earth will be bound in heaven, and whatever you loose on earth will be loosed in heaven" (Matthew 18:18). Notice that the church is doing on earth what the Lord has *already* done in heaven. The will of God is being carried out through the church. The person's impenitent heart has been recognized by the church, and, in removing him from the fellowship, their decision is binding.

Let's look at how the church in Corinth implemented the teaching of Jesus regarding binding and loosing. Within the fellowship a grossly immoral situation was allowed to exist—a man was having an affair with his stepmother. Upon hearing this, Paul immediately instructed the church to deal with the problem. He said, "When you are assembled in the name of our Lord Jesus and I am with you in spirit, and the power of our Lord Jesus is present, hand this man over to Satan, so that the sinful nature may be destroyed and his spirit saved on the day of the Lord.... Expel the wicked man from among you" (1 Corinthians 5:4-5,13). When the church removed the man from the fellowship of the church, they were doing in Corinth what God had already done in heaven. The church had bound the impenitent man. Should he repent, then the church was to accept him back into the fellowship. Their acceptance of him was the church's way of showing their belief that God had forgiven him or that God had loosed him from his sin.

Binding and loosing is understood in this context as forgiving and retaining sins; this squares perfectly with the Lord's words to his disciples before ascending to heaven. "As the Father has sent me, I am sending you.... Receive the Holy Spirit. If you forgive anyone his sins, they are forgiven; if you do not forgive them, they are not forgiven" (John 20:21-23). Binding and loosing is the same as retaining and forgiving sin, and it starts with Jesus himself. The gospel message declares, "In him we have redemption through his blood, the forgiveness of sins..." (Ephesians 1:7). And John said that Jesus "loves us and has freed [the word means to loose] us from our sins by his blood" (Revelation 1:5). The forgiveness of sins was not at the personal discretion of any of the apostles.

Feed My Sheep

The fish weren't biting that night, and the disciples caught nothing (John 21:3). But things were about to change. Instructions from a stranger on the shore brought a catch so great that "they were unable to haul the net in because of the large number of fish" (verse 6). Arriving on the shore, the disciples "saw a fire of burning coals there with fish on it, and some bread" (verse 9). "Come and have breakfast," Jesus said. And when they had finished eating, Jesus said to Peter, "Simon, son of John, do you truly love me more than these?" And without a moment's hesitation Peter replied, "Yes, Lord...you know that I love you." Jesus then commissioned him, "Feed my lambs." Jesus asked the same question again and received the same reply, then said, "Take care of my sheep." This happened again a third time, after which Jesus said, "Feed my sheep" (John 21:15-17).

What purpose did Jesus have for this threefold interrogation and threefold commission? The incident provides an insight into the compassion of Jesus. Peter cannot have been feeling too good about himself. His ego was shattered, his self-confidence was low, and he knew that in spite of his earlier declaration that he would never deny the Lord, he had in fact denied him three times. Whatever flaws the other apostles possessed, none of them had denied the Lord as Peter had. His denial was common knowledge. And Jesus used this incident to give Peter the opportunity to make a public affirmation of his love for the Lord, and Jesus affirmed Peter's appointment to ministry three times.

The Roman Catholic Church claims that "Jesus entrusted a specific authority to Peter…Jesus the Good Shepherd, confirmed this mandate after his resurrection: 'Feed my sheep'…The sole Church of Christ [is that] which our Saviour, after his resurrection, entrusted to Peter's pastoral care…" [551, 816]. This interpretation is out of harmony with the Scriptures. The Roman Catholic Church is reading something into this incident that is not there. Peter was never entrusted with the task of teaching the whole church.

Again, let's examine Scripture as a whole. Before his crucifixion, Jesus told the apostles that upon his return to the Father he would send the Holy Spirit. The Spirit would do three things for them: He would 1) "teach you all things," 2) "remind you of everything I have said," and 3) "guide you into all truth" (John 14:26; 16:13). This leaves no room for Peter to be the supreme authority responsible for teaching the church. Jesus would not have made these statements about the Holy Spirit if he had entrusted to Peter all that the Roman Catholic Church claims.

In addition, the apostle Paul was adamant in stating that his teachings were not given to him by any man, including Peter. What Paul taught was given to him by way of revelation from Jesus Christ. "I want you to know, brothers, that the gospel I preached is not something that man made up. I did not receive it from any man, nor was I taught it; rather, I received it by revelation from Jesus Christ" (Galatians 1:11-12). Paul was one of Jesus' sheep. Who fed him? It wasn't Peter. And all the churches Paul established throughout the Gentile world received their spiritual feeding from Paul, not Peter. In his letter to the church at Ephesus, Paul said that God's plan to save both the Jews and Gentiles in one body, the church, was a mystery that God made known by the Holy Spirit—it was "revealed by the Spirit to God's holy apostles and prophets" (Ephesians 3:5).

Speaking to the leaders of the church in Ephesus, Paul said, "Keep watch over yourselves and all the flock of which the Holy Spirit has made you overseers. Be shepherds of the church of God, which he bought with his own blood" (Acts 20:28). How were these leaders to feed the flock? By teaching the flock what the Spirit had revealed to all the apostles. Peter endorsed this when he said, "To the elders [bishops/pastors] among you, I appeal as a fellow elder.... Be shepherds of God's flock that is under your care, serving as overseers...being examples to the flock" (1 Peter 5:1-3). Peter saw himself as a *fellow* elder with all the other elders who serve in local congregations. Peter made very clear how he understood his role, and it bears no resemblance to the one imposed upon him by the Roman Catholic Church.

Briefly, Peter denied the Lord three times, affirmed his love for the Lord three times, and had his apostolic ministry confirmed three times. To say more than that is to say more than God intended.

Head of the Church

The management structure of most companies resembles a pyramid: there is the chairman at the top, a board of directors, then managing directors, then heads of departments, and so on. That's fine for a company, but the church that Jesus established is not structured along such lines. A search of the Scriptures does not reveal the smallest hint that Peter was appointed head of the church and that provision was made for him to have successors. It simply is not there. If Peter had been made head of the church, we would expect to find ample evidence of it. Two letters that Peter himself wrote do not support the claim that he was the first pope. The extensive writings of Paul, 13 letters in total, and five letters by the beloved apostle John offer no evidence to support the Roman Catholic teaching on this matter.

What we do find in the Scriptures is the church portrayed 1) as a flock of sheep being led by Jesus the Good Shepherd, 2) as a kingdom loyal to Jesus its King, 3) as a bride faithful to her husband, Jesus, and 4) as a body composed of many members connected to Jesus, the head (John 10:16; Ephesians 1:22-23; Revelation 19:16; 21:2). Paul stated very clearly who was appointed the head of the church: "God placed all things under his [Jesus] feet and appointed him to be head over everything for the church, which is his body, the fullness of him who fills everything in every way" (Ephesians 1:22). Surely that has to settle any dispute on the matter.

WHO TEACHES THE CHURCH?

The Roman Catholic Church teaches that Peter and his successors are the head of the church on earth, and that through that office the church is taught. That's the claim, but is it supported by Scripture? Those of us who accept the Bible as our only authority reject this claim. Just because Jesus is in heaven doesn't mean we have been left with no guidance or direction. It is inconceivable to think that Jesus would become a man, die upon the cross, purchase the church with his blood, then return to heaven and leave his children as orphans. The ascended Christ made ample provision for his church to be sustained here on earth and this is the point Paul makes in Ephesians

4:7-16. He said that when Christ returned to heaven, to the church he "gave gifts to men" (verse 8). What are these gifts, and what purpose do they serve? "It was he who gave some to be apostles, some to be prophets, some to be evangelists, and some to be pastors and teachers" (verse 11). The apostles and prophets play a unique role in the life of the church. Their ministry is unrepeatable because it was through them and them alone that the full will of God was made known. The Holy Spirit guided and taught them all that Jesus had said. The truth revealed to them and proclaimed by them is the foundation upon which the church is built. We, the church, are "God's people and members of God's household, built on the foundation of the apostles and prophets, with Christ Jesus himself as the chief cornerstone" (Ephesians 2:19-20). And in succeeding generations the church continues to be built in this way.

As for evangelists, they proclaim the gospel. They are often pioneers who take the gospel to places where Christ is unknown. They are involved in planting churches, training church leaders, and where necessary, resolving difficulties in the local church (1 Corinthians 4:16-17; 16:10; Titus 1:5). Timothy engaged in such service; hence Paul's exhortation to him to "do the work of an evangelist" (2 Timothy 4:5).

The Lord has also given pastors/teachers as gifts to the church. Pastors care for the members of a congregation, teach them, guide them, lead them in God's ways, and protect them from "wolves" who seek to devour them. Pastors are the shepherds of the local congregations, and Jesus is their Chief Shepherd (1 Peter 5:1-4). The church is told that pastors "keep watch over you as men who must give an account" (Hebrews 13:17). We see Paul giving the same instruction to the pastors at Ephesus: "Keep watch over yourselves," he says, "and all the flock of which the Holy Spirit has made you overseers. Be shepherds of [that is, feed] the church of God"

(Acts 20:28). These responsibilities, of course, are endowed by God himself.

One work of pastors is to equip the people through biblical instruction so that the church "will no longer be [made up of] infants, tossed back and forth by the waves, and blown here and there by every wind of teaching" (Ephesians 4:14). The church always needs to be protected from false doctrines, which can create havoc if they get a foothold in the church. It is the responsibility of the pastors to refute such error and keep the flock safe. Error is refuted by the truth found in God's Word. This was true in the days of the apostles, and it is true today. And to ensure that the church he established is nourished, the Lord continues to give gifts in the form of evangelists, pastors, and teachers who proclaim the Word made known by the apostles and prophets.

ERRONEOUS TEACHINGS
ABOUT CHURCH LEADERSHIP

The Error Regarding Papal Infallibility

In June 1989, events in China dominated the world news. Students took to the streets demanding changes in the government. Their hopes were short-lived, for troops and tanks moved in and indiscriminately massacred innocent people. Military courts tried and executed dozens whom Western reporters said were used as scapegoats. The international community was outraged and protested to the Chinese government. The official line fed to a nation that makes up a quarter of the world's population was that only a few people were killed, mainly soldiers. The facts about June 1989 were distorted, and sadly, when people do not know the facts, they are liable to believe just about anything.

Most Catholics are not familiar with the history of their Church. I certainly wasn't. I knew the Church had some dark spots in its history, but there were many so-called facts I had never taken the time to investigate. For example, I thought that papal infallibility had always been a part of the Roman Catholic Church and that it had been securely in place from the time of the apostles. No Catholic today can remember a time when papal infallibility did not exist, so it is automatically assumed that it has always existed. But that's not the case.

The Roman Catholic Church defines infallibility thus: It is

> this Magisterium's [the Church] task to preserve God's people from deviations and defections and to guarantee them the objective possibility of professing the true faith without error.... To fulfill this service, Christ endowed the Church's shepherds with the charism of infallibility in matters of faith and morals.... When the Church through her supreme Magisterium proposes a doctrine "for belief as being divinely revealed," and as the teaching of Christ, the definition, "must be adhered to with the obedience of faith" [890-891].

The Roman Catholic Church maintains that infallibility is necessary in order to keep the truth from being corrupted. It claims that the basis for infallibility is implied in such scriptures as, "You are Peter, and on this rock I will build my church.... Whatever you loose on earth will be loosed in heaven" (Matthew 16:18-19), and, "Feed my sheep" (John 21:17). But as we saw earlier, those passages lend no support to the Roman Catholic position that Peter was appointed the head of the church. One cannot get papal infallibility from those verses, so the Roman Catholic Church has read infallibility into them. The doctrine of infallibility has been imported into Scripture; it certainly did not come out of Scripture.

Far from providing the Roman Catholic Church with a safeguard against error, papal infallibility is a source of embarrassment to those who make a serious investigation of the subject. For example, in 1950, the doctrine of the Assumption of Mary was declared to be an infallible statement. This, according to Pope Pius XII, was "a divinely revealed dogma." (In chapter 12, I will explain how this dogma contradicts God's Word.) Pope Pius IX defined the Immaculate Conception of Mary in an *ex cathedra* pronouncement on December 8, 1854. This was a new doctrine and contradicts the message of Scripture, and a noted group of scholars and Church fathers, including Pope Gregory the Great, are on record as having opposed such a doctrine. Controversy over this issue continued to surround Pius IX. Then in 1870 he issued another *ex cathedra* pronouncement in which he defined papal infallibility. Not only did this new teaching have historical evidence and Scripture stacked against it, but also, there was a time when the Roman Catholic Church did not accept papal infallibility as it is known today. While doing research on this subject, I obtained a copy of Stephen Keenan's *Controversial Catechism,* a Catholic book published in 1860. Consider what it said:

> **Q.** Must not Catholics believe the Pope in himself to be infallible?
> **A.** This is a Protestant invention; it is no article of the Catholic faith; no decision of his can oblige, under pain of heresy, unless it be received and enforced by the teaching body; that is, by the bishops of the Church.[3]

In 1837 Bishop Purcell defended the teachings of the Roman Catholic Church in a public debate. His remarks about infallibility are pertinent, since they were made many years before infallibility was claimed and defined by the Church:

> Appeals were lodged before the bishop of Rome, though he was not believed to be infallible. Neither is he now. No enlightened Catholic holds the Pope's infallibility

to be an article of faith. I do not; and none of my brethren, that I know of, do. The Catholic believes the Pope, as a man, to be liable to error as almost any other man in the universe. Man is man, and no man is infallible, either in doctrine or morals.[4]

Later, Bishop Purcell changed his view. Upon returning from the Vatican Council in 1870 he preached a sermon in which he said, "I am here to proclaim my belief in the infallibility of the Pope, in the words of the Holy Father defining the doctrine."[5]

Many Roman Catholics, unfortunately, know very little or nothing about these developments. They believe that doctrines about matters such as papal infallibility can be traced back to the time of the apostles.

The Error About Apostolic Succession

Is there an unbroken chain of apostolic succession that can be traced from the current pope all the way back to Peter? This is what the Roman Catholic Church teaches—that its bishops are successors to the apostles:

> Q. 16 What are the bishops of the Catholic Church?
> A. They are successors to the apostles.[6]

> But in order to keep the gospel forever whole and alive within the Church, the apostles left bishops as their successors, "handing over their own teaching role" to them.[7]

> The Lord made St. Peter the visible foundation of his Church. He entrusted the keys of the Church to him. The bishop of the Church of Rome, successor to St. Peter, is "head of the college of bishops, the Vicar of Christ and Pastor of the universal Church on earth" [936].

While the Roman Catholic Church asserts that its bishops are the successors to the apostles, not a single verse of Scripture is given to support that claim. The apostles never appointed successors to take their place; neither did they leave provision for that to occur after they died. Both Peter and Paul, as they came to the close of their life on earth, never mentioned appointing successors. Neither did Jesus make provision for successors to his apostles, yet the Roman Catholic Church says that Jesus made such provision. If he did, then where is the evidence?

There are at least four reasons apostolic succession, as taught by the Roman Catholic Church, is not possible:

1. The apostles were eyewitnesses to the ministry of Jesus; they were with him from the beginning until he ascended to heaven. Theirs was a unique and unrepeatable ministry. It was not possible for the apostles to appoint others to be successors to what they themselves had experienced (Luke 24:48; John 15:27; Acts 1:8). For example, in a court of law, testimony will not be admitted if it was told to you by someone else. When Matthias was chosen to replace Judas, who had hanged himself, the apostles said that Matthias had to have "been with us the whole time the Lord Jesus went in and out among us, beginning from John's baptism to the time when Jesus was taken up from us. For one of these must become a witness with us of his resurrection" (Acts 1:21-22). The one to succeed Judas had to have been an eyewitness; he had to have firsthand experience of the Lord's ministry. Anyone claiming to be a successor to the apostles would have to have been an eyewitness of Jesus' ministry and resurrection.

2. The apostolic ministry is unique in that the truth revealed to the apostles by the Holy Spirit provides the foundation upon which the church is built, not only in the first generation, but for all future generations (Ephesians 2:20). Once the foundation of the church was laid through the apostolic office, the need for that office to continue in succeeding generations ceased.

3. God made his full will known through the apostles. Jesus promised

them that he would send the Holy Spirit to empower them for ministry, and said that the Spirit would guide, teach, and recall to their minds all that he had said (John 14:26; 16:13). Through the apostles, God's mystery of saving people in one body, the church, was made known (Ephesians 3:4-6). Jesus gave to the apostles the words the Father had given him (John 17:8). And Jesus prayed "for those [in every generation] who will believe in me through their message" (John 17:20). What was made known through the apostles and then recorded in Scripture was sufficient for people in every generation to be saved. Their ministry was unique and complete.

4. After choosing his disciples, Jesus empowered them and sent them on their first "missionary" journey: "He called his twelve disciples and gave them authority to drive out evil spirits and to heal every disease and sickness" (Matthew 10:1) The miracles, signs, and wonders served as credentials for the apostles, verifying that what they were teaching was indeed the word of God. As their ministry got under way, "The apostles performed many miraculous signs and wonders among the people" (Acts 5:12). And Paul's special ministry to the Gentiles was accompanied by an outpouring of divine power: "God did extraordinary miracles through Paul, so that even handkerchiefs and aprons that had touched him were taken to the sick, and their illnesses were cured and the evil spirits left them" (Acts 19:11-12). And when he had to defend his apostolic position Paul appealed to his miracles: "The things that mark an apostle—signs, wonders and miracles—were done among you with great perseverance" (2 Corinthians 12:12).

In summary, then, the apostles 1) were personally chosen by the Lord, 2) were with him during his ministry and were witnesses to his resurrection, 3) the vessels through which the will of God was revealed, 4) were able to affirm their authority by miracles, signs, and wonders, 5) dispensed teaching that is authoritative and is binding upon us today, 6) and were unique, thus, successors can never be appointed to replace them.

THE TRUTH ABOUT THE APOSTLES

There are several passages in Scripture that refute the Roman Catholic teachings on Peter being the head of the church and on the whole matter of apostolic succession.

1. When Jesus called Peter, he left everything and followed the Lord. Catholics are incorrect when they say this means Peter left his wife. Peter remained a married man throughout his life (Luke 4:38; 1 Corinthians 9:5).

2. Was Peter ever in Rome? There is no suggestion in Scripture that he was ever there. When Paul wrote his epistle to the church at Rome, he sent personal greetings to 27 people, but never mentioned Peter (Romans 16:1-23).

3. The argument is sometimes made that when Jesus changed Peter's name it was because he was giving him a special position. No great significance can be placed on this argument, since Jesus also changed the names of other apostles (Mark 3:16-17; cf. John 1:42).

4. Because Peter's name appears first when the apostles are listed, the Catholic Church believes primacy was bestowed to Peter. However, the lists in the various Gospel accounts are not identical. Obviously the writers of the Gospels did not place any great significance on the order in which the names appeared (Matthew 10:2-4; Mark 3:16-19; Luke 6:13-16; Acts 1:13).

5. Paul speaks about those who were regarded as "pillars" of the church. He names—in this order—James, Peter, and John (Galatians 2:9). Paul's statement shows that he never recognized Peter as standing above any of the other apostles. Peter was one of a number of leaders in the church, not the Vicar of Christ.

6. The fruitful ministry of the apostle Paul was conducted independently of Peter. Paul worked primarily with the Gentiles, while Peter worked with the Jews. Over a period of 17 years, Paul spent only 15 days in Peter's company. Yet Paul insists that the Lord who worked effectually in Peter's ministry worked in the very same way

in his own ministry. Everything the Lord was doing for Peter he was also doing for Paul (Galatians 2:1,7-9). Paul even wrote, "Besides everything else, I face daily the pressure of my concern for all the churches" (2 Corinthians 11:28). Yet Paul never claimed to be the head of the church, and his statements show that neither did he recognize Peter in the role given him by the Roman Catholic Church. None of the apostles did.

7. The New Testament lists the various offices in the church, yet not once is the papal office mentioned. (Neither is there mention of archbishops or cardinals, the princes of the church—see 1 Corinthians 12:28-30; Ephesians 4:11-16). The absence of any reference to the papal office is because it never existed. It didn't appear until centuries after Jesus established his church.

8. The early church had to deal with legalism, the strict adherence to law-keeping for salvation. Legalism was an attack upon the sufficiency of the sacrifice of Jesus Christ, and when the early church met to resolve this problem, it was not Peter who made the final decision about what to do. In fact, he was the fourth from last to speak, followed by Paul and Barnabas. And it was James who drew the meeting to its conclusion. The apostolic group did not defer to Peter (Acts 15:6-23).

9. On one occasion the apostle Paul had to rebuke Peter because he stood condemned by his own actions. Peter had withdrawn himself from Gentile Christians, thereby undermining the gospel. In plain terms, Paul called Peter's behavior "hypocrisy" (Galatians 2:11-14).

10. The apostolic leaders of the church in Jerusalem, upon hearing of the conversion of the Samaritans, "sent Peter and John to them" (Acts 8:14). It is obvious that they did not see Peter as the head of the church.

11. After Peter preached the gospel to the Gentiles, upon his return to Jerusalem he was confronted by the leaders of the church for doing this (Acts 11:1-18). Since they challenged Peter in this way, we can see that they did not see Peter as the infallible head of the church. And Paul speaks of the apostles James, Peter, and John in a manner

that shows he never saw Peter as the head of the church: "As for those who seemed to be important—whatever they were makes no difference to me…those men added nothing to my message" (Galatians 2:6).

TRUSTING GOD'S WORD

What conclusions can we draw? 1) The apostle Peter never recognized himself as being the head of the church on earth. 2) None of the other apostles recognized Peter as the head of the church. 3) There is no mention of the papal office found in the Scriptures. 4) The emergence of the papacy did not occur until several centuries after the church had been established. 5) The apostolic ministry was unique, making it impossible (and unnecessary) to have successors. 6) "Infallible" statements from the pope have been seen to contradict the Scriptures.

There is only one sure road to travel, and that is the one established in the Scriptures. Everything in our world is changing; nothing is constant. Opinions change, views are modified, traditions are abandoned, and practices are updated, but God's Word remains firm, always trustworthy. Peter reminds those early Christians, and us, of the permanence of the living and abiding Word of God: " 'All men are like grass, and all their glory is like the flowers of the field; the grass withers and the flowers fall, but the word of the Lord stands forever.' And this is the word that was preached to you" (1 Peter 1:24-25).

QUESTIONS AND ANSWERS

Q. **Didn't Jesus say he would build his church upon Peter, the rock?**

Jesus said he would build his church "upon this rock," referring not to Peter himself, but to what Peter had said by way of revelation from the Father: "You are the Christ, the son of the living God." The context of Jesus' words, along with the testimony of the rest of Scripture, does not support the Roman Catholic interpretation that the church is built on Peter. Rather, it is built on the truth that Peter spoke: Jesus Christ, the Son of God, is its foundation.

Q. **Didn't the other apostles see Peter as their leader, the head of the church?**

That Peter was prominent in the life of the early church is undeniable, but nowhere in the writings of the apostles is there the slightest hint that they treated Peter as the head of the church, the spiritual head of God's people.

Q. **Didn't Jesus give Peter the keys to the kingdom because he had appointed him the pope?**

The second part of the question must be denied on the basis of the Scriptures: Jesus never made Peter the pope, the head of the church on earth. Jesus did give Peter the keys to the kingdom, and when Peter proclaimed the gospel to the Jews on the day of Pentecost and to the first converts from among the Gentiles, Peter, through the gospel, opened for them the way into the kingdom of heaven. The special privilege given to Peter was that he was chosen to be the first one to proclaim the gospel. This privilege did not make him the head of the church on earth.

Q. Didn't Jesus tell Peter to feed his sheep?

An unwarranted conclusion is drawn by the Roman Catholic Church by isolating Jesus' words to Peter from the rest of what Scripture says. That Jesus told Peter to feed his sheep is undeniable, but to conclude that Peter was put in charge of the whole flock on earth is not supported in Scripture. In fact, it contradicts what Scripture has to say. The care of the sheep was entrusted to *all* the apostles, not just to Peter.

Q. If Peter is not the rock, the head of the church on earth, who is?

The church is built on an unshakeable rock—Jesus Christ, the Son of the living God. The church is the body of Christ, of which Jesus is head. The church is God's flock, and Jesus is the Shepherd. From heaven the Lord guides and directs his church on earth through the Holy Spirit, who resides among the people of God.

Q. If there is no visible head of the church on earth, who then teaches the church?

Paul tells us in Ephesians 4:11-16 that the ascended Christ gives teaching gifts to the church. These teaching gifts are designed to help guide, lead, instruct, and mature the church. Today God continues to call and empower people for this work. Evangelists and pastors/teachers are called and gifted by the Lord to serve his church by building it up in the faith. We have no reason to be afraid; the Lord provides for his church.

5

The One
True Church

. . . .

Catholics, Protestants, and evangelicals all agree that Jesus came to earth to establish his church. But defining the church has been a contentious issue among them. A friend of mine had been speaking with a dear old lady and her comments caused him to wonder if they were speaking about the same thing. Finally, in an attempt to bring clarity to the conversation, he asked her to define her understanding of the blessed Trinity. She confidently replied, "Faith, hope, and charity."

People sometimes use the word *church* in a way that reveals their confusion as to its true meaning. Here are just a few examples:

"I believe in God but not in the church."

"I'm going to the church to say a few prayers."

"He never goes to church anymore."

"We have built a beautiful new church."

The Roman Catholic Church has contributed to the confusion by what it has taught; most Catholics think of the church as an institution, something that speaks on behalf of God through the Magisterium.

> The mission of the Magisterium is linked to the definitive nature of the covenant established by God with his people in Christ. It is this Magisterium's task to preserve God's people from deviation and defections and to guarantee them the objective possibility of professing the true faith without error. Thus the pastoral duty of the Magisterium is aimed at seeing to it that the people of God abide in the truth that liberates. To fulfill this service, Christ endowed the Church's shepherds with the charism of infallibility in matters of faith and morals. [890]

> The infallibility promised to the Church is also present in the body of bishops when, together with Peter's successor, they exercise the supreme Magisterium, above all in Ecumenical Council. When the Church through her supreme Magisterium proposes a doctrine "for belief as being divinely revealed," and as the teaching of Christ, the definitions "must be adhered to with the obedience of faith." [891]

While these quotes are a little technical, they do make clear how the Roman Catholic Church sees herself: The bishops are the successors to the apostles, and collectively, with the pope, their teachings on matters of faith and morals are infallible. These teachings are binding upon all the faithful. A church whose teachings are infallible is seen as necessary to ensure that error or heresy does not find its way into the Church. Once Rome has spoken, there is no further discussion.

Yet if one were to search through Scripture to seek the model of the Roman Catholic Church, it would be in vain, for it's simply not there. The church Jesus came to build bears no resemblance to the definition of the church given by the Magisterium. While they are claiming infallibility, the Bible says that only Scripture is infallible, not the church (2 Timothy 3:16-17). Furthermore, the church revealed in the Bible continuously receives gifts from the Lord in the form of evangelists, pastors, and teachers to instruct the church in what God has revealed in his infallible Word (Ephesians 4:11-16).

A correct understanding of the church Jesus came to build can be seen only by returning to the Bible and taking our definition from there. So let us begin by looking at the ministry of Jesus to see what we can learn.

WHAT IS THE CHURCH?

From the moment of his conception, Jesus' mission was tied to our spiritual recovery. An angel told Joseph that the child Mary was carrying was from the Holy Spirit. The child was to be named Jesus "because he will save his people from their sins" (Matthew 1:21). This redemptive theme was echoed during his public ministry. He said he had come "to seek and to save what was lost" and "to give his life as a ransom for many" (Luke 19:10; Matthew 20:28). The mission of Jesus involved securing forgiveness of sins through the sacrifice of himself upon the cross.

"Didn't Jesus come to build his church?" you might ask (Matthew 16:18). Yes. Is the church, then, something in addition to Christ's redemptive mission? No. The Greek word for church is *ekklesia,* which literally means "called out." Jesus would build his church by calling out a people to be his own, forgiving their sins, and reconciling them to God by his death and resurrection. When people heard Jesus saying that he would build his church, they didn't respond, "You're what?!" He didn't shock anyone when he used the word *church*. It was not a word he invented, it was a word in common usage in his day. And it is not an exclusively religious word either. The word *church* can refer to any group of people who are "called out" for a specific purpose—a trade union, a council meeting, etc. When we are talking about God's "called out" people, then, we need to understand how the word was intended to be understood.

Comparing scripture with scripture, the church emerges as a community of people whom Jesus has saved. It is not a place, it is people. For example, Paul says that Jesus bought the "church of God...with his own blood" (Acts 20:28). In Revelation 5:9 some creatures sing to Christ, saying, "With your blood you purchased men for God from every tribe and language and people and nation." On Pentecost, 3,000 people were saved and added to the company of the redeemed. What, then, is the church? The church is comprised of people whose sins have been forgiven; it is a community of redeemed people who belong to the Lord Jesus Christ. That's what the church is.

Note also that before his conversion to Jesus, Paul persecuted the church. That doesn't mean he vandalized holy buildings or attacked a religious institution. Rather, he persecuted holy people: "Saul began to destroy the church. Going from house to house, he dragged off men and women and put them in prison" (Acts 8:3). Later he recalled how "intensely [he] persecuted the church of God and tried to destroy it" (Galatians 1:13). When Paul was persecuting the church, his attack was specifically against people who were disciples of the Lord Jesus Christ. *That's* the church Jesus came to build.

More specifically, the church does not include all people, not even all religious people. The church is made up of those whose sins have been forgiven, whose faith rests in Jesus alone for salvation. This is what Jesus came to bring into existence—a redeemed people, the one true church.

CONVERTED TO CHRIST

According to the New Testament, through the preaching of the gospel, people were converted to the Lord Jesus Christ. In various towns and cities these Christians formed local churches—congregations of God's people. This was certainly the apostolic practice: "For a whole year Barnabas and Saul met with the church and taught a great number of people. The disciples were called Christians first at Antioch" (Acts 11:26). Later Paul returned to some of the congregations he had helped establish and "appointed elders for them in each church" (Acts 14:23). When he finished his missionary journey, he and his companions "gathered the church together and reported all that God had done through them" (Acts 14:27).

Though there is only one universal church over which Jesus is the head (Ephesians 1:21-22), the universal church is composed of local congregations. We read of "the churches of God" (1 Corinthians 11:16). Paul speaks of "the churches of Christ" (Romans 16:16). And those converted to the Lord in Thessalonica are simply referred to as "the church" (1 Thessalonians 1:1). The size of these congregations varied, but in general they seem to have been small enough to meet in the homes of members. Two outstanding servants of God were Priscilla and Aquila, whom Paul greeted along with "the church that meets at their house" (1 Corinthians 16:19). Greetings were also sent to "Nympha and the church in her house" (Colossians 4:15). Finally, when Peter was arrested, "the church was earnestly praying

to God for him.... Many people had gathered and were praying"
(Acts 12:5, 12).

In every case, it's clear that the church refers to God's people.
Who exactly are these people, and how did they become a part of
the church?

FOR GOD SO LOVED THE WORLD

As a Roman Catholic, I had been taught that God loved me, yet
I had a very poor grasp of what God's love really meant. While God
was real to me, he was also remote and not very approachable. The
mention of his love did not strike a responsive chord in my heart.
What contributed to my lack of understanding about God's love was
my failure to see the connection between my sins and the death of
Christ, which was the ultimate expression of the love of God. Yes,
I believed I was a sinner and that Jesus died because he loved me.
But what exactly did all this mean? These were religious terms that
did not translate well into everyday understanding. Like so many
other Catholics, I had a sentimental view of the death of Jesus; I was
moved to pity when I thought about him having to die such a cruel
death. Yet there upon the cross God was exhibiting the depth of his
love for all of us. To understand and appreciate that love, we need
to have a clear understanding of sin.

The Bible describes all of us as being lost, separated from God,
and unable to save ourselves. Ours is a hopeless condition indeed.
And there's another dilemma. How could God forgive our sins and
also see that justice was carried out? God could not simply forgive
us and ignore the fact that we had broken his holy law, which carries a severe penalty. Who would pay for our crime against God? In
his only begotten Son, Jesus Christ, the Father found the One whose
death would fully satisfy the demands of justice, thereby enabling

him to forgive our sins. This is how the apostle Paul expressed the thought:

> God presented him as a sacrifice of atonement, through faith in his blood. He did this to demonstrate his justice, because in his forbearance he had left the sins committed beforehand unpunished—he did it to demonstrate his justice at the present time, so as to be just and the one who justifies those who have faith in Jesus (Romans 3:25-26).

The cross of Christ vindicates God: It shows God to be just, in that he did what his own law demanded; he is also the one who justifies/pardons all those who have faith in Jesus. Jesus became our substitute when he took our sins upon himself: "He himself bore our sins in his body on the tree" (1 Peter 2:24). The debt incurred by our sins could be paid only by an adequate sacrifice offered on our behalf. Though two other men died along with Jesus on that Good Friday, only Jesus' death was able to cancel our debt. Peter captures the concept of Christ as our substitute and Savior in these words: "Christ died for sins once for all, the righteous for the unrighteous, to bring you to God" (1 Peter 3:18).

THE CROSS: THE POWER OF GOD

The sacrifice of Jesus is inseparable from the church Jesus came to build. The early Christians spoke exclusively of Jesus as the Savior of sinners. They never entertained the idea that a person could be right with God apart from Christ. "Salvation is found in no one else," said Peter, "for there is no other name under heaven given to men by which we must be saved" (Acts 4:12). Paul was equally adamant when he said, "I resolved to know nothing while I was with you except Jesus Christ and him crucified" (1 Corinthians 2:2).

Strange as it may seem, the cross of Christ displays neither weakness nor failure, but God's mighty power. And it was that power that purchased the church.

When I think of God's power, I think of some of the Lord's miracles. He brought the dead back to life. He restored the sight of the blind. He removed the dreaded disease of leprosy. He calmed a howling storm on the sea of Galilee. And he saved us from our lost condition, undoing the damage brought by our sins—this demanded nothing less than the power of God. "The message of the cross...is the power of God," said Paul (1 Corinthians 1:18). Elsewhere he wrote, "I am not ashamed of the gospel, because it is the power of God for the salvation of everyone who believes" (Romans 1:16).

The gospel not only tells us that God forgives our sins, but it also tells us that there is no one whom God doesn't love. God's love is seen in sacrificial action. God did more than just talk about love. According to Paul, "God demonstrates his own love for us in this: While we were still sinners, Christ died for us" (Romans 5:8). Though God was the offended party, he was the One who came in loving pursuit of each one of us, loving us unconditionally. He never asked that we show an interest in him and his ways before he would love us. He never demanded that we promise to turn over a new leaf and try a little harder. His love never laid down any conditions. The only reason any of us are in the church today is because Jesus loved us when we were outside the church. And the love we now have for God springs from the fact that he first loved us (1 John 4:19).

A Living Faith

Forgiveness is a free gift from God and cannot be earned by any deeds we do. Neither is forgiveness a reward for achieving an acceptable standard of holiness. It's common for people to think forgiveness can be earned or received as a reward, but both views are contrary to the teachings of Scripture. If we are to be part of the church Jesus came to build, we need to have a correct understanding of faith. Jesus pointed out the folly of trying to earn one's way to heaven when he told the parable of the Pharisee and the publican (Luke 18:9-14). The lesson was directed to "some who were confident of their own righteousness." Two men, Jesus said, went up to the temple to pray. The Pharisee began his prayer by parading all his good deeds before God. Pride filled his heart as he thanked God that he was not like those around him: robbers, evildoers, adulterers, or even the tax collector, whose profession was notorious for dishonesty. He continued his prayer with a reminder to God that he fasted twice each week and gave ten percent of his income to the Lord.

The publican also prayed, but in a different tone. Jesus said that he stood at a distance and would not even raise his eyes to heaven. In true repentance he said, "God, have mercy on me, a sinner." Which of these two people was forgiven? It was the publican who found favor with God, Jesus said, not the Pharisee. What was wrong with the Pharisee? After all, he believed in God, said his prayers, and lived a good life. So why was he not forgiven? Because he was trusting in the performance of his religious duties to save him. The Pharisee felt that his good deeds, which were many, would tip the scales of God's justice in his favor.

Not by Our Deeds

People today are still trying to get to heaven by their own efforts. They are trusting that their lives are good enough, that they have done enough religious duties and have lived a pretty decent life overall. They entertain the idea that God will inspect their lives and, based on how they did while on earth, either let them into heaven or banish them for eternity.

But forgiveness is not obtained on the basis of our deeds, no matter how honorable they are. Forgiveness comes from God, and we accept it by faith. As a Catholic, I believed that my good deeds contributed toward my salvation; these included various acts of charity, participating in novenas, attendance at weekly Mass, frequent confession, and other religious duties. I understood loyalty to the Church as loyalty to God, and therefore all that the Church commanded I tried to obey. I believed that all my good deeds would count for something, producing a certain amount of credit that would be taken into account on the day of judgment.

Yet an inescapable conclusion arises from this line of thinking: If we are contributors to our own salvation, then we must affirm that the death of Jesus was not only inadequate but unnecessary. The apostle Paul put it this way: "If righteousness could be gained through the law, Christ died for nothing!" (Galatians 2:21).

There are many wonderful Catholics who live their lives on a religious treadmill because of what they are taught about salvation. For years I was spiritually frustrated, weary of making new promises to God, only to fail yet again. I didn't know (because I was never taught) that forgiveness is a free, unmerited gift from God, and that there is absolutely nothing we can do to earn it or deserve it. Furthermore, this gift is not maintained by our deeds. We cannot save ourselves, nor can we keep ourselves saved. Jesus alone is the Savior.

Jesus came into the world to set us free and to give us new life, not to supply us with a new set of rules and regulations to be obeyed in order to get to heaven. The last thing any of us need is a religion based upon our performance; what we need is someone to give a perfect performance for us. Listen to how clearly the Word of

God speaks on this important subject: "It is by grace you have been saved, through faith—and this not from yourselves, it is the gift of God—not by works, so that no one can boast" (Ephesians 2:8-9).

Our response to God's offer of pardon cannot have any overtones of having earned or deserved the free gift of eternal life. For example, when you become sick, you take medicine to help you get better. If you use a syrup, then two or three times a day you pour the medicine into a spoon and drink it. When you recover, what do you credit with making you well—the medicine or the spoon? The medicine of course! You would never think of writing the spoon manufacturer to thank them for your speedy recovery. Let me state it one more time: There is nothing we can do to save ourselves; we must simply "turn to God in repentance and have faith in our Lord Jesus" (Acts 20:21).

REPENTANCE TOWARD GOD

As a Roman Catholic I understood repentance as being sorry for sin and then promising never to sin again, but that is quite different from what the Bible calls repentance. For example, suppose a person were to spend an evening consuming a large quantity of alcohol. The next morning, with head throbbing and nerves jumping, he stumbles toward the medicine cabinet vowing, "Never again. I'll never touch another drop as long as I live!" Though he may never take another drink, if he doesn't turn his life over to God, he has not truly repented before God. What he has expressed is deep remorse and regret, but that is not godly repentance.

It is very easy to turn "repentance" into yet another good deed to be performed in order to obtain forgiveness. The danger is very subtle but real: We sin, we repent, we are now back in God's favor, and our repentance is credited with having achieved that result. Once repentance takes on the overtone of a savior, we tend to have faith in our repentance, or in the performance of our religious duty. Unless that misunderstanding is corrected, a life on the religious treadmill follows quickly: We sin, we are lost, we repent, we are saved, we sin…. And so the cycle continues.

Repentance and turning to God are inseparably linked. When we repent, we make a conscious decision to turn away from sin because it offends God and to turn our life in God's direction; we determine to live in obedience to him. Godly repentance involves a change in our behavior. Scripture says, "Godly sorrow brings repentance that leads to salvation and leaves no regret, but worldly sorrow brings death" (2 Corinthians 7:10).

Zacchaeus was a wealthy tax collector who heard about Jesus' miracles and his claim to be the promised Messiah. Anxious to see Jesus, but prevented because of his short physical stature, Zacchaeus climbed a sycamore tree in order to catch a glimpse of Jesus as he passed by. When Jesus saw him in the tree he called out, "Zacchaeus, come down immediately. I must stay at your house today" (Luke 19:5). Zacchaeus came down and welcomed Jesus, and this encounter moved his heart to repentance. "Here and now," he said, "I give half of my possessions to the poor, and if I have cheated anybody out of anything, I will pay back four times the amount" (verse 8). That is godly repentance. Because of his penitent heart and obvious faith in Jesus, the Lord said to Zacchaeus, "Today salvation has come to this house" (verse 9).

Salvation comes to those who repent and have faith in Jesus. Without repentance there is no salvation. The call to repentance is a recurring theme in the Scriptures. John the Baptist insisted that his listeners "produce fruit in keeping with repentance" (Matthew 3:8). John wanted the people not only to believe in Jesus the Messiah, but to demonstrate that they had turned their lives away from sin by displaying the evidence of true repentance. Jesus commanded that "repentance and forgiveness of sins…be preached in his name to all nations, beginning at Jerusalem" (Luke 24:47). Peter told one large crowd that they were to "repent and be baptized." Later he told others, "Repent, then, and turn to God" (Acts 2:38; 3:19).

Repentance decides to change the direction of one's life and walk toward God. And because repentance involves turning to God, it cannot be separated from faith. Paul said, "I have declared to both Jews and Greeks that they must turn to God in repentance and have faith in our Lord Jesus" (Acts 20:21).

FAITH IN JESUS

Faith means to trust, to believe. Abraham is the man whose faith is held up as the model for us (Romans 4:16). Abraham's life was marked by significant demonstrations of his faith. For example, God told him to leave his home and go to a foreign land. "By faith Abraham, when called to go to a place he would later receive as his inheritance, obeyed and went, even though he did not know where he was going" (Hebrews 11:8). That's faith!

Another example is God's promise of a son to Abraham. Time passed, and the promise remained unfulfilled. Abraham was 99 years old and his wife, Sarah, was 90 when God spoke to him again about the promise of a son. Though surrounded by physical impossibilities, Abraham still had faith that what God had said would come to pass. "By faith Abraham, even though he was past age—and Sarah herself was barren—was enabled to become a father because he considered him faithful who had made the promise" (Hebrews 11:11). That's faith!

Later, God commanded Abraham to take his son Isaac and offer him as a sacrifice. Abraham responded in faith when God tested him (Hebrews 11:17), yet God never allowed Abraham to take the young man's life, though Abraham was prepared to do so. For this reason, Abraham is called "God's friend" (James 2:23). That's faith!

The type of faith that Abraham displayed is the kind of faith that

God wants us to have. When God tells us something, he wants us to believe it to be true and to respond accordingly. When he asks us to obey him, he expects obedience. Lip service is not what the Lord wants from us. Jesus asked a group of religious people, "Why do you call me, 'Lord, Lord,' and do not do what I say?" (Luke 6:46). True faith will always do what God commands.

BAPTISM: A RESPONSE TO THE CROSS

A few days after I was born, I was christened in the Roman Catholic Church. This sacrament of baptism supposedly regenerated my soul and removed the stain of original sin. By that one act I was now part of the one true Church. Not until my mid-twenties did I learn that baptism is always accompanied by faith in the sacrifice of Jesus. Having come to see what Scripture was saying, I believed in Jesus and was baptized.

This is affirmed in Acts 2, where we see Peter preaching the gospel to thousands. The people were convicted of their sin by the Holy Spirit and cried out, "Brothers, what shall we do?" Peter said to them, "Repent and be baptized, every one of you, in the name of Jesus Christ for the forgiveness of sins. And you will receive the gift of the Holy Spirit.... Those who accepted his message were baptized, and about three thousand were added to their number that day" (Acts 2:37-38,41). Those who were baptized had faith in the sacrifice that Jesus offered for the remission of their sin. They did not trust in what they were doing, but trusted in what Jesus had done for them. Their faith was not in a sacrament, but in a wonderful Savior. They trusted Christ crucified, not the church, for their forgiveness. In their baptism they were identified, by faith, with Jesus in his death, burial, and resurrection (Romans 6:1-6).

From Pentecost onward the apostles proclaimed forgiveness of sins in the name of Jesus Christ. Those who believed that message were baptized in his name. We read that when the Samaritans "believed Philip as he preached the good news of the kingdom of God and the name of Jesus Christ, they were baptized, both men and women" (Acts 8:12). "And many of the Corinthians who heard [Paul] believed and were baptized" (Acts 18:8). When the gospel was preached to the Gentiles and they came to believe in Jesus, Peter "ordered that they be baptized in the name of Jesus Christ" (Acts 10:48). When Paul taught the gospel, many believed and were "baptized into the name of the Lord Jesus" (Acts 19:5). In all these situations, the apostles were carrying out Jesus' command to go and make disciples of all people, and to baptize those who come to belief in him (see Matthew 28:18-20).

The same pattern is repeated again and again in the Bible. Those who were baptized were believers whose faith was in Jesus to save them. Infants do not have such faith. As a Catholic, when I first read this connection between faith and baptism in the Bible, it was all new to me. Yet it was clear to me that when Jesus commanded the gospel to be preached and believers to be baptized, he excluded anyone who did not have faith. The teaching of Scripture is that baptism must be accompanied by faith in the sacrifice of Christ—otherwise it is a meaningless act, an empty ritual.

In baptism we are identified with Christ in his death, burial, and resurrection. We consciously make a break from the world and its ways and commit our life to the Lord for as long as we live. In a sense, baptism is like marriage. When a couple makes their wedding vows, they commit themselves to each other for life. From that point onward they enter into a new relationship as husband and wife. Likewise, baptism marks the beginning of a new believer's relationship with the Lord.

By the way, in the Bible, baptism is depicted by a person's full immersion in water. The practice of pouring or sprinkling water on the head of the one being baptized is a departure from the biblical command. In the original Greek text of the New Testament, the word "baptize" means "immerse." Note that after Philip taught the Ethiopian, "both Philip and the eunuch went down into the water and Philip baptized him. When they came up out of the water..." (Acts 8:38-39). Jesus himself was immersed at his baptism: "As soon as Jesus was baptized, he went up out of the water" (Matthew 3:16). Obviously he had to have been in the water to come up out of it. We are right when we take our definition of baptism directly from what God has said in Scripture.

THE LIVING CHURCH

After Jesus ascended to heaven, he left the church to be his witness in the world. To ensure that the church in every generation would become mature in the faith, the risen Lord gave evangelists, pastors, and teachers to help build up the body of Christ for the work of service (Ephesians 4:11-16). When these gifted people teach the Scriptures to the people of God, it ensures that the church will be equipped to fulfill its God-ordained role in the world.

Conversion to Jesus is a supernatural occurrence and results in a radical change in the lifestyle of those converted. Some prominent distinctions of the early Christians were enjoyment in fellowship together, meeting to receive instruction in the Word of God, and time spent in prayer and praise to the Lord (Acts 2:42-47). They gathered together each Sunday to express thanks to their Savior and to remember his sacrifice by partaking of the Lord's Supper (Acts 20:7; 1 Corinthians 11:17-34).

Along with faithfulness to the Lord, the early church was marked by an extraordinary spirit of generosity. Christians sold their property and shared their possessions with those in need. "All the believers were together and had everything in common" (Acts

2:44). Even the poor shared out of their deep poverty in order to relieve the needs of those less fortunate than themselves. The explanation for their spirit of liberality is that "they gave [of] themselves first to the Lord" (2 Corinthians 8:5).

Today's church must also be marked by that spirit of generosity and must "not forget to do good and to share with others, for with such sacrifices God is pleased" (Hebrews 13:16). It is to the praise of God that generous people are still found in his church. These are the people who capture the true meaning of Jesus' words, "It is more blessed to give than to receive" (Acts 20:35). Their lives are a clear testimony that the church is alive and well and serving in this world.

The church must also be a caring community of people. There is a reason why the church is called the body of Christ. The apostle Paul argues that just as the physical body is dependent on each member to enable the body to function correctly, so the church is dependent on its members to work together as one body (1 Corinthians 12:15-26). A spirit of indifference has no place among God's people. The attitude that says "It's none of my business" is unacceptable because it is unlike Jesus' attitude. We are instructed to "remember those in prison as if you were their fellow prisoners, and those who are mistreated as if you yourselves were suffering" (Hebrews 13:3). Within the church there will be some who are strong and others who are weak and struggling. The battle of life is hard on the struggling, and they often grow discouraged and downhearted. We all know people who have had more than their share of tough breaks in life. Even for those with the strongest will in the world, continuous trials can wear them down. All of us in the body of Christ have an obligation to help such people. They are our wounded brothers and sisters, members of God's family, and we are to be their strength and hope—the arm they can lean upon, the shoulder they can cry on, and the ear that is open to hear their pain.

What attracted the worst of sinners to Jesus was his kind and compassionate spirit. They had heard him often enough to know that they had found a true friend in him. It didn't make any difference which side of the city they came from, and it didn't matter if their lives had been steeped in sin—he had time for them. Jesus came to mend their broken lives, to restore their dignity, and to give them hope. Everyone was welcome.

The goal of every congregation of God's people must be to become imitators of their Lord and Savior, ministering to the needs of all, spreading the joyful news of the gospel and worshiping God in spirit and in truth. There is life beyond the grave for the obedient because Jesus died and rose from the grave on the third day. Because Jesus lives, his church is a living body. This is the true church of the living Christ.

TRUE ALLEGIANCE TO CHRIST

I cannot close this chapter without answering a question that some might be inclined to ask me at this point: "Are you trying to *reform* the Roman Catholic Church, or are you *calling people out* of the Roman Catholic Church?"

I don't believe the Roman Catholic Church as we know it will ever be reformed along biblical lines. The structure of the Church makes this impossible. The noble attempts of men such as Luther proves that point. More importantly, Jesus said you cannot put new wine into old wineskins because old wineskins are brittle, and when new wine is poured into them, the wine ferments and the old wineskins cannot contain the new wine (Matthew 9:17). The point Jesus was making is this: The gospel that frees us from our sins cannot be contained within a legalistic religious system such as the Roman

Catholic Church. The gospel that frees us from our sins is not the gospel preached by the Roman Catholic Church. (Why do you need indulgences and purgatory if the gospel alone can save you?) Therefore, those whom the Lord calls through the gospel of his Son will see that they cannot remain in a church whose fundamental message of salvation does not harmonize with the ancient message of Christ and his apostles. And why would anyone who has been truly converted to Christ want to remain in a church whose doctrines undermine the glorious sacrifice of the Lord Jesus Christ? In making this statement it is not my intention to make people anti-Catholic but pro-Christ. Our allegiance must never be to the church, Catholic or otherwise, but to the crucified Christ.

QUESTIONS AND ANSWERS

Q. **What is the church?**

The church is comprised of a "called out" people who have put their faith in the message that Jesus died for our sins and rose again. The church is a collection of people who belong to the Lord Jesus Christ, not a building or a religious system.

Q. **Are all religious people in the church?**

No. There are many religious people who have never confessed faith in the Lord Jesus Christ and been baptized in his name as a response of faith. Granted, they are religious in that they say their prayers, do their religious duties, live decent lives, etc. Many people are in that category yet are not in the church.

Q. **Can you be saved and not be in the church?**

No. If you are saved then you are in the church, which belongs to Jesus. The Bible does not talk about the saved as if they were different or apart from the church. The saved and the church are one and the same. For Jesus to save the lost and for him to build his church are the same thing.

Q. **Can you "go to church" each Sunday and not be in the church?**

Yes. Many people attend a church service each Sunday and are not part of the church Jesus came to build. These are people who have never been converted to the Lord Jesus Christ, though they probably would not deny him. Though they may have been born into a Christian family, they themselves have not been "born again." They have not received the true grace of God that alone sets sinners free from their sins.

Q. What is the connection between the church and the death of Jesus?

The church exists because of the death of Jesus. Without his death there would be no church. He said that he came to seek and to save the lost and gave his life as a ransom. It was through his death upon the cross that he purchased the church with his blood. Through his death he redeemed a people to be his very own.

Q. Should we be looking for the church Jesus built?

Since the church is the redeemed people of God, I see no value in "looking for the true church." Sick people should be looking for a doctor, not for healthy people. Sinners should be looking for the Savior, not the saved; they should be looking for the crucified Christ, not the church.

Q. Is there only one true church?

Absolutely. And that one true church embraces "all those everywhere who call upon the name of our Lord Jesus Christ—their Lord and ours" (1 Corinthians 1:2). Every day the gospel of Jesus is being spread throughout our world and many believe and are being baptized. All these people are in the church Jesus came to build. Not one saved person is outside of his body, the church. Remember, Jesus builds his church when he saves sinners.

Q. Did Jesus establish the Roman Catholic Church?

I have no hesitation in answering no, for this reason: The structure of the Catholic Church, along with many of her doctrines, contradicts the message set forth in the Word of God. The Roman Catholic Church cannot be produced simply from Scripture; it has to rely on sources other than the Bible. Since the Word of God cannot produce the Roman Catholic Church, I conclude that it has not been established by Jesus.

6
Unity: That They May Be One

. . . .

T
he call to unity has been at the fore of Christian discussion for several decades. The Roman Catholic Church's invitation for greater cooperation between Roman Catholics and evangelicals is growing in popularity. This is being hailed as a positive move in bringing about the fulfillment of the Lord's prayer for unity in John 17. But note carefully what Jesus was praying for: "I pray also for those who will believe in me through their [the apostles'] message, that all of them may be one, Father, just as you are in me and I am in you. May they also be in us so that the world may believe that you have sent me" (verses 20-21). Can evangelical Christians be united with the Roman Catholic Church? Should evangelicals even be giving consideration to such a possibility?

The unity Jesus speaks about can exist only among those who are converted to him, those who have been redeemed by the precious blood of the Lamb. Unity between the forgiven and the unforgiven is impossible. There can be union and uniformity among religious people, but not unity as defined by Jesus. In his prayer, Jesus is praying specifically for those who have come to believe in him through the apostolic message; when that message has not been accepted, there can be no conversions to Jesus and therefore no unity. How can there be unity between the Roman Catholic Church and evangelical churches when the doctrines of the Roman Catholic Church—the teachings regarding Mass, purgatory, indulgences, baptismal regeneration—undermine the one sacrifice of Jesus that forever secured the remission of sin? There cannot be unity. I don't say that because I'm against unity, but because the facts need to be stated in the interest of truth and the gospel. The Roman Catholic Church does not teach the saving gospel as set forth in the Word of God. The gospel states that the atoning death of Jesus paid in full the penalty of all our sins, rendering us sinless before God, free of all condemnation, and assuring us that upon death we will join the Lord in heaven. Furthermore, Jesus offers that forgiveness as a gift; it cannot be earned by the performance of good and noble deeds as if they possessed "spiritual collateral."

What all this means is that forgiveness cannot be received through some power alleged to exist in a sacrament. Forgiveness is not given in exchange for obedience. The proper response to God's free offer of pardon is to believe and be baptized into him in whom salvation is found. The Roman Catholic Church, in its doctrines of the Mass and purgatory, demonstrates that it sees the sacrifice of Jesus as needing to be supplemented. The Roman Catholic Church will vigorously deny this, but their practice confirms it. The Roman Catholic teaching on this subject is not what the Bible teaches. So how could evangelicals and Roman Catholics have unity? They can't. However, evangelicals and Catholics can function together in certain joint ventures, such as collective opposition to abortion, gay marriages, pornography, and injustice. When such joint ventures take place, evangelicals are not making a statement that we are all "one in Christ."

INVISIBLE AND VISIBLE UNITY

Only God knows who is truly saved and who isn't. His church is comprised of all the redeemed, who are perfectly united together in Christ. This unity is not always visible to us, but it is to God. Church directories are not a carbon copy of the Lamb's book of life. Unity embraces all redeemed believers and no one else. They alone are the object of our Lord's prayer for unity in John 17:20-21. Jesus was praying only for those who have believed in him and responded in faith to the gospel message. The scope of the unity Jesus prayed for is seen in Paul's opening remarks in his first letter to the Corinthians: "To the church of God in Corinth, to those sanctified in Christ Jesus and called to be holy, together with all those everywhere who call on the name of our Lord Jesus Christ—their Lord and ours" (1 Corinthians 1:2). Paul addressed "the church of God at Corinth," which was composed of all the "Corinthians who...believed and were baptized" (Acts 18:8). But numbered along with the redeemed at Corinth were "all those everywhere who call upon the name of the Lord Jesus Christ" to save them from their sins. Though the redeemed people of God are a scattered people, in the eyes of God, they are perfectly united together in Christ Jesus.

The reality of what the Lord has done by making us one with the Father and himself must be reflected in the life of all God's people. The church must reflect unity to the world. When we live out the reality of that truth in our life, we witness to the world that the Father did send his Son. God's people living together in harmony send a powerful message to the world that something extraordinary must have happened to us. The explanation is that the Father sent his Son into the world to redeem us and the Son now lives among his people.

Paul's words to the believers in Ephesus throw additional light upon the subject of unity. He said, "Make every effort to keep the unity of the Spirit through the bond of peace" (Ephesians 4:3). The church is not charged with the responsibility of creating unity among the members; that is not our assignment. We are charged with maintaining the unity created by the Spirit. This is where so much of the talk about Christian unity today goes astray. People are trying to create unity, but unity can only be created by the Spirit. Our responsibility is to "make every effort" to keep that unity in the church. This is the visible unity we display to the world. Maintaining this unity is not easy, hence the instruction to "make every effort." The opposite of unity is disharmony, discord, rivalry, contention, and so on. These must not be allowed to go unchecked within the church.

The church is a mixture of people from all walks of life. We are all very different, yet in spite of our differences, there are common denominators that bind us together. We have the same Father, who has given us a new birth. We have the same Savior, who has redeemed us. And we have the same Holy Spirit, who resides in us.

Unity Misunderstood

The Roman Catholic Church looks at evangelical churches and sees widespread division. There is a church on every corner that has a different name from the one across the street. And each church has its own set of distinct beliefs and practices. Roman Catholics see this as division, and it reinforces their own belief that an infallible church is needed to ensure that such division does not occur. However, the multiplicity of churches does not necessarily prove that division exists or that Jesus' prayer for unity is going unheeded. As I have already stated, Scripture portrays the scattered people of God as perfectly united in Christ Jesus.

Unity can exist even in the midst of disagreement. For example, in the early church, it was not the common understanding among the believing Jews that the Gentiles could become fellow heirs with them in the church. The conversion of the household of Cornelius, the first Gentile, proves this. Peter had been praying when he saw a vision—a sheet being let down from heaven containing all kinds of animals. He was told, "Get up, Peter. Kill and eat" (Acts 10:13). He refused, contending that he could never eat anything that was "unclean." Meanwhile, Cornelius had received a vision in which he was told to send someone to Joppa to get Peter. Upon Peter's arrival, Cornelius told Peter about his vision, and Peter began to tell Cornelius about Jesus. While they were talking, the Holy Spirit came upon them all, just as on Pentecost in Acts chapter 2. Convinced that God had accepted the Gentiles, Peter commanded that they be baptized (verse 48). Upon his return to Jerusalem, Peter was severely criticized for having gone to the Gentiles. But when he explained what had happened, the Jewish believers "had no further objections and praised God" (Acts 11:18).

Was there unity among the apostles and elders of the church in Jerusalem? Yes, in the sense that they were perfectly united together in Christ. But they were poles apart on their understanding that the Gentiles were to be accepted into the body of Christ. The Jewish believers didn't change their position until after Peter's explanation. This point needs to be emphasized for Catholics: There can be unity (among redeemed people) even when there are differences of understanding on some issues, and that is what we see among some of the evangelical churches today. The differences are not on what we would call "the essentials." Not every doctrine is of equal importance, says the apostle Paul: "For what I received I passed on to you as of first importance: that Christ died for our sins according to the Scriptures, that he was buried, that he was raised on the third day according to the Scriptures" (1Corinthains 15:3-4).

When there is agreement among evangelicals on matters that are of "first importance," namely the atoning death of the Lord Jesus Christ, his burial and victory over death, and our response to it, then there is agreement on the essentials. This doesn't mean that as long as you believe in the death, burial, and resurrection of Jesus, nothing else matters. That is not true. For example, the worship of Almighty God must be in accordance with his will, "in spirit and in truth" (John 4:24). The sanctity of marriage must be maintained along with the protection of the unborn child. A godly standard of living must be maintained. And through prayer, study, and discussion with each other, we can come to a better understanding on these matters. But we stand united on the essentials.

The Roman Catholic Church cannot point its finger at the "divisions" in other churches without recognizing the divisions that exist within its own ranks on some of its foundational doctrines. For example, in other chapters we have mentioned the strong disagreement within the hierarchy over infallibility and other major doctrines that set the Roman Catholic Church apart from other churches. Infallibility, when first defined in 1870, was not unanimously accepted by the bishops. It traveled a very rough road in the course of becoming an official teaching of the Church. Even today infallibility is not accepted by some leading theologians; I'm thinking specifically of Roman Catholic priest and theologian Hans Kung, whose views are contained in his book *Infallible?: An Unresolved Enquiry* (London: Continuum International Publishing Group, 1994). The writings of this man cannot be dismissed lightly.

Celibacy among the clergy is without any support in Scripture
and is openly criticized by many, including clergy. They see it as an
unjust rule. Divorce is another area where there is disagreement
among the clergy. As for birth control, which was prohibited by
Pope Paul VI, the majority of Catholics today ignore the prohibi-
tion. This is undeniable. The ordination of women to the priesthood
has definite support even though the official teaching of the Roman
Catholic Church is that only men can be candidates for the priesthood. All of this proves conclusively that the Catholic Church is not
the united Church it portrays itself to be. There is definite diver-
gence of belief on many core doctrines.

VISIBLE UNITY

Our Lord's prayer for unity in John 17 finds its fulfilment among
those whom the Lord Jesus has saved. He prayed: "that all of them
may be one" (21), "that they may be one as we are one" (22), and
"[that all may] be brought to complete unity" (23). God sees complete unity in his church. However, we don't always display the
reality of this unity. We need to make every effort to exhibit something of the wonder of what the Lord has done. And we should see
this as being possible because Jesus prayed that the unity of the
church would be like the unity existing between the Father and the
Son.

However, unity cannot be accepted at any price. The unity of
which the Bible speaks was secured by the atoning sacrifice of Jesus.
That's the price that was paid for unity. And that is why there can
be no compromising on the gospel. There will be times when we will
need to take a strong stand in defense of the gospel of Jesus Christ.
This can become difficult, especially in the current religious climate
that encourages fellowship between Roman Catholic and Protestant
and evangelical churches. The gospel is the only way of salvation

and there is nothing we can contribute toward our redemption. It's grace from beginning to end. This brings us into immediate conflict with the teachings of the Roman Catholic Church, which supplements the gospel with sacraments and works.

The refusal to compromise may result in being accused of destroying all the good ecumenical work that has been done over recent years. However, we must be prepared to let the accusations come our way and heed Paul's words to the church at Philippi. He said he wanted them to be "contending as one man for the faith of the gospel" (Philippians 1:27). Jude, in his short letter, gave this exhortation: "I felt I had to write and urge you to contend for the faith that was once for all entrusted to the saints" (Jude 3). The importance of the defense of the gospel cannot be overstated. Paul, who said that every effort must be made to keep the unity of the Spirit, was not shy in saying, "If we or an angel from heaven should preach a gospel other than the one we preached to you, let him be eternally condemned" (Galatians 1:8). It gives me no pleasure in saying this, but the Roman Catholic Church, on the basis of her teachings so clearly set forth by the Magisterium, does not preach the saving message of the cross of Christ. Granted, the Roman Catholic Church uses evangelical words: cross, death, blood, atonement, and so on. But then it contradicts the gospel with, for example, its doctrines of the Mass, purgatory, and indulgences.

Evangelicals, whether individually or as churches, can display visible unity even though they have differences over secondary issues; this is made possible because of their being united in Christ Jesus. This is not to say that we can ignore secondary issues. We need to spend a lifetime learning God's will more fully through open dialogue, study, and prayer so that the will of God becomes fully formed in our lives. The church in Corinth failed to be an influence upon the world because of the lack of unity among the members.

The behavior in the church was a scandal to society because of the division, the petty jealousy, and the mistreatment of one another. As a result, their Christian witness was diminished.

The same is true today. All the wrong signals are being sent to the world—the very world Jesus wants us to influence by our unity—when we behave in an ungodly fashion toward one another. Unkind criticisms, unfair comments, and careless actions against fellow Christians do nothing to influence the world for Jesus. The bitterness that resides in churches due to church splits ensures that the lost will not come seeking spiritual refuge there. When churches exhibit disunity it is because they have not heeded the instruction of the Lord Jesus Christ or his apostles. Paul was forever instructing the churches to live united. "I urge you," he said, "to live a life worthy of the calling you have received" (Ephesians 4:1). "Whatever happens," he wrote to the saints at Philippi, "conduct yourselves in a manner worthy of the gospel of Christ" (Philippians 1:27).

There will always be differences of opinion and understanding among the people of God as we continue to learn more about God and his will. But what makes us one in Christ is not our agreement on everything, but our adoption as sons and daughters into the Lord's family, all made possible because of what Jesus did on the cross. That is why we must not exclude anyone whom the Lord includes, even those with whom we disagree on secondary issues. If God is pleased to extend fellowship to them then so should we.

But how are we to handle the differences that are among us? We will go a long way toward resolving our doctrinal differences if we become a more prayerful and humble people. None of us is right about everything. Jesus is the only one who taught perfect theology, and the rest of us are struggling pilgrims on this journey. When there is disagreement, we must not circulate rumors that question the sincerity or honesty of those with whom we disagree. Neither must we brand them with unkind labels simply because we differ with them. There are areas where all of us will feel outside our comfort zone. We may not be able to get involved in some churches because of this. But what we must do is affirm that we are brothers and sisters in Christ. Our differences must not allow us to behave as if we were not brothers and sisters in Christ. If that happens, we will lose our opportunity to be a good witness to this unbelieving world.

The disunity sometimes found among evangelical churches is not because we are divided on the essentials of the faith, but because we have not loved each other as we ought. Genuine unity, even among those who have differences, can be displayed if we take to heart the words of Paul: "Let the peace of Christ rule in your hearts, since as members of one body you are called to peace" (Colossians 3:15). The word "rule" gives us our English word *umpire*. Peace is the umpire in our life because we are "members of one body," the church.

ONE IN CHRIST JESUS

I believe in one, holy, catholic, and apostolic church. The church is one in that it embraces all those who have been justified by faith in Christ Jesus. It is a community united in Christ Jesus. It is holy because the redeemed people of God are holy as God is holy. It is catholic in that it is universal and not regional. Its gospel message is for every nation. And it is apostolic in that it is based upon the foundation of the apostles' teachings. Only churches that preach the true gospel are the spiritual heirs to this ancient creed.

QUESTIONS AND ANSWERS

Q. How would you define the unity Jesus prayed for?

On his last night with his disciples, Jesus prayed for the unity of all his people throughout the ages. This unity is to reflect the unity that exists between the Father and the Son. In Christ, we are all perfectly united in his body, the church. The reality of this must then be displayed in our behavior as we interact one with another. Through our loving care, support, and encouragement of each other we show to the world that we are disciples of Jesus.

Q. Can we create this unity?

No. The unity of which Jesus speaks cannot be created by human effort. Unity exists because of the redemptive work of the Lord in our lives. The apostle Paul does not tell us to create unity, but rather to "maintain the unity of the Spirit in the bond of peace." In other words, maintain that which the Spirit has already created.

Q. Is there unity among the many different evangelical churches?

All who have been redeemed by the atoning sacrifice of Jesus Christ by being born again of water and the Spirit are unified in Christ.

Q. Were the apostles and early church united?

Yes, because they all belonged to the Lord Jesus Christ. However, that is not to say there was agreement on everything. Besides, unity is not based upon everyone agreeing on every single issue. If that were the case, no two people could ever be united because no two people see everything the same. Where disagreement exists, differences must be resolved in a manner that honors the Lord and with reference to his Word. Respect, love, and patience are essential when Christians are endeavoring to resolve their differences.

Q. Can there be unity between evangelical churches and the Roman Catholic Church?

This is not possible since their views on authority are fundamentally different. Evangelicals hold that the Bible is the Word of God, the final authority in all matters of belief and practice. The Roman Catholic Church is emphatic in that it considers the Church to have authority in these matters. Furthermore, evangelicals hold that the one sacrifice of Jesus was sufficient to secure full pardon of all our sins, whereas this is denied by Roman Catholic teachings and practices such as the Mass, indulgence, and purgatory. So there cannot be unity between the two groups.

Q. Should Protestants and evangelical Christians not put aside their differences and join hands with the Roman Catholic Church?

Much of the hostility that once existed is almost gone, having been replaced with open dialogue and discussion. A spirit of tolerance and acceptance is now the norm. But the tough questions still have to be addressed: Where do we receive our authority from— the Bible alone, or the Roman Catholic Church? Is justification by faith, or must it be supplemented by works? These and other fundamental questions must be resolved before there can be true biblical unity.

7

Made Right
with God

. . . .

I was a very contented Roman Catholic. I believed I was in the
church Jesus had come to build. I believed the full expression
of Jesus' will was contained in the Roman Catholic Church,
so there was no need to look further than the Church in pursuit of
truth. Seeking truth in other churches was unthinkable—after all,
they were apostate churches that had broken away from the Roman
Catholic Church. What they needed to do was return to Rome. The
priests in these apostate churches were not validly ordained because
the Roman Catholic Church had not laid hands upon them. I was
taught that all those who were not Roman Catholics needed to join
us; only then would they be right.

I have always been struck by the similarities that exist between the Jews of Jesus' days and the Roman Catholic Church. The Jews were God's chosen people and were raised up by God for the purpose of bring the Savior into the world, but they read more into their claim than was warranted. They had the attitude that they alone were right and everyone else was wrong. True, God had blessed them as he had no other nation. "You only," God said, "have I chosen of all the families of the earth" (Amos 3:2). He promised them the Messiah and gave them the covenants and the prophets. The Jews wrongly concluded that because of God's gracious dealings with them their special status automatically made them right with God.

This "we are right" attitude flourished in the days of Jesus. For example, the Jews claimed "Abraham is our father" (John 8:39), implying that because God made promises to Abraham and they were his descendents, they automatically qualified to inherit those promises. While Jesus never denied that the Jews were Abraham's physical descendants, he strenuously denied that they were Abraham's spiritual heirs, for they did not possess the same faith as their illustrious ancestor (John 8:36-47).

In his discourse with the Jewish leader Nicodemus, Jesus exposed the Jews' false sense of security when he told Nicodemus that he needed to be born again. Physical connection to Abraham was insufficient to secure a place in heaven. Nicodemus needed a second birth—not another physical birth, but a spiritual birth given by the Father (John 3:1-7). Being born into a race of people known as "the chosen people" would never make a person a son of God. Similarly, being christened into the Roman Catholic Church by the sacrament of baptism, no matter how sincere one's parents are, will have no effect upon one's eternal destiny. No one can be right with God without having a personal relationship with God. One must choose to follow the Lord, to place faith in him. This is a conscious decision all must make. Sacraments can't make us right with God, and the Roman Catholic Church can't make us right. Only God can make us right with himself. For years I believed I was right with God because I was in the Roman Catholic Church, but salvation is by choice, not by circumstance.

LIVING IN ERROR

Let's look in the Bible at three examples of people who sincerely thought they were right with God when, in fact, they were not. These examples will help Roman Catholics to see some of the same errors that reside in their teachings.

The Rich Young Ruler

The rich young ruler's encounter with Jesus illustrates how many Roman Catholics think. Whether or not he realized it, the young man had asked Jesus the most important question anyone can ever ask: "What must I do to inherit eternal life?" (Luke 18:18). Not only did he ask an important question, he also asked the only One who could give him the correct answer. Jesus told him that he needed to keep the commandments, to which the man confidently replied: "All these I have kept since I was a boy" (verse 21). Jesus told him that he lacked one thing: "Sell everything you have and give to the poor, and you will have treasure in heaven. Then come, follow me" (verse 22). The instruction was not received with joy: "When he heard this, he became very sad, because he was a man of great wealth" (verse 23). Jesus had exposed a key barrier to faith: This inquirer was involved in a love affair with a god called money, and he was not prepared to discontinue the affair. Yet he could confidently say that he kept all the commandments: "Do not commit adultery, do not murder, do not steal, do not give false testimony, honor your father and mother" (Luke 18:20). Granted, he was a man who kept all the *externals* of the law of God. He had never committed the physical act of adultery, or strangled the life out of another human being. As far as observing the *externals* of the law of God, he was blameless. But beneath the pious exterior a sinful heart resided.

Similarly, as a Catholic, I once lived (for a time) a blameless life. I conformed to what the Church required in the belief that I was doing the will of God. I went to confession, received Holy Communion, observed the regulations of Lent, and believed all the teachings of the Church. I believed that I was right with God because I was faithfully doing my religious duty. Even today I hear appeals being made by the Church urging lapsed Catholics to return to Mass. Religious duty seems to be the yardstick by which faithfulness to God is measured.

The rich young ruler in Luke 18 was a good, moral, upright man. He was religious and was confident he was right with God. But he didn't have a heart committed to God alone, a heart that had no room for anything but God. The tragedy for him, and for many religious people, is that he went through the external rituals of religion. He resembled those of whom Jesus said, "These people honor me with their lips, but their hearts are far from me" (Matthew 15:8). Many Catholics are in the same category, believing that faithfulness to the Church makes them right with God.

The Pharisee and Tax Collector

Luke 18:9 tells us, "To some who were confident of their own righteousness and looked down on everyone else, Jesus told this parable." This parable highlights the futility of an external religion, a religion that relies upon compliance to rules and regulations. The parable revolves around two men, one a self-righteous Pharisee and the other a tax collector. The Pharisee went to the temple to pray

and paraded before God all his good deeds. He recounted his strict
adherence to the details of the law. He fasted twice a week (that
puts me to shame), something the law did not require, and he gave
a tenth of his possessions. He was also a prayerful man. On the
moral side of the ledger, he declared that he was grateful not to be
like other people and proceeded to identify them: robbers, evildoers, and adulterers, and he was especially pleased that he was not
like the tax collector. Then Jesus turned to the prayer offered by the
tax collector, who "stood at a distance. He would not even look up
to heaven, but beat his breast and said, 'God, have mercy on me, a
sinner'" (verse 13). Right away we can see a difference between the
two men. The tax collector knew he deserved nothing from God,
he could not negotiate a settlement with God, he could not trade in
his good works and religious duties in exchange for forgiveness. All
he could do was acknowledge the truth about himself before God
and throw himself upon God's divine mercy. Did the tax collector
have any commendable qualities he could have spoken about? I'm
sure he did, but they were overshadowed by the fact that he was a
sinner unable to save himself. He knew he needed God to deal graciously with him.

It is interesting to see how Jesus concluded the parable. He said
it was the tax collector, not the Pharisee, who went home justified,
forgiven, pardoned of sin. Why was the Pharisee not pardoned?
After all, he was a good, moral, upright man who fulfilled his religious duties. Wherein lay his problem? The Pharisee was trusting
in his own personal goodness to save him. He believed that all his
good works, his obedience to duty, would tip the scales in his favor.
Catholics do the very same thing. I make that statement because
I've stood in the place of the Pharisee, thinking that obedience to
my duty was saving me. I was taught that if I was good I would
go to heaven, so I tried even harder to be good. I sought refuge in
the fact that my pious life had accumulated countless indulgences

that would be placed on the scales to help balance my account. I did works of charity so that credit would accrue to me and would be taken into consideration on the day of judgment. The Second Vatican Council, with its sweeping changes, did not change this specific teaching. Today when I ask a Catholic if they think they will go to heaven, their reply reveals where their faith is: "I hope I'll make it. I do my duty, I go to Mass and confession, I give to charity, I try to be a good neighbor, I don't do anything wrong." These sentiments are expressed by good, decent people, but none of these things can save a sinner.

The sheer hopelessness of trying to get to heaven by my own efforts was brought home to me not long after my conversion to Jesus. I was sitting in the lobby of a bank and in front of me was an escalator. Two children were playing on the escalator, doing what children do—they were trying to go up an escalator that was moving down. They made several heroic attempts, but every time, the escalator brought them down again. They were never able to reach the top, even though they really tried. They then moved to the escalator that moved up, and it took them to the top. What happened before my eyes was the perfect illustration of what Catholics are doing: They are trying to get to heaven on a religious system that cannot take them there. Every effort fails to achieve the goal. In contrast to that, God, in his mercy, has provided a way to take us to heaven. Peter captures this great doctrine of grace in these words: "Christ died for sins…to bring you to God" (1 Peter 3:18). That's God's escalator. We need to let God take us to heaven.

The Life of Saul

There is much in the life of Saul of Tarsus (as the apostle Paul was known before he became a Christian) that is parallel to the Roman Catholic way of thinking. All the sincerity with which he strove to serve God and all his efforts to live a good life are also present in the lives of many Roman Catholics. Yet what is astonishing is that this godly, sincere, zealous man was not right with God. A fatal flaw in his belief system kept him a prisoner of sin and barred from heaven. Saul was not a pagan or an atheist; he was a man whose faith was focused on what he thought God wanted him to do and he trusted in his performance to gain him his place in heaven. The similarities between Saul's way of thinking and the Catholic way of thinking are striking. Let's survey the life of this sinner who became one of God's greatest saints.

Saul was one of the most unlikely people to embrace the gospel of the Lord Jesus Christ. Scripture shows him as a man violently opposed to the message that through a crucified Christ God had reconciled the world to himself, and that only through faith in Jesus could one be saved. Also, Saul did not hold the view that it doesn't matter what you believe as long as you are sincere. The infant church soon found that persecution was to become their daily companion, and the first Christian martyr was Stephen. He had proclaimed that Jesus was the promised Messiah whom the Jews had rejected. "When [the Jews] heard this, they were furious and gnashed their teeth at him....they covered their ears and, yelling at the top of their voices, they all rushed at him, dragging him out of the city and began to stone him" (Acts 7:54,57-58). Saul would later recall: "When the blood of your martyr Stephen was shed, I stood there giving my approval and guarding the clothes of those who were killing him" (Acts 22:20). At Saul's instigation a wave of persecution against the church broke out. "On that day a great persecution broke out against the church at Jerusalem, and all except the apostles were scattered throughout Judea and Samaria. Godly men buried Stephen and mourned deeply for him. But Saul began to destroy the church. Going from house to house, he dragged off men and women and put them in prison" (Acts 8:1-3). Saul's fanaticism against the gospel was recorded by Luke: "Meanwhile, Saul was still breathing out murderous threats against the Lord's disciples. He went to the high priest and asked him for letters to the synagogues in Damascus, so that if he found any there who belonged to the Way, whether men or women, he might take them as prisoners to Jerusalem" (Acts 9:1-2). These were the actions of a man who was repulsed by the idea that one could be reconciled to God through a man who was crucified as a common criminal.

After Saul became a Christian, he confessed his wrongdoing. At his trial before King Agrippa he said, "I too was convinced that I ought to do all that was possible to oppose the name of Jesus of Nazareth. And that is just what I did in Jerusalem. On the authority of the chief priests I put many of the saints in prison, and when they were put to death, I cast my vote against them. Many a time I went from one synagogue to another to have them punished, and I tried to force them to blaspheme. In my obsession against them, I even went to foreign cities to persecute them" (Acts 26:9-11). His remark, "I too was convinced" revealed he understood the thinking of his accusers at his trial, for that is exactly how he once thought—the gospel must be opposed for God's sake.

FROM FLAWED RULES TO TRUE RIGHTEOUSNESS
Living by Tradition and Rules

Before he became a Christian, Paul was a Pharisee who practiced a legalistic religion. He had received his education from the leading authority at that time, Gamaliel. "Under Gamaliel," he said, "I was thoroughly trained in the law of our fathers" (Acts 22:3), and "I was advancing in Judaism beyond many Jews of my own age and was extremely zealous for the traditions of my fathers" (Galatians 1:14). Paul was not boasting about his scholastic achievements;

he was simply stating facts about himself that provide an insight into what he was like before his conversion to Jesus. He further expounded upon this in his letter to the church at Philippi:

> If anyone thinks to base his claims on externals, I could make a stronger case for myself: circumcised on the eighth day, Israelite by race, of the tribe of Benjamin, a Hebrew born and bred: in my attitude to the law, a Pharisee; in pious zeal, a persecutor of the church; in legalistic rectitude, faultless (Philippians 3:4-6 NEB).

He was confident that his lineage from Abraham, the father of the nation of Israel, coupled with his meticulous observance of the law, was sufficient to secure his place in heaven. He, along with other Pharisees, had developed this line of thinking to a fine art.

Trusting a False Righteousness

After Paul received Christ, he tirelessly shared the saving message of Jesus with his fellow Jews. He lamented their lost condition, knowing that they trusted a religious system that could never save them. What they wanted—to be right with God—could not be achieved by human effort. He said,

> My heart's desire and prayer to God for the Israelites is that they may be saved. For I can testify about them that they are zealous for God, but their zeal is not based on knowledge. Since they did not know the righteousness that comes from God and sought to establish their own [righteousness], they did not submit to God's righteousness (Romans 10:1-3).

Paul knew exactly where these people were coming from, for he had been there. If there were ever a place in the Word of God that would hold out hope that people will be saved because they are good and sincere it would be found here, but no such hope is given. Look at the type of people Paul had just described (he could well be describing many good Roman Catholics). How could such good people, such zealous people, such believers in God, not be right with God? Many would find it outrageous to say that these very religious people were not right with God. However, their protests only serve to show that they too do not know how it is that God accounts sinners right with him. Many Roman Catholics today are in this very category; they believe they will be accepted by God because they are good, decent, God-fearing people. They are sincere, genuine, and zealous for God, but they have been taught incorrectly.

To the Jewish people of Jesus' day, the Pharisees were the most upright observers of the law. Yet Jesus made this interesting comment: "I tell you that unless your righteousness surpasses that of the Pharisees and the teachers of the law, you will certainly not enter the kingdom of heaven" (Matthew 5:20). Was Jesus saying that we need to outperform the Pharisees? In other words, if they fasted twice a week then we should fast three times, and if they donated 10 percent of their income we need to donate 11 percent. Is that what Jesus was teaching? No. Jesus was pointing out that the Pharisees believed their righteous acts would get them to heaven. Theirs was a righteousness based on human works. The only righteousness that can save us is that which became available to us through Christ on the cross.

Only after his conversion could Paul see the futility of trusting in religious performance. That which was once "very important" he now considered to be "garbage" because his works could not do the one thing he trusted them to do—save him from his sins and secure his place in heaven. I can identify with what Paul was saying, for when I was a practicing Roman Catholic I too trusted in the performance of my religious duties, believing that my obedience to the

Church's rules would save me. Like many Roman Catholics I too was very sincere in my convictions; but later I realized that the way of salvation lay elsewhere and the obedience I rendered, the rosaries I said, the novenas I did, and my devotion to the saints could not save me.

Paul stated that it is only through faith in the death of Jesus that we can be saved and "not because of righteous things we have done" (Titus 3:5). This is hard to accept, but it's a biblical truth: We cannot save ourselves; we need to be saved. The tenor of Scripture is clear: We cannot make ourselves righteous before God no matter how hard we try. And this is the specific point at which Roman Catholics are going wrong. So how then can we be right with God?

RIGHTEOUSNESS

Depending on True Righteousness

For clarity's sake we are going to delve into some "heavy" theology here that will require some careful thinking. However, the reward that comes from understanding the doctrine of imputed righteousness is more than worthwhile and can change our eternal destiny. So together, let's launch out into the deep.

If we are to be righteous before God, then God will have to impute his very own righteousness to us. In the book of the Romans, Paul spent three chapters explaining the sinfulness of man and his inability to alter his situation. Against that background Paul introduces the theme of grace: "But now," he said, "a righteousness from God, apart from the law, has been made known, to which the Law and the Prophets testify. This righteousness from God comes through faith in Christ Jesus to all who believe" (Romans 3:20-21). Throughout his early life Paul had tried to produce a standard of righteousness God would accept. Yet he was attempting the impossible. The righteousness that comes from God is not earned by a flawless performance; rather, it comes as a gift and is accepted by faith.

This is not a doctrine invented by Paul, it is a doctrine enshrined in the Old Testament. David, Israel's great king, "speaks of the blessedness of the man to whom God credits righteousness apart from works" (Romans 4:6). There are three facts to note here: 1) This righteousness comes from God, 2) it is credited, or imputed to the believer, and 3) it is independent of works; that is, it is not a reward for having done anything. Neither is it imputed to us because God was obligated to us in some way. Later Paul stated, "It is because of him that you are in Christ Jesus" (1 Corinthians 1:30). He was saying that a right standing with God is attributed entirely to Jesus, for he "has become for us…our righteousness" (verse 30). Who is our righteousness? The Lord Jesus Christ himself. In yet another amazing passage Paul said, "God made him who had no sin to be sin for us, so that in him we might become the righteousness of God" (2 Corinthians 5:21). This is the doctrine of substitution: The sinless Jesus took our sins upon himself so that "in him" we could be accounted righteous before God with a righteousness that comes from God.

Paul has a very sympathetic heart for those sincere people who seek to be right with God through their own pious efforts. Yet they have been misguided by their teachers. So when Paul wrote on the theme of God's amazing grace he drew from his own life as a self-righteous person who tried to save himself by his works and said, "It is by grace you have been saved, through faith—and this not from yourselves, it is the gift of God—not by works, so that no one can boast" (Ephesians 2:8-9). If we could be saved by our works, then we could boast about having saved ourselves. We could become our own savior. But because we are saved not by our works but by our faith, we conclude that faith is not a work of merit. Faith does not earn anything for us. If it did, then it would no longer be faith but a work. There is no saving power in our faith; it is the crucified Christ who saves us. While faith and works of merit are incompatible, faith and obedience are compatible.

AN EXAMPLE TO ALL

Paul's life before his conversion is very similar to that of many Roman Catholics. Like Paul, Catholics try to be right with God through their good works. (If I do good works, God will accept me. If I am faithful to the Church, I am being faithful to God.) But later, Paul realized his works could not save him. So his conversion to Jesus is the model for all Roman Catholics. He realized that no one is righteous before God and that all must trust in God's mercy and grace for their salvation. What's more, Paul said, "I was shown mercy so that in me, the worst of sinners, Christ Jesus might display his unlimited patience as an example for those who would believe on him and receive eternal life" (1 Timothy 1:16). Paul was saying that if God could save him, then God can save anyone.

After Paul became a Christian, his former friends persecuted him. Now that Paul had "deserted" the cause, other Jews took up the mantle he had left and started persecuting him. When Paul proclaimed that Jesus is the Christ, the fulfillment of ancient prophecies, instead of rejoicing at this news, "the Jews conspired to kill him.... Day and night they kept close watch on the city gates in order to kill him" (Acts 9:23-24). Saul the persecutor had now become Paul the persecuted.

THE PRICE OF FOLLOWING TRUTH

Catholics who leave the Roman Catholic Church often find themselves facing a similar dilemma. Through the study of the Bible they come to an understanding of the gospel of Jesus and embrace it. At this point they realize they cannot remain in the Church because its fundamental doctrines conflict with those of the Bible. They leave to join a church committed to the authority of Scripture. This may cause friction within their family, and it's an awkward situation because no one wants to cause conflict. No one wants to upset loving parents, brothers, and sisters. But conversion to Christ often brings persecution.

Those who leave are often asked hard questions that are not easy to answer. What do we say, for instance, about all the good, sincere, zealous Catholic men and women who have given their lives on foreign mission fields bringing education, hospitals, and orphanages to people in need? There are many who have given up the comforts of this world in order to serve those for whom life is a daily struggle. And what about the many good, decent, God-fearing Catholics who can be found among our friends and colleagues? Are they all wrong? Are we saying that their wonderful lives count for nothing? And are we saying that we alone have discovered the truth and others remain in darkness?

These are hard questions that need to be answered. The sincerity, the honesty of Catholics who ask these questions must not be doubted unless you have evidence to the contrary. But truth is not determined by how many people have signed up for it; truth comes by way of revelation from God. It is not negotiable. It is not up for discussion. It is not subject to modification so that it conforms to the particular persuasion of any person or church. The Bible calls us to proclaim the message of how God sets people right with him. All of us are sinners in need of God's forgiveness. Our works cannot make us right with God. If they could, then Jesus didn't need to die on the cross.

QUESTIONS AND ANSWERS

Q. **What is faith?**

Faith has nothing to do with our feelings. Faith is trusting in God, believing in what God has said, acting upon what God has revealed. This faith comes from hearing the Word of God (Romans 10:17).

Q. **How does our faith save us?**

There is no saving power in our faith. Our faith is not in our faith, but in Jesus, who saves us. Faith looks to him and trusts in him to save us. Without Jesus we could not talk about a saving faith.

Q. **Do our good works play any part in saving us?**

The Roman Catholic Church teaches that good works contribute toward salvation, but this contradicts the plain teaching of Scripture. There is nothing we can contribute toward our salvation. Attempting to make a contribution belittles the perfect, saving sacrifice of Jesus.

Q. **What does the Bible say about baptism?**

Baptism, by definition, is the immersion into water of those who have put their faith in Jesus to save them. The Bible speaks of baptism as a faith-response to the sacrificial death of Jesus for the remission of our sin. The one being baptized is being identified by faith with Jesus' death, burial, and resurrection. He is being "born again." The Roman Catholic sacrament of baptism is not what the Bible teaches on this important subject.

Q. **When we die, can we be certain of going to heaven?**

The Bible tells us that because Jesus died and paid in full the penalty for all our sins, the righteousness of God himself is imputed
to us. Because of Christ's substitutionary action on our behalf, we
can know that when we die we will go to heaven.

8

The Sacrifice
of the Mass

. . . .

Some of my earliest childhood memories have to do with going
to Mass with my family in Saints Michael's—a drafty, cold church
on Dublin's west side. In spite of the discomfort, attendance at Mass
was a duty I faithfully discharged into my mid-twenties.

For me, the Mass was a minor spectacle because of what was
happening on the altar. *This is what religion is all about,* I thought.
My interest in the Mass was enhanced by the multicolored vestments worn by the priest, the altar decorated with candles and
flowers, and the proceedings that were uttered, at that time, in Latin.
And if it was a high Mass, the smell of incense made the occasion all
the more solemn. The incense hung in the air long after the priest
had said, *"Ite missa est,"* or "Go, it is the dismissal."

I was taught that the Roman Catholic Mass was instituted
by Jesus on Holy Thursday night, and that the Roman Catholic

Church is the only faithful custodian of that night's proceedings. I was grateful to belong to "the one true, holy, catholic and apostolic church" and not to have suffered the misfortune of being born a Protestant! It was in Saint Michael's that I made my first Holy Communion, and whenever I was asked about the happiest day of my life, like every other Catholic child in Ireland I would reply, "The day I made my first Holy Communion." That answer ensured financial reward, so I used it often.

As I was prepared to make my first communion, I was taught about the real presence of Jesus in the bread and wine, and that I needed to be in "a state of grace" before receiving communion and have fasted before receiving the blessed Eucharist. There were discussions as to what constituted "breaking your fast." For example, could I brush my teeth before receiving communion since there was always the possibility I might accidentally swallow some toothpaste? Being overly scrupulous about such matters, I put dental hygiene on hold until after communion. I was also taught about the correct posture when receiving communion. Since I would be receiving the actual "body, blood, soul, and divinity" of the Lord Jesus Christ, holy protocol had to be observed. After receiving communion I would clasp my hands and walk reverently back to my seat. Such fine-tuned legalism was taken to new heights by some "very holy people" in the church who always proceeded to their seat in a slow, contemplative walk, hands clasped, head slightly tilted to one side, and a mournful expression on their faces.

For some years I served Mass as an altar boy. In those days only the priest was allowed to touch the host. When the communicants came, my task was to place the paten under their chin to catch any particles from the host lest they fall to the floor. The priest would then clean the paten into the chalice. These proceedings reinforced for me the Roman Catholic teaching about the Mass, and I happily subscribed to the teaching. For example, I would have accepted as true the following statement:

> At the last Supper on the night which he was betrayed, our Savior instituted the Eucharistic Sacrifice of His Body and Blood. He did this in order to perpetuate the sacrifice of the Cross throughout the centuries until He should come again, and so to entrust to His beloved spouse, the Church, a memorial of His death and resurrection: a sacrament of love, a sign of unity, a bond of charity, a paschal banquet in which Christ is consumed, the mind is filled with grace and a pledge of future glory is given to us.[1]

Changes began occurring for me when I started reading the Bible in my mid-twenties. This was a new experience for me—one that answered many of my questions while also raising areas of conflict with my Catholic beliefs. The Word of God was challenging me to return to the apostolic belief and practice of the early church and providing me with the perfect starting place for examining the original meaning of the Lord's words in the Upper Room when he instituted the Eucharist. I discovered that none of us has to fear exposing our beliefs to the teachings of God's Word. If what we believe is correct, the Bible will confirm it. And if what we believe is in conflict with the Word, then we must decide which to follow. Let's now examine what the Bible says about the Eucharist. (The word *Eucharist* is the Greek word for *thanksgiving* and is found in the phrase, "Is this not the cup of thanksgiving which we share?")

THE CONTEXT: JESUS' LAST EVENING

The Lord's time with his apostles was coming to an end and the purpose for which he came into the world was fast approaching, yet he still had much to share with them. Their last evening together would be memorable. Jesus had spoken often to his apostles about his death, but during the Passover meal he astonished them by announcing that one of them would betray him. In unison they all declared their innocence and asked Jesus to identify the betrayer. He said, "It is the one to whom I will give this piece of bread when I have dipped it in the dish," and he gave the bread to Judas and added, "What you are about to do, do quickly" (John 13:26-27). Judas got up and left. The remaining disciples did not know the significance of what Jesus had said to Judas and assumed that because he was the treasurer he was going out to buy some food for the poor (verse 29). This was not so. Judas was putting the finishing touches onto a plan he had been harboring for some time. The religious authorities had long wanted to get rid of Jesus because his teachings were at odds with theirs. They knew that only death would stop him.

So when Judas came to the religious leaders and offered to betray Jesus, they must have been thrilled. In fact, Mark tells us that "they were delighted to hear this and promised to give him money" (Mark 14:11). They would have seen their good fortune as nothing other than divine intervention. Judas was an answer to their prayers. This could only be the hand of God. Who would ever have thought that they would get their big break from one of Jesus' own group!

THE SETTING: THE PASSOVER MEAL

Some of us look back on our school days and rate history as one of the more boring subjects we had to study. If you happened to be one of those unfortunates, I apologize, but we must indulge for a moment in a short history lesson about the Passover because it is against that background that Jesus instituted the Eucharist. While enslaved in Egypt, the children of Israel experienced a population explosion and grew in number to about two million. The Egyptians saw them as a threat and reduced them to the status of slaves. However, God was not deaf to their cries, nor had he forgotten his covenant with Abraham, a covenant that promised them the land of Canaan, a land "flowing with milk and honey." God raised up Moses to lead his people to the Promised Land, but because Pharaoh refused to allow the people to leave, God sent ten plagues upon Egypt. God's repeated call to Pharaoh, "Let my people go," failed to move his sinful heart. One by one the plagues demonstrated to Pharaoh that God is the one true God and there is no other God beside him. The plagues were the judgement of God "on all the gods of Egypt" (Exodus 12:12). The tenth and final plague secured freedom for the Hebrew slaves, and after that they began their journey to the Promised Land.

THE EVENT: THE TENTH PLAGUE

Because the Lord's Supper was instituted within the context of the Passover meal, we need to revisit the original Passover so we can better understand the Lord's Supper. In preparation for the final plague, Moses instructed the people,

> Go at once and select the animals for your families and slaughter the Passover lamb. Take a bunch of hyssop, dip it into the blood in the basin and put some of the blood on the top and on both sides of the doorframe. Not one of you shall go out the door of his house until morning. When the LORD goes through the land to strike down the Egyptians, he will see the blood on the top and sides of the doorframe and will pass over that doorway, and he will not permit the destroyer to enter your houses and strike you down. Obey these instructions as a lasting ordinance for you and your descendants. When you enter the land that the LORD will give you as he promised, observe this ceremony (Exodus 12:21-25).

Israel did as God instructed: Each family killed a lamb and sprinkled its blood upon the doorpost of their home to protect themselves from the coming judgment of God. Then "at midnight the LORD struck down all the firstborn in Egypt, from the firstborn of Pharaoh, who sat on the throne, to the firstborn of the prisoner, who was in the dungeon, and the firstborn of all the livestock as well." That night, the Bible says, "There was loud wailing in Egypt, for there was not a house without someone dead" (verses 29-30). That night Pharaoh summoned Moses with instructions to take the people out of Egypt, and "six hundred thousand men on foot, besides women and children," left Egypt (verse 37). This event was not lost in the annals of history but became the centerpiece of the Hebrew calendar, for God said,

> This is a day you are to commemorate; for the generations to come you shall celebrate it as a festival to the LORD—a lasting ordinance.... When you enter the land that the LORD will give you as he promised, observe this ceremony. And when your children ask you, "What does this ceremony mean to you?" then tell them, "It is the Passover sacrifice to the LORD, who passed over the houses of the Israelites in Egypt and spared our homes when he struck down the Egyptians." Then the people bowed down and worshiped (Exodus 12:14,25-27).

The food eaten by the Israelites at the Passover is significant: The slain lamb recalled how God's judgement was diverted by a slain lamb whose blood was sprinkled upon their doorposts, the bitter herbs spoke of their slavery in Egypt, and the unleavened bread was called the bread of affliction (Deuteronomy 16:3). Jews today still celebrate the Passover, remembering this very event in their history when, as a nation, God delivered them from slavery.

THE CEREMONY: THE LAST SUPPER

Israel's deliverance from bondage in Egypt provides the backdrop against which the Eucharist was instituted:

> While they were eating, Jesus took bread, gave thanks

and broke it, and gave it to his disciples, saying, "Take and eat; this is my body." Then he took the cup, gave thanks and offered it to them, saying, "Drink from it, all of you. This is my blood of the covenant, which is poured out for many for the forgiveness of sins. I tell you, I will not drink of this fruit of the vine from now on until that day when I drink it anew with you in my Father's kingdom" (Matthew 26:26-30).

How are we to understand what Jesus said? How have Catholics and evangelicals arrived at such different understandings of the Last Supper? How can we both look at the same text and come to different conclusions?

Here's an illustration you might find helpful. Have you written a letter, proofread it several times, and then sent it, only to discover later that you had overlooked a misspelled word? How did you miss seeing the error even though you read the letter several times? Simple—you expected the word to be correct and chose to see it that way. We've all done this—we see things as we expect them to be. That's how it is with the Lord's Supper. When Roman Catholics approach the words of Jesus at the Last Supper, they expect to see what their Church officially teaches, and so they see in his words the Mass, transubstantiation, and a propitiatory sacrifice. They don't realize that these concepts are not in the text. They don't realize these teachings are foreign to apostolic understanding and absent from the life of the early church. They "see" this doctrine in our Lord's words even though it is not in Scripture.

Now, another important detail is the fact that throughout his ministry, Jesus spoke of liberation. For example, he said, "You will know the truth, and the truth will set you free.… If the Son sets you free, you will be free indeed" (John 8:32,36). In relation to his atoning death on the cross, Jesus spoke of freedom, deliverance, redemption, and forgiveness. And at Passover, Jesus took the bread and said, "Take and eat; this is my body" (Matthew 26:26). Then he took the wine and said, "This is my blood of the covenant, which is poured out for many for the forgiveness of sins" (verse 28). Through his death, Jesus would bring about a new exodus. Through the cross, those in bondage would be set free. And just as Israel had commemorated their freedom from slavery with the Passover meal, so the church, through the memorial of the Eucharist, would commemorate its freedom from the bondage of sin and its consequences. This was the apostolic understanding and practice in the early church, and it has been common practice in Christian churches ever since (Acts 20:7).

What the Apostles Heard

When the apostles heard the words of Jesus, they would not have concluded that Jesus has just celebrated the first Mass, as the Catholic Church teaches. Nothing remotely similar to Catholic doctrine would have crossed their minds. I know that such a statement might sound harsh, but I cannot avoid saying what needs to be said. While the apostles did not have a totally clear understanding of the events leading up to Good Friday, we can see in Scripture and in the practices of the early church that from the time the Spirit came on the day of Pentecost, the apostles' understanding of what Jesus meant that night in the Upper Room had not included the slightest hint of Roman Catholic doctrine.

When Jesus gave the apostles the bread and said it was his body, and when he said the cup contained his blood shed for the forgiveness of sins, the apostles didn't understand him literally. Jesus had not yet died upon the cross. Are we expected to believe that the apostles believed the Catholic doctrine of transubstantiation and the real presence when at the very same time in the Upper Room the apostles were still very unclear that Jesus' atoning death was required? (Peter even tried to prevent it from happening by coming to Jesus' defense when Jesus was arrested.) To see the Roman Catholic doctrine of the Mass in the Last Supper requires that this teaching be imported into the text.

Furthermore, it is difficult to believe that the apostles, who held to strict dietary laws, one of which prohibited eating anything that contained blood, took the cup and drank the literal blood of Jesus without objection. Let's refresh our minds on just how strict the apostles were regarding eating anything that was classified as unclean. In Acts chapter 10, some time after Jesus' crucifixion, resurrection, and ascension, God gave Peter a vision that meant all people, irrespective of race, were acceptable to him on the basis of the death of Jesus:

> [Peter] saw heaven opened and something like a large sheet being let down to earth by its four corners. It contained all kinds of four-footed animals, as well as reptiles of the earth and birds of the air. Then a voice told him, "Get up, Peter. Kill and eat." "Surely not, Lord!" Peter replied. "I have never eaten anything impure or unclean." The voice spoke to him a second time, "Do not call anything impure that God has made clean." This happened three times, and immediately the sheet was taken back to heaven (Acts 10:11-16).

Remember, this reaction—"I have never eaten anything impure or unclean"—came from an apostle who, according to Roman Catholic teaching, believed he was drinking the Savior's blood and eating his literal flesh in the Upper Room.

As the church grew and the gospel message reached the Gentiles, the apostles realized some guidelines needed to be put in place for the sake of the Gentiles. After the church met in Jerusalem it was decided that the following instructions be given to the Gentiles: "You are to abstain from…blood, from the meat of strangled animals…. You will do well to avoid these things" (Acts 15:29).

Such statements could not be made by the apostles if they believed that, in eating the bread in the Eucharist, they were actually eating the body of the Savior and in drinking the wine they were literally drinking his blood.

The Lack of Evidence

Roman Catholic teaching speaks of the Mass as a miracle because the bread and wine are changed into the body, blood, soul, and divinity of the Lord Jesus Christ. Though the elements themselves have not changed, nevertheless, the Church says they become the actual body of Christ. Yet this "miracle" cannot be verified. When Jesus worked miracles, people could see that something supernatural had occurred—which is why "a great crowd of people followed him because they saw the miraculous signs he had performed on the sick" (John 6:2). Even the enemies of Jesus—and he had many—could not deny his miracles. After he raised Lazarus from the dead, "the chief priests and the Pharisees called a meeting of the Sanhedrin. 'What are we accomplishing?' they asked. 'Here is this man performing many miraculous signs' " (John 11:47). And when Jesus changed the water into wine in John 2, the miracle could be verified by the senses: The liquid looked like wine, it had the smell of wine, and it tasted like wine. Everyone who drank it confirmed that it was wine (verses 9-10). What's more, Jesus knew the difficulty people had in believing in him, so he said to them, "At least believe on the evidence of the miracles themselves" (John 14:11). Miracles that could be verified were the credentials that supported Jesus' claims. Yet in the so-called "miracle" of the Mass, nothing resembling any of the miracles of Jesus is evident.

In spite of the lack of evidence for transubstantiation, the Roman Catholic Church insists that Christ is literally present in the bread and the wine. This is "the real presence." That Christ is present with his people is an undeniable biblical truth. He said, "I will ask the Father, and he will give you another Counselor to be with you forever—the Spirit of truth. The world cannot accept him, because it neither sees him nor knows him. But you know him, for he lives with you and will be in you. I will not leave you as orphans; I will come to you" (John 14:16-18). Jesus does not dwell in holy buildings or tabernacles on altars. Rather, through his Spirit, his real presence resides in his holy people, the church. He said, "If anyone loves me, he will obey my teaching. My Father will love him, and we will come to him and make our home with him" (John 14:23). The Lord takes up permanent residence in the lives of those who love him. His real presence can be seen in the life of one who loves God. This is clearly stated by Paul when he says that all God's people are "members of God's household....[and] the whole building is joined together and rises to become a holy temple in the Lord. And in him you too are being built together to become a dwelling in which God lives by his Spirit" (Ephesians 2:19-22). There's the real presence—the Lord living in his people through the Spirit.

Note specifically what Jesus said at the Last Supper: "Do this in remembrance of me" (Luke 22:19). The Eucharist is a *memorial* of what Jesus did for us in his death upon the cross. It is a continuous *reminder* of a past event that we celebrate each time we share in the Supper.

Consider this illustration: Every country has a flag. When a foreign head of state visits that country, he shows respect by saluting the flag because that flag represents the nation he is visiting. We've seen news reports on television of protesters burning a country's flag. When they do this, they are doing much more than burning a piece of colored material; they are displaying their opposition to that country by burning the very thing that is symbolic of that nation— its flag. In a similar way, the Lord's Supper is a symbolic reminder of what Jesus did for us. The saving event occurred on Calvary, and the bread and wine are a memorial of that event.

Finally, our Lord stated, "I will not drink again of the fruit of the vine until the kingdom of God comes" (Luke 22:18). This is a reference to that time when we will be together with the Lord in the kingdom of heaven. This unbroken fellowship with him for eternity will have been made possible by his atoning death upon the cross. Those who have received the blessing issuing from his death commemorate this when they partake of the bread and the wine. We not only look back to what he did on the cross; we also look forward in certain hope of what is to come. "Do this" Jesus said, "in remembrance of me" (Luke 22:19).

THE INTERPRETATION: A KEY PROOF TEXT

The words of our Lord in John chapter 6 have been called upon by the Roman Catholic Church to support their teaching of the Mass. They see in the words of Jesus a direct connection to his words spoken in the Upper Room on the night when he was betrayed. But is the discourse in John 6 really speaking about the Mass? I believe it is speaking about eternal life, which is received through faith in his death. This discourse, while fascinating, can be a little difficult to follow. Let's look at it carefully.

Jesus said, "Unless you eat the flesh of the Son of Man and drink his blood, you have no life in you" (John 6:53). How are we to understand these words? Catholics hold that they are to be understood literally. Others, including myself, hold that his words are to be understood figuratively. While some Scriptures can be misunderstood without affecting our relationship with God, these words of Jesus are not in that category. If we want the "life" Jesus is referring to, a correct understanding of his words is imperative. We will proceed by examining the Scripture within its context and comparing scripture with scripture, looking carefully at the entire sixth chapter of John to ensure a correct interpretation of our Lord's words.

The Feeding of the 5,000

A large crowd followed Jesus because of the miracles he performed on all who were sick (verse 2). The crowd needed to be fed, and Jesus said to Philip, "Where shall we buy bread for these people to eat?" (verse 5). Philip calculated that even eight months' wages would not be enough to feed such a large crowd (verse 7). Andrew stepped forward with his solution to the problem: "Here is a boy with five small barley loaves and two small fish" (verse 9). Apparently he expected Jesus to work a miracle. So Jesus had the people sit down, took the boy's loaves and fish, gave thanks to the Father, and then miraculously multiplied the loaves and fish for distribution among the 5,000 people. After everyone had eaten, there were still 12 baskets filled with food (verse 13). The well-fed people responded, "Surely this is the Prophet who is to come into the world" (verse 14). They were referring to the Prophet whom Moses said would come (Deuteronomy 18:15-18). Jesus' response to their overtures is interesting: "Jesus, knowing that they intended to come and make him king by force, withdrew again to a mountain by himself" (verse 15). Jesus knew the people's motives for attempting to make him king. They saw Jesus as the solution to their problems: He met their material needs, and they had hopes that he would rid their country of Roman rule. The common view among the people was that this is what the promised Prophet, the Messiah, would do.

The Journey to Capernaum

That evening the disciples were making their way by boat across the lake to Capernaum. Partway across, Jesus joined them in the boat for the remainder of the journey, having walked on the water to reach the boat. The following day the crowd Jesus had fed realized that Jesus was no longer in the vicinity and concluded he must have gone to Capernaum, so they journeyed there. When they caught up with Jesus he said to them, "I tell you the truth, you are looking for me, not because you saw the miraculous signs, but because you ate the loaves and had your fill" (verse 26). What did Jesus mean? He was telling them they had not sought him because they believed the miracles that confirmed he was the Son of God, the Savior of the world, and the One foretold by the prophets. Rather, they sought him because of the material benefits he could provide. How do we know this? By what he said next: "Do not work for food that spoils, but for food that endures to eternal life, which the Son of Man will give you" (verse 27). In other words, Jesus knew what motivated the people to seek him, and he told them they had made a poor choice. They pursued him for food that would spoil. Instead, they needed to pursue him for the food he could give that would impart eternal life. Jesus was contrasting the material with the spiritual, and he continues to do this throughout the rest of his discourse.

Upon hearing Jesus speak about working for food that endures, the crowd responded in typical legalistic fashion: "What must we do to do the works God requires?" (verse 28). They were asking Jesus to give them a list of duties—works to perform, goals to achieve so that they could make themselves right with God. Jesus corrected them, saying that a relationship with God is not based upon performance. "The work of God is this: to believe in the one he has sent" (verse 29). Jesus was teaching that for one to do the works of God, then a person must believe in the one whom God had sent. All who believe are enabled to believe because of the work of God in their hearts (Romans 10:14). The faith to believe is a gift from God. The only acceptable response to "the food that endures to eternal life" is not works or performances, but faith, trust, belief, obedience.

The people then asked Jesus, "What miraculous sign then will you give that we may see it and believe you? What will you do? Our forefathers ate the manna in the desert; as it is written: 'He gave them bread from heaven to eat'" (verses 30-31). (Apparently the previous day's miracle of feeding 5,000 had not convinced them!) What they were saying is this: God met the needs of our forefathers; what are you going to do for us? Jesus picked up on their words and said, "It is my Father who gives you the true bread from heaven. For the bread of God is he who comes down from heaven and gives life to the world" (verses 32-33). Jesus, unknown to them, was moving the conversation in a direction that would allow him to teach about his atoning death. He personalized his comments about the bread of life: "For the bread of God is he who comes down from heaven and gives life to the world" (verse 34). "'Sir,' they said, 'from now on give us this bread'" (verse 34). Did the people really want what Jesus had to offer? No; they had misunderstood him. They thought he was offering to meet their physical needs for the rest of their lives. That's why they said, "From now on give us this bread." The attitude was, "In the way you met our needs yesterday, continue meeting our needs from now on."

It's important to note that Jesus identified himself as "the bread of life" (verse 35). He is the giver and sustainer of life. "He who comes to me will never go hungry, and he who believes in me will never be thirsty" (verse 36). To "come" and "believe" in Jesus is to satisfy one's spiritual needs. Jesus then said, "My Father's will is that everyone who looks to the Son and believes in him shall have eternal life, and I will raise him up at the last day" (verse 40). The crowd responded negatively: "At this the Jews began to grumble about him because he said, 'I am the bread that came down from heaven'" (verse 41). Jesus' statement didn't square with the facts they possessed. They knew his family and where he came from. "Is this not Jesus the son of Joseph, whose father and mother we know?

How can he now say, 'I came down from heaven?'" (verse 42). They had expected Jesus to say he was from Nazareth, not heaven.

Jesus continued, "He who believes has everlasting life. I am the bread of life" (verses 47-48). Jesus reinforced the point by saying that the manna God had provided to their ancestors had sustained them physically, but eventually they all died. "Your forefathers ate the manna in the desert, yet they died" (verse 49). In other words, that miracle had done nothing for their spiritual life. It merely met their physical needs.

In contrast to that, Jesus said, God has provided bread from heaven that will give eternal life. "Here is the bread that comes down from heaven, which a man may eat and not die. I am the living bread that came down from heaven. If anyone eats of this bread, he will live forever. This bread is my flesh which I will give for the life of the world" (verses 50-51). In other words, Jesus is the bread of life, and all who eat of this bread will never die. This bread differs from the bread that provided physical nourishment only. The bread of heaven, however, provides spiritual nourishment. All who eat the bread that has come down from heaven will 1) "not die" and 2) "will live forever." What kind of bread can this be? Jesus said that this bread "is my flesh, which I will give for the life of the world"— a clear reference to his atoning death upon the cross.

A Hard Saying

The crowd still didn't understand. They argued, "How can this man give us his flesh to eat?" (John 6:52). Because they thought Jesus was speaking literally, their question was natural. (Remember, they had already been confused by Jesus' words that he came down from heaven when they knew he came from Nazareth.)

The theme of Jesus' teaching all through this dialogue is the giving of himself as the perfect sacrifice, which results in eternal life for all who believe. Jesus continued, "I tell you the truth, unless you eat the flesh of the Son of Man and drink his blood, you have no life in you. Whoever eats my flesh and drinks my blood has eternal life, and I will raise him up at the last day" (verses 53-54). Those words harmonize with what he said earlier: "My Father's will is that everyone who looks to the Son and believes in him shall have eternal life, and I will raise him up at the last day" (verse 40). Both these scriptures, then, are saying the same thing. "Eternal life" and being "raised up at the last day" come from eating and drinking Jesus' flesh and blood, which is done through faith, through trusting his sacrifice.

As sinners we look, in faith, to the sacrifice of Jesus for eternal life. Our trust, our faith, is in what he has done for us. "For my flesh is real food and my blood is real drink" (verse 55). Jesus was affirming that he was the perfect sacrifice. All the animal sacrifices previously offered could never do what the sacrificed body and blood of Jesus would do. "Whoever eats my flesh and drinks my blood remains in me, and I in him" (verse 56). In other words, the closest possible fellowship will exist between the Savior and the saved ("[he] in me and I in him").

Jesus then said, "Just as the living Father sent me and I live because of the Father, so the one who feeds on me will live because of me" (verse 57). How does one "feed" on Jesus? The Lord provided the answer: "He who comes to me will never go hungry, and he who believes in me will never be thirsty" (verse 35). We feed on Jesus by coming to him in faith, by believing in him as the perfect Lamb of God whose death secured eternal life for us. We live a life of faith in him from the moment of our conversion until we die; that is how we are nourished spiritually.

"This is the bread that came down from heaven. Your forefathers ate manna and died, but he who feeds on this bread will live forever" (verse 58). Jesus was declaring that his real place of origin is heaven, not Nazareth, as some had supposed. And unlike the crowd's ancestors, who ate the bread in the wilderness and eventually died, Jesus has come down from heaven as the bread of life, and all who eat this bread will live forever. The new life they will have is not physical, but spiritual.

Even if it were possible literally to eat Jesus, one would not have obtained eternal life from doing so. We eat and drink his body and blood through faith, by believing, by trusting in his death upon the cross. Knowing that his listeners misunderstood him, Jesus gave further clarification: "The Spirit gives life; the flesh counts for nothing. The words I have spoken to you are spirit and they are life" (verse 63). The question had been asked earlier, "How can this man give us his flesh to eat?" (verse 52). They were thinking, incorrectly, that Jesus would literally distribute himself for them to eat and drink. Such a literal understanding was incorrect, for "the flesh counts for nothing." What flesh counts for nothing? The literal flesh which they thought Jesus would give them and which they must eat if they are to have eternal life. But eternal life cannot be imparted in this way. Rather, it is "the Spirit [that] gives life."

Many turned and walked away. Jesus didn't call them back. Why? Because "Jesus had known from the beginning which of them did not believe" (verse 64). It is not that they were offended by the Catholic doctrine of transubstantiation and so departed from Jesus as the Catholic Church states. On the contrary, there were no honest seekers among those who walked away that day.

In John 6, then, Jesus' words make it clear that man's spiritual need can be satisfied only through his sacrifice on the cross. All who believe in Jesus, all whose faith embraces his sacrifice, are said to eat the flesh and drink the blood of Jesus, and it is this faith in him that gives in eternal life. I have no hesitation, then, in concluding that there is nothing in our Lord's words that supports the Roman Catholic teaching about the Mass.

THE CONCERN: A CONTINUAL SACRIFICE

I recall my school days, and how each day began with religious instruction. We were taught from a little red book called *A Catechism of Christian Doctrine*. To its credit, it gave clear, unambiguous answers to the questions it posed. For example, in answer to the question, "What is the Mass?" the following answer was provided: "The Holy Mass is one and the same sacrifice with that of the Cross, inasmuch as Christ, who offered Himself, a bleeding victim, on the Cross to His Heavenly Father, continues to offer Himself in an unbloody manner on the altar, through the ministry of His priests."[2] There was no room for maneuvering or sidestepping the plain and obvious meaning of the answer: The Roman Catholic Church teaches that the Mass is a continual sacrifice. And the teachings of the Council of Trent (1545–1564), which are still binding today, are equally clear:

> If anyone says that in the mass a true and real sacrifice is not offered to God…let him be anathema (Canon 1).

> If anyone says that by these words, "Do this for a commemoration of me," Christ did not institute the Apostles priests, or did not ordain that they and other priests should offer his own body and blood, let him be anathema (Canon 2).

> If anyone says that the sacrifice of the mass is one only of praise and thanksgiving; or that it is a mere commemoration of the sacrifice consummated on the cross but not a propitiatory one, let him be anathema (Canon 3).[3]

If the tone of the Council's remarks seems a trifle strong for our modern day, given that we live in an age of tolerance and relativism, note that the decibel level is maintained in two recent papal encyclicals.

"Pius XI in *Ad Catholici Sacerdotti* (1935) described the mass as being in itself "a real sacrifice…which has a real efficacy." Moreover, "the ineffable greatness of the human priest stands forth in its splendour," because he "has power over the very body of Jesus Christ." He first "makes it present upon our altars" and next "in the name of Christ himself he offers it a victim infinitely pleasing to the Divine majesty" (pp. 8-9). In *Mediator Dei* (1947) Pius XII affirmed that the Eucharistic sacrifice "represents," "re-enacts," "renews," and "shows forth" the sacrifice of the cross. At the same time he described it as being itself "truly and properly the offering of a sacrifice" (para. 72), and said that "on our altars he [Christ] offers himself daily for our redemption" (para. 77).[4]

These papal encyclicals are official statements made by the Roman Catholic Church and are said to reflect the will of God. If this teaching on the Mass is from God, then it should agree with the Word of God. But does it?

THE QUESTIONS: WHAT THE BIBLE TEACHES

Is the Mass a propitiatory sacrifice? To answer this, we need a clear understanding of sin and God's forgiveness.

Because of sin, we all have incurred the wrath of God. Our sin separates us from God and we stand self-condemned, unable to alter our situation. It is not God's desire that we perish, but the reality of our sins cannot be ignored. For God to be truly holy and just, he must deal with our sin justly. And a propitiatory sacrifice is one that satisfies God's justice.

For centuries the people of Israel offered animal sacrifices up to God for their sins. The book of Hebrews tells us that these sacrifices could never satisfy God's justice and were unable to secure forgiveness. Though the number of animals sacrificed over the centuries is incalculable, not a single sin was forgiven as a result of these sacrifices. "It is impossible," the Bible says, "for the blood of bulls and goats to take away sins" (Hebrews 10:4). Therefore, they could not serve as propitiatory sacrifices.

Now, if the animal sacrifices were so ineffective, then why were they offered? Imagine, if you will, that you are an Israelite. Because of your sin, you select a lamb from your flock and take it to the priest, who kills the animal and offers it to God as a sacrifice. The exercise would illustrate to you how serious sin is in that it demands 1) death and 2) the death of an innocent victim.

The sacrificial system God gave to Israel served as a shadow of what was to come: It pointed to a future time when God himself would provide the perfect sacrifice whose death would satisfy his holy justice. It was John the Baptist who identified Jesus by saying, "Look, the Lamb of God, who takes away the sin of the world!" (John 1:29). The Lamb was provided by God himself, and this Lamb's sacrificial death secured forgiveness of sin. In the death of Jesus 1) God is seen to be just because he met the demands of his own law, which calls for the death of the guilty one, and 2) God can now offer forgiveness to all who have faith in his Lamb. The magnificence of what Jesus accomplished in his death is contrasted with the futility of Israel's sacrificial system: "Unlike the other high priests, he [Jesus] does not need to offer sacrifices day after day.... He sacrificed for their sins once for all when he offered himself" (Hebrews 7:27). Furthermore, the Bible speaks clearly when it says, "When this priest [Jesus] had offered for all time one sacrifice for sins, he sat down at the right hand of God" (Hebrews 10:12). His sacrificial work was finished forever. Only the once-for-all-time sacrifice on the cross of an innocent victim, Christ, can satisfy God's justice.

Now we're ready to ask our question again: Is the Mass a real and propitiary sacrifice? Earlier we saw that Pope Pius XII said, "On our altars he offers himself daily for our redemption." How does that compare to the great epistle to the Hebrews? The writer said this about the sacrifice of Christ: "Just as man is destined to die once... so Christ was sacrificed once to take away the sins of many people" (Hebrews 9:27-28). What did the writer mean by this? Clearly he meant that Jesus is offered as a sacrifice as often as man dies—once! Furthermore, "By one sacrifice he made perfect forever those who are being made holy" (Hebrews 10:14). Since this one sacrifice made us perfect and complete in Christ, to speak of the Mass as a continual sacrifice being offered for our redemption contradicts the plain teaching of Scripture. This is reinforced again in the book of Hebrews: "Where these have been forgiven, there is no longer any sacrifice for sin" (Hebrews 10:18). Because our sins have been forgiven, there is no longer any need for a sacrifice.

The Roman Catholic Mass, then, has taken on a meaning foreign to what Jesus instituted in the Upper Room. A Roman Catholic Mass is offered for the living and the dead, for those who are sick, for one's special intentions, for wedding anniversaries, and for success in school examinations. That is not what Jesus instituted. The Roman Catholic Mass would never be endorsed by the apostles.

I remember nearly 40 years ago reading the book of Hebrews for the first time and wondering how any Catholic priest could read what it said and continue saying Mass. Even today, many years later, I am still deeply affected by the sheer wonder of Jesus' sacrifice, and I am jealous to defend that. Having been a faithful Catholic, I know that many Catholics are sincere about their faith. I certainly was! But when teachings, though sincerely held, contradict the Word of God, those beliefs must be abandoned and the truth of God's Word embraced.

QUESTIONS AND ANSWERS

Q. **At the Last Supper, did Jesus not say, "This is my body… this is my blood"?**

Yes, Jesus did use those words at the Last Supper. However, the construction placed on these words by the Roman Catholic Church is in conflict not only with what our Lord said, but also with the clear teaching of Scripture. Jesus was not speaking literally for he had not yet died upon the cross; the perfect sacrifice had not yet been offered for the remission of sins.

Q. **Is not the Roman Catholic teaching on transubstantiation to be found in Jesus' words—"this is my body… this is my blood"?**

Transubstantiation has no support in the Scriptures. The bread and wine do not change into the body and blood of Jesus. Jesus promised that his holy presence would be with his people for all time— not in the bread and wine, but through the Holy Spirit, who lives in his people, the church. The real presence is Christ living in his people through the Spirit.

Q. **Jesus said in John 6 that we must eat his flesh and drink his blood in order to have eternal life. Isn't that a clear reference to the words Jesus spoke at the Last Supper?**

Those words were not spoken at the Last Supper; they are found in an entirely different context. The context speaks of providing eternal life through his sacrificial death upon the cross. Jesus' body and blood would be offered as a perfect sacrifice for the remission of our sins. To be saved, we must accept his sacrifice, by faith. When we, in faith, trust his death for the remission of our sins we are indeed eating and drinking the body and blood of Jesus.

Q. **Is not the Mass a holy sacrifice offered by the priest for the sins of the living and the dead?**

The book of Hebrews states clearly that Jesus offered himself once and for all as the perfect sacrifice for the remission of our sins. This one sacrifice satisfied in full the justice of a holy and righteous God. This point is reinforced by Paul with an unanswerable argument when he says that the death of Jesus occurs as often as man dies— once. And because that one perfect sacrifice accomplished our forgiveness, there is no need for another sacrifice or for the one perfect sacrifice to be offered again and again.

Q. **What did Jesus intend by his words at the Last Supper?**

Jesus spoke about his body and blood with the Passover meal in mind. The Passover was celebrated by the Jewish people each year to recall God's deliverance of Israel from the bondage of Egypt. This redemptive event pointed to a time when God would provide the Passover Lamb to redeem his people from the bondage of sin. This redemption was accomplished through the death of Jesus. When we partake of the Eucharist, we look back to Jesus' death, an event that secured our redemption, and forward to the time when the Lord will return for his church and bring us to be with him forever.

9

The Souls
in Purgatory

. . . .

The family, a father and his young children, occupied the front seat in the church. Before them lay the coffin containing the remains of a beloved wife and caring mother. She had been a good and kindly lady, respected by all who knew her. Death, that uninvited intruder, had taken her life, shattering the fragile world of her family. Their gentle sobbing echoed around the large church. The ringing of the altar bells announced that the priest was ready to say Mass on behalf of the deceased. He spent a few moments with the family, then announced to the congregation that this Mass was being offered for the repose of the soul of their departed loved one. Through the holy sacrifice of the Mass, her soul would eventually be released from the fires of purgatory.

The doctrine of purgatory is woven into the teachings of the Roman Catholic Church. I was taught in school that the fire of purgatory was the same as that of hell, with the difference being that one could escape from purgatory. Because we were taught that most of us were going to have to spend some time in purgatory, we were given regular lectures on the subject. For example, our spiritual director once told us the story of an old priest who was dying. The priest called the young curate to his bedside and made him promise that the moment he died the curate would go immediately to the church and say Mass on his behalf. The curate promised he would. He was with the old priest the night he died, and remembering his promise, went immediately to the church (which was next to the priest's home), put on his vestments, and went to the altar to celebrate Mass. He was confronted with a vision of the old priest, who was infuriated with the curate. "You promised that when I died you would immediately say a Mass for me." The young curate replied, "You died just a few moments ago and I came immediately." "Nonsense," the old priest replied. "I've been dead for forty years and you left me to suffer in purgatory!" The story was meant to convey that the pains of purgatory are so terrible that a few moments seems like 40 years. If our spiritual director's point was to scare us half to death, he succeeded. Such stories have great shock value when told to young, impressionable boys.

The Roman Catholic Church is not shy in teaching about purgatory and attaching an anathema on those who dare to disbelieve. Here is a sampling from the Catholic Catechism:

> All who die in God's grace and friendship, but still imperfectly purified, are indeed assured of their eternal salvation; but after death they undergo purification, so as to achieve the holiness necessary to enter the joy of heaven.

> As for lesser faults, we must believe that, before the Final Judgement, there is purifying fire.

> The Church also commends almsgiving, indulgences and works of penance undertaken on behalf of the dead.

Let us not hesitate to help those who have died and to offer our prayers for them. [1030, 1032]

If any says that after the reception of the grace of justification the guilt is so remitted and the debt of eternal punishment so blotted out to every repentant sinner, that no debt of temporal punishment remains to be discharged, either in this world or in Purgatory, before the gates of Heaven can be opened, let him be anathema.[1]

During the Eucharist, through the general intercessions and the Memento for the dead, the assembled community presents to the Father of all mercies those who have died, so that through the trial of purgatory they will be purified.... The Church believes that the souls detained in purgatory "are helped by the prayers of the faithful and most of all by the acceptable sacrifice of the altar" (Council of Trent, *Decree on Purgatory*), as well as by "alms and other works of piety" (Eugene IV, *Bull Laetantur coeli*).... I therefore encourage Catholics to pray fervently for the dead, for their family members and for all our brothers and sisters who have died, that they may obtain the remission of the punishments due to their sins and may hear the Lord's call: "Come, O my dear soul, to eternal repose in the arms of my goodness, which has prepared eternal delights for you" (Francis de Sales, *Introduction to the Devout Life*, 17, 4).[2]

A BIBLICAL RESPONSE TO PURGATORY

We will look at the Roman Catholic Church's "proof texts" in defense of purgatory shortly, but first let us look carefully at the redemptive power of the cross of Christ, for then the repercussions of the doctrine of purgatory will become clear. Purgatory does nothing to honor the achievements of Christ's death. It says, in effect, that his death did not achieve a full pardon of our sins and that it must be supplemented by suffering in purgatory. By contrast, the great apostle Paul said that Jesus "is able to save completely those who come to God through him, because he always lives to intercede for them" (Hebrews 7:25). Save completely! "Completely" doesn't mean partially, which is the implication of purgatory. When Jesus saves you completely, there is no need for purgatory.

Furthermore, Hebrews 10:10, says that "we have been made holy through the sacrifice of the body of Christ once for all." Because we are made holy by a holy God, there is no need for purgatory. And again, "By one sacrifice he has made perfect forever those who are being made holy" (Hebrews 10:14). Why would you need to go to purgatory when your sins have been forgiven, when Jesus' death has made you holy, and when you are said to be made perfect before God by the one sacrifice of Jesus? I believe a key difficulty for Catholics is that they don't understand what the death of Jesus accomplished. When the sacrifice of Christ is understood, then purgatory becomes redundant. And knowing that Jesus paid our debt in full should stir in us a spirit of worship and adoration of Christ the Lord. It certainly does for me.

The apostle John wrote that Jesus "freed us from our sins by his blood" (Revelation 1:5), and that "the blood of Jesus...purifies us from all sin" (1 John 1:7). The sins that once awaited punishment have been pardoned. God now treats us as if we had never sinned. One of my favorite verses of Scripture is 1 Peter 3:18: "Christ died for sins once for all, the righteous for the unrighteous, to bring you to God." I love that expression "to bring you to God." Our lost condition made it impossible for us to find our way back to God. We were lost and needed to be found. We were blind and needed to receive sight. We were guilty of sin and needed to be pardoned. We were separated from God and needed to be restored. We were enemies of God and needed to be reconciled. We were dead in sin and needed to be given life. And the whole purpose of the atoning death of Jesus was to accomplish this—"to bring you to God." Because of Jesus' death, "Mission Accomplished" can be written over the cross of Christ. Divine justice has been fully satisfied. Purgatory, then, has no place or purpose. Nor is it biblical.

The Truth About Ourselves

There is an unpalatable truth about ourselves that we find hard to accept. None of us see ourselves as God sees us. We compare ourselves to others and conclude that we are not so bad after all; in fact, we are rather good. That's fine when humans compare themselves to humans. But God's evaluation of us presents an entirely different picture:

> You see, at just the right time, when we were still powerless, Christ died for the ungodly. Very rarely will anyone die for a righteous man, though for a good man someone might possibly dare to die. But God demonstrates his own love for us in this: While we were still sinners, Christ died for us. Since we have now been justified by his blood, how much more shall we be saved from God's wrath through him! For if, when we were God's enemies, we were reconciled to him through the death of his Son, how much more, having been reconciled, shall we be saved through his life! (Romans 5:6-10).

God's verdict is that we are powerless, ungodly, and his enemies. Not very flattering, but true nevertheless. Yet in his infinite love Jesus laid down his life for us so we could have eternal life. As a result of his death we are now "justified by his blood"—that is, we are put right with God. Through Jesus' death we are "saved from God's wrath." The sword of God's justice will not fall upon us because divine justice was fully satisfied in the sacrificial death of God's Lamb.

Paul reminded the Colossian Christians of their spiritual condition both before and after their conversion to Jesus: "Once you were alienated from God and were enemies in your minds because of

your evil behavior. But now he has reconciled you by Christ's physical body through death to present you holy in his sight, without
blemish and free from accusation" (Colossians 1:21-22). Isn't that
wonderful? We are "free from accusation." This is true about all
who belong to Jesus. Three points highlight Paul's remarks: 1) God
does the reconciling; 2) the death of Christ makes reconciliation
possible; and 3) reconciliation enables Christians to be presented
to God holy, without blemish, and free from accusation. Certainly
this leaves no room for purgatory.

These blessings are not of our own making: "All this is from God,"
Paul says, "who reconciled us to himself through Christ" (2 Corinthians 5:18). Reconciliation is the result of God "not counting men's
sins against them" (verse 19). Every taint of sin that once offended
God and kept us separated has been removed by Jesus. I would ask
every Roman Catholic reading this to embrace the wonderful truth
of a crucified Christ and let nothing—absolutely *nothing*—distract
from the achievements of Christ's death.

Over almost four decades of ministry, I have heard many people
express astonishment at what the gospel says. It has not been unu-
sual for them to say, in effect, "It's too good to be true; there must
be a catch to it." If such blessings were the result of our own efforts,
then I could understand people's hesitation to believe them. But
when our faith is focused on Jesus, doubt is replaced with a blessed
assurance. The certainty of our forgiveness and our home with God
in heaven is captured in these words: "Christ did not enter a man-
made sanctuary that was only a copy of the true one; he entered
heaven itself, now to appear for us in God's presence" (Hebrews
9:24). We need to pause a little to draw our breath at the wonder of
what this scripture teaches us. Unlike the sacrifices offered by the
priests in the temple in Jerusalem, Jesus, who is both our high priest
and sacrifice, has entered into the very presence of God in heaven
"for us." It is those two small words "for us" that guarantee our home

in heaven the moment we die. Because I belong to Jesus, I know that when I die he will take me to heaven to be with him. I know I am a sinner, but I also know that I have a Savior, a fact I can never deny. My certainty of going to heaven when I die rests on those two words, "for us." When the Father accepted Christ, he accepted all those who belong to Christ.

Why, then, should there be a need for purgatory? What purpose does it serve? Jesus has provided "purification for sins," and once that purification was accomplished by his death, "he sat down at the right hand of the Majesty in heaven" (Hebrews 1:3). The seated position of the Lord Jesus Christ declares that his sacrificial work has been accomplished. Listen to what he uttered from the cross: "It is finished" (John 19:30). It is through his death that we are now "holy and blameless in his sight" (Ephesians 1:4). And a day will come when Jesus will "present her [the church] to himself as a radiant church, without stain or wrinkle or any other blemish, but holy and blameless" (Ephesians 5:27). What makes the bride of Christ, the church, spotless and perfect is the atoning death of Jesus. The purification needed to enter heaven was achieved by Christ's death, not by the flames of purgatory.

No Condemnation in Jesus

In Romans 8:1 the apostle Paul wrote that "there is now no condemnation for those who are in Christ Jesus." No condemnation! Our sins and their consequences have been dealt with at the cross. Before God we are innocent. In reinforcing this wonderful truth, Paul asked a series of rhetorical questions, one of them being, "Who will bring any charge against those whom God has chosen? It is God who justifies" (Romans 8:33). Every charge that can be brought against one who belongs to Christ is answered by pointing to a crucified Christ who paid in full the penalty of all our sins.

Let me illustrate the certainty of our full pardon by sharing about an incident that happened to me. I entered into a business transaction with a company and promptly paid them for their services. Yet over the next several weeks I received invoices requesting payment. Friendly reminders were soon replaced with not-so-friendly reminders. Eventually the threat of legal proceedings arrived. During the entire time I was not worried. Why? I knew the company had no case against me, no matter what they said, for I had in my possession a cancelled check proving that payment had been made.

Likewise, we as Christians possess a receipt that says full payment for our sins has been made by God's Lamb. Our debt is paid in full—nothing, absolutely nothing, remains outstanding!

THE CATHOLIC REPLY

What proof does the Roman Catholic Church offer from Scripture in support of the doctrine of purgatory, with its anathema on those who do not accept it? A text in 2 Maccabees is cited: "It is therefore a holy and a wholesome thought to pray for the dead that they may be released from sins" (2 Maccabees 12:46 NEB). There are three important points that need to be made about 2 Maccabees.

First, 2 Maccabees was never recognized as part of the canon of Scripture. We have the authority of Jesus for this. He endorsed only the 39 books of the Old Testament as canonical: "Beginning with Moses and all the Prophets, he explained to them what was said in all the Scriptures concerning himself.... Everything must be fulfilled that is written about me in the Law of Moses, the Prophets and the Psalms" (Luke 24:27,44).

Second, the book of 2 Maccabees never made any pretense of being inspired of God. In fact, the writer quite openly said that he hoped his work didn't have too many flaws in it: "At this point I will bring my work to an end. If it is found well written and aptly composed, that is what I myself hoped for: if cheap and mediocre, I could only do my best" (2 Maccabees 15:38-39 NEB). These are not the words of a man writing by the inspiration of the Holy Spirit. No wonder this book was never regarded as Holy Scripture! Yet the Roman Catholic Church clings to it in order to justify purgatory.

Finally, the book contradicts the Roman Catholic doctrine of purgatory. The writer says of Israel's slain soldiers, "It is therefore a holy and wholesome thought to pray for the dead that they may be loosed from sins" (2 Maccabees 12:46 DRV). Those who died were found with idols in their possessions (verse 40). According to Roman Catholic teaching, idolatry is a mortal, not a venial, sin. Since these people had committed mortal sin, they would have gone to hell (and not purgatory), from which there is no escape.

It is obvious that the Catholic Church's key proof text in relation to the doctrine of purgatory is unreliable. But there are some texts in the New Testament that are called upon to support purgatory. For example, Paul's words in 1 Corinthians 3:12-15: "If any man builds on this foundation using gold, silver, costly stones, wood, hay or straw, his work will be shown for what it is, because the Day will bring it to light. It will be revealed with fire, and the fire will test the quality of each man's work. If what he has built survives, he will receive his reward. If it is burned up, he will suffer loss; he himself will be saved, but only as one escaping through the flames." It is not my intention to be impolite in my remarks here, but some straight talking is called for because of the consequences of this doctrine. Simply taking a text that has the words "flames" and "saved" and imposing on it the doctrine of purgatory is an appalling use of Scripture. There is absolutely nothing in this passage that remotely hints of purgatory. In context, Paul is giving instruction to those engaged in ministry. Ministers must take care to build with the right types of material because the quality of their work will one day be tested. The use of figurative language is plain to see, for no one actually builds the work of God with literal gold, silver, costly stones, wood, hay, or straw. All this passage is saying is that our works will be tested to see what survives. Fire tests a man's work. If it is built with quality material, it will survive; otherwise it will be destroyed. To import purgatory into Paul's words is a great injustice.

The Catholic Church also calls upon Jesus' words to lend support to purgatory. They quote Matthew 12:32, which says, "Anyone who speaks a word against the Son of Man will be forgiven, but anyone who speaks against the Holy Spirit will not be forgiven, either in this age or the age to come." Again, the context of the passage must be respected. Here's the background: Jesus had been working miracles "by the Spirit of God" (verse 28). The religious leaders were unable to deny that miracles were happening, yet were reluctant to acknowledge Jesus as the Messiah. The only way they could explain the miracles was to say Jesus was in league with the devil. In so doing they were denying the clear evidence before them and attributing demonic power to Jesus. The passage has to do with those who totally reject God's revelation, not with having sins purged from us at some point in the future. The Roman Catholic Church interprets the unforgiven sins in "the ages to come" as sins that will be forgiven in purgatory. This is a terrible abuse of Jesus' words.

The Roman Catholic Church teaches that there is "purifying fire" through which the departed soul must pass before entering heaven. And, if purgatory can prepare a soul for heaven, is not purgatory in some way a savior? Do you see what is happening here? Do you see the implication this teaching has on the sacrifice of Christ? The Roman Catholic Church might cite the words, "God disciplines us for our good, that we may share in his holiness" (Hebrews 12:10), and Roman Catholics may want to say that since God punishes his children to make them holy, he will continue to punish them in purgatory in order to make them ready for heaven. But to use this scripture in this way is to abuse it. The context of Hebrews 12:10 is

God's discipline of his children who are now living in this world and has absolutely nothing to say about God's discipline in the afterlife.

I recall a discussion I had with a Roman Catholic priest on the subject of purgatory. This took place in the month of November, the month the Church sets aside for observing the suffering souls in purgatory. Earlier that day he had said Mass for those suffering souls. I asked him, "If Jesus the Lamb of God took away our sins, why is there a need for purgatory?" Either Jesus took away our sins, or he didn't. If purgatory is necessary, then Jesus' pardon was not complete. Yet Scripture says he paid in full the penalty for our sins. (By the way, the priest could never answer my question.)

DOES PURGATORY EXALT JESUS' DEATH?

Even the most fervent advocate of purgatory doesn't look forward with enthusiasm to joining the ranks of the suffering souls. And knowing that just one venial sin can send you there is a frightening prospect. When I was a Catholic, I felt that my best hope of minimizing my stay in purgatory was to accumulate enough indulgences to offset my sentence. (Seriously, I kept a close eye on the religious duties that brought the most indulgences. For example, making the sign of the cross granted 100 days' indulgence, whereas making the sign of the cross with holy water granted 300 days' indulgence.)

To believe in purgatory is to believe that the death of Jesus did not remit all punishment due to our sins. In other words, his death was insufficient. When a Roman Catholic says Jesus' death achieved our forgiveness, I ask, "Why then do you still need purgatory?" The typical answer is "to remove the temporal punishment due to sin." To which I reply, "But didn't Jesus' death take care of that?" I'm sorry, but you can't have it both ways. To say that purification in purgatory is also necessary is to heap an insult (unintentionally, but wrong nevertheless) upon the atoning sacrifice of Jesus. It is to nullify the gospel. I am fully convinced this is not what Roman Catholics intend, but that is the consequence of what they believe. Roman Catholics may try to tone down the problem by saying that not everyone goes to purgatory. But even if only *one* soul went to purgatory, the doctrine belittles the atoning sacrifice of Christ. Why would even one soul need to go to purgatory?

In summary, purgatory is a denial of all that the Bible teaches about the full and complete redemption achieved by the death of Jesus, the Lamb of God.

WORTHY IS THE LAMB

My objective in this chapter has not been to be anti-Catholic but to be pro-Christ—to exalt the blessed and wondrous sacrifice of God's Lamb and to highlight his divine accomplishments. I hope I have done that. What better way to conclude this chapter than with the words of the apostle John, who in a vision of heaven heard these glorious words:

> Worthy is the Lamb, who was slain, to receive power and wealth and wisdom and honor and glory and praise.... To him who sits on the throne and to the Lamb be praise and honor and glory and power, for ever and ever. The four living creatures said, "Amen," and the elders fell down and worshiped (Revelation 5:12-13).

QUESTIONS AND ANSWERS

Q. **Is not the Roman Catholic doctrine of purgatory taught in the Bible?**

No. This doctrine is found nowhere in the Bible. The Roman Catholic Church appeals to the book of 2 Maccabees for support but 1) this book never formed part of the canon of Scripture; 2) the book does not claim to be inspired of God (in fact, it states the opposite); and 3) the book contains contradictions. Furthermore, the Catholic Church's appeals to passages in the New Testament to support the doctrine of purgatory require one to take scripture out of context.

Q. **Is not purgatory necessary to purge us of sin?**

No. All the punishment we deserved was paid in full by the atoning sacrifice of the Lamb of God. His death satisfied in full God's holy justice. Nothing was left outstanding. Hence Paul's words, "There is now no condemnation for those who are in Christ Jesus" (Romans 8:1).

Q. **Because we are not good enough to enter heaven, isn't there a need for purgatory to prepare us for heaven?**

No one deserves to go to heaven; we all deserve to go to hell. That's an unpleasant fact, but it's true. But because God is gracious we receive what we never deserved—a full pardon of all our sins. This is made possible through what Jesus did upon the cross. The perfect sacrifice of Jesus makes purgatory unnecessary.

Q. **Is not the holy sacrifice of the Mass beneficial for the suffering souls in purgatory?**

There is no such place as purgatory; there is no suggestion of it in the Bible. The Bible speaks of full and total forgiveness to those who receive Jesus as their Savior, which makes the Mass for souls in purgatory unscriptural and unnecessary.

Q. **What are the implications of believing in purgatory?**

The doctrine of purgatory, in effect, says that the one perfect sacrifice of Jesus Christ did not achieve our full pardon. Purgatory does nothing to honor the perfect and complete sacrifice of Jesus Christ.

10

The Royal Priesthood

. . . .

The Roman Catholic priesthood is indispensable to the sacramental life of the Church, for without an ordained priest, the sacrifice of the Mass cannot be offered, and the sacrament of penance cannot be received. The Roman Catholic Church has always affirmed that Jesus, on the night he instituted the Lord's Supper, appointed the apostles to be priests and that the apostles, in turn, passed on their authority to forgive and retain sins and to say Mass to succeeding generations. Whatever misgiving one may have about the Council of Trent (1545–1564), the council must be credited with speaking in terms that are unambiguous. On the priesthood the Council of Trent says:

> If any says that by those words, "Do this for a commemoration of me," Jesus did not institute the Apostles priests or did not ordain that they and others priests

should offer his own body and blood, let him be anathema (Canon 2).

On Holy Orders and the priesthood the Catholic Catechism has this to say:

> Christ, whom the Father hallowed and sent into the world, has, through the apostles, made successors, the bishops namely, sharers in his consecration and mission; and these, in their turn, duly entrusted in varying degrees various members of the Church with the office of this ministry…[the priest] in virtue of the sacrament of Holy Orders, after the image of Christ, the supreme and eternal priest, they [priests] are consecrated in order to preach the gospel and shepherd the faithful as well as to celebrate divine worship as true priests of the New Testament [1562-1564].

These statements show the Roman Catholic Church's firm conviction that its priesthood is ordained of God. I believe that this view is held in all sincerity and that many of those who serve as priests do so with honest conviction. But the criteria for determining truth must be the Word of God. What does Scripture say about the priesthood?

PRIESTS IN THE OLD TESTAMENT

To understand the origins of the Catholic priesthood, we need to have an understanding of the priesthood among the people of God in the Old Testament. After the Israelites left Egypt and were on their way to the Promised Land, God began revealing instructions as to how his people were to worship him. From the 12 tribes that composed the nation of Israel he chose the tribe of Levi as the priestly tribe. This meant genealogy alone determined who would be priests.

These priests served first in the tabernacle, and later, in the temple. They fulfilled a variety of functions and ministered to the people. They wore special clothing when ministering before the Lord, and a clear description of the nature of their work is given throughout the Old Testament (see Exodus 27–29; 38:21; Leviticus 6:12; 10:11; Numbers 3:10; Nehemiah 8:7-9; 9:3-5; 12:27-47). There were some periods during which the priests, along with the prophets, engaged in idolatry and departed from what God had commanded. There was also a high priest, and his "job description" is found in Hebrews: "Every high priest is selected from among men and is appointed to represent them in matters related to God, to offer gifts and sacrifices for sins. He is able to deal gently with those who are ignorant and are going astray, since he himself is subject to weakness" (Hebrews 5:1-2). The high priest represented the people in his ministry before God.

THE SACRIFICIAL PRIESTHOOD

In the Hebrew epistle we get a clear insight into what the Old Testament priests did. Their most important duty was to offer animal sacrifices to God on behalf of the people, and yet these sacrifices were totally ineffective in securing remission of sin. The ineffectiveness of this priesthood, along with the sacrifices they offered, is stated thus: "Day after day every priest stands and performs his religious duties; again and again he offers the same sacrifices, which can never take away sins. But when this priest [Jesus] had offered for all time one sacrifice for sins, he sat down at the right hand of God. Since that time he waits for his enemies to be made his footstool, because by one sacrifice he has made perfect forever those who are being made holy" (Hebrews 10:10-14).

This leads to a key question: Why did God institute such a priesthood and an ineffectual sacrificial system? They served as a shadow of what was to come. Let me explain that: When you stand in the sunlight, your body casts your shadow on the ground. The shadow is not real, it is merely indicative of something that is real—in this case, yourself. The priesthood and sacrifices were shadows of real things that were yet to come; they were announcements of the coming Jesus, who would be both the high priest and a sacrifice. The ineffectual system with priests and sacrifices was not intended to last forever; it would cease with the coming of Jesus, who is God's perfect sacrifice and high priest.

THE HIGH PRIESTHOOD OF CHRIST

Hebrews chapter 7 talks about Melchizedek the priest, and it's interesting to read that "this Melchizedek was king of Salem and priest of God Most High.... Without father or mother, without genealogy, without beginning of days or end of life, like the Son of God he remains a priest forever" (Hebrews 7:1,3). Why are we not told anything about Melchizedek's parentage? This silence helps present Melchizedek as a type of Christ. He sets the stage for the introduction of the high priesthood of Christ, who "has become a priest not on the basis of a regulation as to his ancestry but on the basis of the power of an indestructible life" (verse 16). God then added, "You are a priest forever, in the order of Melchizedek" (verse 7:17).

Verses 23-25 continue, "Now there have been many of those priests, since death prevented them from continuing in office; but because Jesus lives forever, he has a permanent priesthood. Therefore he is able to save completely those who come to God through him, because he always lives to intercede for them." Because of Jesus' endless life "the ministry Jesus has received is as superior to theirs [the Old Testament priests'] as the covenant of which he is mediator is superior to the old one, and it is founded on better promises" (Hebrews 8:6).

BEHIND THE VEIL

The superiority of Jesus' priesthood is clearly seen when it is contrasted to the ministry of Israel's high priests. Once a year on the Day of Atonement the high priest entered the Holy of Holies in the temple to seek God's forgiveness for the people (Hebrews 9:7). The curtain separating the Holy of Holies from the rest of the temple symbolized the people's inability to come into God's presence. Remember, when Adam and Eve sinned and were driven from the Garden of Eden, their intimate fellowship with God was broken. But when Jesus died, "at that moment the curtain of the temple was torn in two from top to bottom" (Matthew 27:51), demonstrating that the way into God's presence had been restored through the atoning death of Jesus, the High Priest. Unlike the high priest who entered the Holy of Holies on the Day of Atonement with the blood of a slain animal, Jesus provided himself as the perfect sacrifice. Having accomplished our redemption, "he sat down at the right hand of God" (Hebrews 10:12). The Old Testament priesthood, which was only a shadow, is now redundant. The shadow yields to the reality, the ineffectual priesthood yields to the effectual.

A ROYAL PRIESTHOOD

The New Testament speaks of a new priesthood distinctly different from the old priesthood, which was based entirely on ancestry and served in a temple where animal sacrifices were offered. If you were not from the tribe of Levi, you could not be a priest. But the criterion to be a priest in the church of Christ is not based on whether your father is a Levite, but whether God is your Father through a new birth (John 1:12; 3:1-16). Racial, cultural, social, and sexual distinctions do not exist in the new community of the Spirit, "for all of you who were baptized into Christ have clothed yourselves with Christ. There is neither Jew nor Greek, slave nor free, male nor female, for you are all one in Christ Jesus" (Galatians 3:27-28).

This means everyone in the church is a priest. Former distinctions have been abolished. Collectively we who are in the church compose the "holy priesthood" of which Peter speaks and are "priests" who serve God (1 Peter 2:5; Revelation 1:6). We don't have to have a vocation or special calling to be a priest. A priest in the church does not hold a position distinct from other believers in the community of faith. That is foreign to the New Testament. Nowhere in the New Testament do you read of anyone being ordained to be a priest.

What we do see is the appointing/ordaining of men to serve as *spiritual leaders* in the churches (Acts 14:23; 1 Timothy 3:1-7; Titus 1:5). They are referred to by titles such as elders, pastors, bishops, overseers—all of which refer to the same office (Acts 20:17,28). They are charged with looking after the spiritual welfare of the local church (1 Peter 5:1-5). These are spiritual, trustworthy men who are chosen by the local church because they can give mature spiritual leadership to the church. It is incorrect to think that these elders were ordained as priests, as the Roman Catholic Church maintains. Their appointment to serve the church was accompanied by the "laying on of hands" (1 Timothy 5:22; see also 4:14). This was the accepted manner of giving approval or endorsement. This is not the sacrament of Holy Orders, something the Bible never speaks about.

The role of the Catholic priest resembles the role of priest in the Old Testament, who wore special vestments and offered sacrifices for the sins of the people. Yet we have seen that Israel's priesthood served its purpose and that now there is a new priesthood composed of every believer. The clergy-laity arrangement in the Catholic Church is not seen in the church we read about in the Bible.

PRIESTHOOD OF ALL BELIEVERS

Christ's priests now offer a new kind of sacrifice. No longer is there a need for sacrifices to be offered for our sins. Instead, we are given this instruction: "Offer your bodies as living sacrifices, holy and pleasing to God—this is your spiritual act of worship" (Romans 12:1). Everything we do with our bodies—our hands, feet, eyes, ears, tongue, etc.—is to be holy, a living sacrifice offered unto to God. Knowing that everything we do, even the most menial task, can be offered up to God gives great dignity to all we do: "Whatever you do, whether in word or in deed, do it all in the name of the Lord Jesus Christ, giving thanks to God the Father through him" (Colossians 3:17).

Further examples of the priestly sacrifices we can offer to God are seen in Paul's words to the Christians at Philippi. Paul had established that church on one of his missionary journeys. From the beginning this church sustained a wonderful relationship with Paul, supporting his evangelistic work. When Paul was imprisoned in Rome, the church sent gifts to meet his needs. Courteous as always, Paul thanked them for their kindness, referring to their generosity as "a fragrant offering, an acceptable sacrifice, pleasing to God" (Philippians 4:18). Paul's words are rich in liturgical meaning. He is thanking them for the priestly ministry they had rendered—a ministry accepted by God as an act of holy worship.

On another occasion Christians are encouraged to continue engaging in their priestly work of prayer because God views this as a sacrifice offered to him: "Through Jesus, therefore, let us continually offer to God a sacrifice of praise—the fruit of lips that confess his name" (Hebrews 13:15). Then the next verse adds, "Do not forget to do good and to share with others, for with such sacrifices God is pleased" (Hebrews 13:16). Emerging from the Scriptures is a lovely picture of what a Christian is: a priest whose body is the temple of the Holy Spirit and who offers spiritual sacrifices to God (1 Corinthians 6:19; Hebrews 13:15-16; 1 Peter 2:9). Wherever there is a Christian, there is a priest and a temple in which spiritual sacrifices are offered to God. This is the priesthood in the church Jesus built.

An Unbiblical Burden upon Priests

Celibacy is a gift from God. Jesus taught that some have been given this gift for the benefit of the kingdom of heaven (Matthew 19:11-12). Those who remain celibate for the sake of the kingdom of God have a distinct advantage, in some areas, over those who are married with families. Paul wrote, "An unmarried man is concerned about the Lord's affairs—how he can please the Lord. But a married man is concerned about the affairs of this world—how he can please his wife—and his interests are divided" (1 Corinthians 7:32-34).

Let us suppose, for example, that an opportunity arises for preaching the gospel in a remote and difficult area of the world and there are two suitable candidates: one is single, and the other is married with a young family. The obvious choice in this case is the one who will not be burdened with the responsibility of having to care for a family. The one who is celibate is free from the responsibility of having to help a family adjust to a new and difficult environment. Will there be suitable schooling for the children? Will his wife get homesick? These concerns do not exist for the unmarried man. This is not to say that celibacy is a superior gift to marriage; it is not. The ministry I am engaged in has been blessed tremendously through the support of a godly wife. And in the early church, the apostles were married—a fact that is never denied by the Roman Catholic Church. However, when I was a Catholic, I recall being taught that when the apostles said to the Lord, "We have left everything to follow you!" that included their wives (Matthew 19:27). I am amazed to think how naively so many of us accepted this as fact, never considering the grave injustice such a decision would have had on the wives of the apostles, not to mention the fact such a teaching contradicts the evidence in Scripture.

Peter and the other apostles, along with the brothers of the Lord, remained married throughout their lives, and their wives often accompanied them on their journeys: "Don't we have the right to take a believing wife along with us, as do the other apostles and the Lord's brothers and Cephas [Peter]?" (1 Corinthians 9:3-5; cf. John 1:42). When Peter wrote about marriage he said, "Husbands, in the same way be considerate as you live with your wives, and treat them with respect" (1 Peter 3:7). That statement would carry no weight if it came from a man who had left his wife.

A PRIESTHOOD IN CONFLICT

As noted earlier, the Roman Catholic priesthood is without divine authorization. It is a priesthood in conflict with the epistle to the Hebrews. Furthermore, the Roman Catholic Church's insistence that priests be celibate cannot be supported from Scripture. Consider Paul's instructions to those who would serve in the church as bishops (remember, the word *bishop* is used interchangeably with *elder/pastor/overseer/presbyter*). Guided by the Holy Spirit, Paul wrote that a bishop must be "the husband of but one wife.... He must manage his own family well and see that his children obey him with proper respect. (If anyone does not know how to manage his own family, how can he take care of God's church?)" (1 Timothy 3:2,4-5; cf. Titus 1:5-9). Bishops/elders/pastors were family men with a proven record of domestic stability, spiritual maturity, and wisdom. You can tell a lot about a man by how he treats his wife and from the behavior of his children. Elders were appointed by those who knew and trusted them to be their spiritual guides.

The cover story for the February 23, 1970 issue of *Time* magazine was titled, "The Catholic Exodus: Why Priests and Nuns Are Quitting." Many of those who left expressed frustration with the Catholic Church, and celibacy figured prominently in their dissatisfaction. Since those days, the number of priests who have left is in excess of 100,000. According to these figures, a Catholic priest resigns his ministry every few hours.

Some Roman Catholic priests who left the priesthood have found their spiritual life in the church of Christ. I am personally acquainted with a number of such men. They are not the first men to have left the priesthood. Luke records how "the number of the disciples in Jerusalem increased rapidly, and a large number of priests became obedient to the faith" (Acts 6:7). These were Levitical priests who had offered up daily sacrifices for the people. But upon hearing the good news that the one sacrifice offered by Jesus achieved the forgiveness of all our sins, they became obedient to the Lord. They discontinued their former ministry as priests, seeing in Jesus Christ a superior priesthood and a superior sacrifice. Saved from their sins, they became part of the "holy priesthood" in the church of Christ.

Roman Catholic priests do not take their commitment lightly. Personal sacrifices and tough decisions accompany their choice to pursue the priesthood. I would be less than honest if I did not say that, based on the Word of God, these priests, like those mentioned by Luke, need also to become "obedient to the faith." It is my prayer that this will happen—for the glory of God alone.

QUESTIONS AND ANSWERS

Q. What does the Bible say about priests in the Old Testament?

The nation of Israel was composed of 12 tribes, and the priests were chosen from the tribe of Levi. Their function was to offer sacrifices to God on behalf of the people. There was also a high priest who represented all the people before God. The whole sacrificial system pointed to a future time when God would provide the perfect high priest and the perfect sacrifice to atone for the sins of the world—Jesus Christ.

Q. What was deficient in the Old Testament priesthood?

The sacrificial ministry did not remove even one sin committed because a perfect sacrifice was required. Only God could provide that, and he did, in his Son, the Lamb of God, who takes away the sin of the world. Furthermore, the high priest's ministry lasted only as long as he lived. Then another high priest had to be found to replace him. What was needed was a sacrifice that would achieve forgiveness and a high priest who would never die. Only Jesus could meet these demands.

Q. Who are God's priests today?

Peter is emphatic that every Christian is part of the royal priesthood. No longer is priesthood linked with tribal ancestry as under the old covenant; in the new covenant, every believer is a priest, male or female. As priests we offer to God "a sacrifice of praise—the fruits of lips that confess his name" (Hebrews 13:15).

Furthermore, we offer our lives in service to him, "for with such sacrifices God is pleased" (verse 16). The Bible speaks clearly, then, about the priesthood of all believers.

Q. **Where, then, did the Roman Catholic priesthood come from?**

It is modeled in the lines of the Old Testament priesthood. To be a Roman Catholic priest, one must be male, as in the Levitical priesthood. By contrast, the Bible speaks of male and female priests in God's priesthood of all believers. There is no clergy-laity distinction in the church. Furthermore, Roman Catholic priests are like Israel's priests in that they are engaged in offering the same sacrifice day after day, when, in fact, Jesus already offered one perfect sacrifice for all time, putting an end to the need for repeated sacrifices.

11

Confess Your Sins

. . . .

Do you remember making your first confession? I do. For months we received instruction on this sacrament in preparation for making our first Holy Communion. The priest assured us there was nothing to fear; confession would be a wonderful experience. And so, at the age of seven, our class formed two lines and marched from school to the parish church. I entered the confession box with a mental list of all my sins.

"Bless me, Father, for I have sinned. This is my first confession." I proceeded, "I often talk in church; I look around me during Mass when I should be paying attention; I fight with my sisters."

"You have made a very good confession," said the priest, "and for your penance, say three Hail Marys."

That was the first of many confessions I made. As I grew older and my sins moved from "venial" (minor) to "mortal" (serious) sins, confession became more arduous. The occasion of the sins and their frequency had to be recalled: I committed this sin eight

times, that sin twice, and the other sin 16 times. The practice of
confession was reinforcing to me that the Church held in its power
the keys to unlock the way to heaven, and without the Church
and its sacraments—especially the sacrament of penance—all that
awaited me after death was an eternity in hell. I was left in no
doubt that the Church was indispensable; it was my lifeline to
heaven.

What the Church Teaches

Many Catholics find confession difficult. In fact, it is often
neglected, even though the Church teaches that confession must be
made at least once a year. Confession is one of the seven sacraments
of the Roman Catholic Church, and the proof text the Church uses
in support of this practice is John 20:19-23:

> On the evening of that first day of the week, when
> the disciples were together, with the doors locked for fear
> of the Jews, Jesus came and stood among them and said,
> "Peace be with you!" After he said this, he showed them
> his hands and side. The disciples were overjoyed when
> they saw the Lord. Again Jesus said, "Peace be with you! As
> the Father has sent me, I am sending you." And with that
> he breathed on them and said, "Receive the Holy Spirit. If
> you forgive anyone his sins, they are forgiven; if you do not
> forgive them, they are not forgiven."

The Roman Catholic Church stands alone in its understanding
of these words from Jesus. On December 2, 1973, Pope John Paul VI
authorized the publication of "Rite of Penance," which states,

> Our Savior, Jesus Christ, when he gave to his Apostles
> and their successors power to forgive sins, instituted in his
> Church the sacrament of penance. Thus the faithful who

fall into sin after baptism may be reconciled with God and renewed in grace.[1]

Moreover, the teaching of Trent and of the Church today is that "absolution is given by a priest, who acts as judge."[2]

The Church teaches that it is necessary by divine law to confess to a priest each and every mortal sin—and also circumstances which make a sin a more serious kind of mortal sin—that one can remember after careful examination of conscience.[3]

These statements show the unique claim being made by the Roman Catholic Church—the claim that it was entrusted by Christ with the power to forgive and retain sins through the sacrament of penance. But is the Bible filled with examples of people confessing their sins to a priest, as practiced by the Roman Catholic Church? Surely if this is what Jesus meant in John 20, then we should expect to see convincing evidence of the practice in Scripture. Since the apostles were the ones to whom Jesus addressed the words in John 20, we need to see how they understood the words. In order to do this, we need to look at two aspects of forgiveness: 1) how our sins are forgiven initially, and 2) how we are forgiven of sins committed after our conversion to Christ.

WHY JESUS CAME TO EARTH

Before Christ's birth, nearly four centuries had gone by with no direct word from God. Malachi was the last of the Old Testament prophets, and through him God had foretold the coming of Israel's deliverer, the Messiah. God finally broke his silence to announce, through the angel Gabriel, that Mary would give birth to the promised Messiah, the Son of God. His mission was clear: Jesus would

196 Answers to Questions Catholics Are Asking

"save his people from their sins" (Matthew 1:21). The theme of forgiveness figures prominently in Jesus' ministry. "The Son of Man
came," he said, "to seek and to save what was lost" and "to give his
life as a ransom for many" (Luke 19:10; Matthew 20:28). Writers
of the New Testament linked the coming of Jesus with our forgiveness. The apostle John says that God sent his Son "that we might
live through him....[to be] an atoning sacrifice for our sins....to be
the Savior of the world" (1 John 4:9-10,14). And Paul says, "Here
is a trustworthy saying that deserves full acceptance: Christ Jesus
came into the world to save sinners—of whom I am the worst"
(1 Timothy 1:15). Jesus spoke of us being sheep who had gone astray
and that he was the Good Shepherd who "lays down his life for the
sheep" (John 10:11). Because of our spiritual condition we were lost
and needed to be found, were blind and needed sight, were dead in
sin and needed new life, were sinful and needed forgiveness. And
only Jesus could meet our need.

Before Jesus offered himself as the sacrifice for our sins, he demonstrated his power to forgive sins. The gospel of Mark records how
a crowd came to the house where Jesus was staying. The house was
filled to overflowing. A paralytic man was brought by his friends to
Jesus, but they were unable to gain access. Undaunted, they climbed
onto the roof and made an opening, lowering the paralytic into the
Lord's presence (not a very dignified entrance, but when you know
the miracle worker is present, then nothing stands in your way).
Jesus was amazed by their display of faith. He turned to the paralytic man and said, "Son, your sins are forgiven" (Mark 2:5). This
is not what the man and his friends were expecting; that's not why
they had come. They wanted Jesus to heal the man. The religious
leaders who had been listening to Jesus were horrified at what they
heard and retorted, "He's blaspheming! Who can forgive sins but
God alone?" (verse 7). Jesus didn't correct what they had said; he
allowed their statement to stand—only God can forgive sins and it

is blasphemy for anyone to assume that they can forgive sins. He asked them, "Which is easier, to say to the paralytic, 'Your sins are forgiven,' or to say, 'Get up, take your mat and walk'?" (verse 9). No theological training is required to answer that question—it is easier to say your sins are forgiven; the harder thing to do would be to enable the man to walk. And to show that he had authority to forgive sins, Jesus then told the paralytic man to "get up, take your mat and go home" (verse 11). Immediately the man, having been restored to perfect health, stood up and walked. The wide-eyed leaders exclaimed, "We have never seen anything like this!" (verse 12). The miracle confirmed who Jesus was—the Son of God, who had the power to forgive sins.

Irrespective of the age in which we live, the forgiveness of our sins is based upon the atoning sacrifice of Jesus. Those who were forgiven their sins before Jesus died were forgiven on the basis of his death. For example, the paralytic man was forgiven because Jesus would lay down his life as the payment for his sin. This is the message of forgiveness, the gospel that Jesus told the apostles to proclaim to all nations: "Go into all the world and preach the good news to all creation" (Mark 16:15). And just as Jesus had been sent by the Father with a mission to accomplish, he sent his apostles out to proclaim that the mission had been accomplished.

THE APOSTLES' ROLE

Before ascending to heaven Jesus said to his apostles that "repentance and forgiveness of sins will be preached in [my] name to all nations, beginning at Jerusalem" (Luke 24:47), and he entrusted them with this mission. How did the apostles understand these words from Jesus? How did they forgive sins? We need go no further than the day of Pentecost for our answer. On that day the glorified Christ sent the Holy Spirit to empower the apostles for their ministry. The message was that Jesus who was rejected, crucified, and buried had risen from the dead and ascended to the Father in heaven. Through the ministry of the Spirit, those who heard what the apostles proclaimed were convicted in their hearts of their sinfulness. Jesus, whom they had rejected, was indeed both Lord and Christ. So they cried out to the apostles, "What shall we do?" (Acts 2:37). What were they asking? They realized they had rejected the promised Messiah, the One foretold by the prophets. And they saw themselves as sinners in need of forgiveness. Peter commanded them, "Repent and be baptized, every one of you, in the name of Jesus Christ for the forgiveness of your sins. And you will receive the gift of the Holy Spirit.... Those who accepted his message were baptized, and about three thousand were added to their number that day" (Acts 2:38,41).

What does this example teach us about how the apostles forgave sins? Did they hear the confessions of any of these people and give them absolution? Or did they point sinners to the One who alone can forgive sins? The good news heard by the sinners in Acts 2 was that forgiveness of sins is to be found in Jesus. He died for the remission of their sins. That was the message consistently proclaimed by the apostles. We never read in the Bible of a distinction being made between venial and mortal sins. This teaching is not apostolic. Furthermore, we never read in Scripture of the Roman Catholic practice of confession. A Roman Catholic priest cannot forgive sin, even though he claims to do so by the authority of the Church; only God can forgive sins, for only God knows the heart of man.

THE CALL TO CONFESSION

Even after our conversion to the Lord we still sin. So how are those sins forgiven? The Roman Catholic Church says that all mortal sins must be confessed to a priest in order to receive absolution. This sacrament of penance is an indispensable part of Roman

Catholic teaching, though a search through the Word of God for evidence to support this teaching reveals nothing. On the contrary, the Bible presents a very different picture.

The apostle John heard Jesus speak about forgiving and retaining sins, and speaks about the need to confess the sins we have committed—but our confession is to be made to God, whom we have offended. "If we walk in the light," John says, "as he is in the light, we have fellowship with one another, and the blood of Jesus, his Son, purifies us from all sin. If we claim to be without sin, we deceive ourselves and the truth is not in us. If we confess our sins, he is faithful and just and will forgive us our sins and purify us from all unrighteousness" (1 John 1:7-9). According to the Bible, we confess our sins not to notify God of something he would not know otherwise, but to acknowledge our sinfulness and our dependence upon him for mercy. Through our conversion we are a forgiven people, but we must also be a penitent people.

Let's consider another apostolic instruction about confession. Simon the sorcerer believed the good news about Jesus and was baptized (Acts 8:13). He was impressed by the ministry of Peter and John, and when he saw that through the laying on of hands upon people spiritual gifts such as tongues and prophecy were given, he offered them money to give him this type of power. This was a grievous request and Peter told him, "Repent of this wickedness and pray to the Lord. Perhaps he will forgive you for having such a thought in your heart. For I see that you are full of bitterness and captive to sin" (Acts 8:22-23). Simon answered, "Pray to the Lord for me so that nothing you have said may happen to me" (verse 24). Here we have a baptized believer who sinned, yet Peter never told Simon to confess his sin to him or to John or to some priest. Instead Peter told Simon to repent—that is, to personally seek forgiveness from God, whom he had offended. If Peter and John had understood the words of Jesus as the Roman Catholic Church understands them, they would have instructed Simon accordingly. But they did not do that. Why? Because the sacrament of penance, the practice of confessing sins to a priest for absolution, is not to be found in the words spoken by Jesus or in the practice of the apostles or early church. Nothing in the ministry of the apostles remotely resembles the Roman Catholic sacrament of confession.

Three Types of Confession

The Scriptures speak of three categories of confession: 1) secret confession between God and man alone, 2) private confession between two people, one of whom has been sinned against by the other party, and 3) public confession requiring the exercise of church discipline. This is borne out by what Jesus said about confession of sins:[4]

> If your brother sins against you, go and show him his fault, just between the two of you. If he listens to you, you have won your brother over. But if he will not listen, take one or two others along, so that "every matter may be established by the testimony of two or three witnesses." If he refuses to listen to them, tell it to the church; and if he refuses to listen even to the church, treat him as you would a pagan or a tax collector. I tell you the truth, whatever you bind on earth will be bound in heaven, and whatever you loose on earth will be loosed in heaven. Again, I tell you that if two of you on earth agree about anything you ask for, it will be done for you by my Father in heaven. For where two or three come together in my name, there am I with them (Matthew 18:15-20).

Secret confession. When God alone has been sinned against, then he alone is the one to whom confession must be made. There are "secret sins" (Psalm 90:8) we commit; they do not involve anyone else. We think evil thoughts, we covet what another person has, we attribute false motives. These are all sins committed in the heart.

Jesus spoke of this kind of sin: "I tell you that anyone who looks at a woman lustfully has already committed adultery with her in his heart" (Matthew 5:28). The physical act of adultery does not need to take place in order to commit a sin; having committed adultery in the heart is enough to make it a sin. Such secret sins must be confessed only to God because no one else was involved in the sin. Confession of such sins does not require the presence of a third party. This is the clear teaching of Jesus.

Private confession. Not all sins are secret sins; some sins directly affect other people. What are we to do in such cases? This is where private confession comes in. Consider this scenario: John spreads lies about Tom and causes great distress to Tom. It is not enough that John seek God's forgiveness; he must also seek Tom's. This is one of the most neglected areas in the Christian life, though Jesus spoke clearly on the issue: "If you are offering your gift at the altar and there remember that your brother has something against you, leave your gift there in front of the altar. First go and be reconciled to your brother; then come and offer your gift"(Matthew 5:23-24). In this case, John needs to obey what Jesus said and go and be reconciled with Tom, whom he has sinned against. Then, and only then, can he return to worship.

What if someone who has sinned against you seeks reconciliation? Jesus said, "If your brother sins, rebuke him, and if he repents, forgive him. If he sins against you seven times in a day, and seven times comes back to you and says, 'I repent,' forgive him" (Luke 17:3-4). You are to forgive the offender when the offender repents. The brings about reconciliation, and it's the biblical manner in which confession is to take place. The Roman Catholic practice of confession to a priest finds no support here.

Public confession. What is Tom to do if he confronts John about his behavior, and John won't repent? Again, Jesus gives clear instructions: Witnesses are to be brought along. The matter has now moved from being private to being semiprivate. If John still won't repent even after being confronted, then the final step is to be invoked: The matter is to be taken to the church at which John and Tom are members. If after the matter is presented to the leaders of the church John still refuses to repent, then the church is to remove John from the assembly. No longer is the fellowship of the church to be extended to him. As long as he is impenitent, his sin is retained. The church is doing on earth what the Lord has already done in heaven. In the church in Corinth, a man was living with his father's wife (his stepmother). Paul instructed the church to discipline the impenitent man by removing him from the church; in so doing, the church was retaining his sin until the man repented. Not until after he repented could the church once again extend fellowship to him (1 Corinthians 5).

The Roman Catholic practice of confession cannot be found anywhere in the teachings of Jesus. Look closely again at what Jesus taught. He said that if your brother sins against you, you yourself are to reprove him privately. If he repents, then the matter is to go no further. The only time someone else is to hear about the sin is when that person refuses to repent and witnesses are needed. The Roman Catholic teaching says that even if the two people are reconciled, the "mortal" sin must also be confessed to a priest. But there is no scriptural support for such a teaching. Any teaching about confession of sins—including the words of James, "confess your sins to each other" (James 5:16)—must be understood within the boundaries set forth in Scripture.

Confession in James 5

The Roman Catholic Church has called upon James 5:14-16 to support its practice of having people confess their sins to a priest:

> Is any one of you sick? He should call the elders of the church to pray over him and anoint him with oil in the name of the Lord. And the prayer offered in faith will make the sick person well; the Lord will raise him up. If he has sinned, he will be forgiven. Therefore confess your sins to each other and pray for each other so that you may be healed. The prayer of a righteous man is powerful and effective.

Is James advocating the Roman Catholic practice of confessing sins to a priest? A careful examination of this passage shows quite the opposite.

This person who is sick, James says, is to call for the elders of his church. These are the spiritual leaders entrusted by God to care for his people. "They keep watch over you as men who must give an account" (Hebrews 13:17). The elders are not told to come and heal the sick person, but to come and pray for him.

Why is the person sick? We know that God sometimes disciplines his children for their spiritual benefit, and this discipline can come in the form of sickness. For example, the sinful behavior of some believers in Corinth brought discipline from God: "That is why many of you are weak and sick" (1 Corinthians 11:30). The person James speaks about may well have been engaged in sin and may have been experiencing discipline from the Lord. The discipline has had its desired effect and compelled the sick person to call for the elders of the congregation, his spiritual shepherds. This is not a social visit he has requested; they have come so that he can tell them that he has sought God's forgiveness and now seeks their prayers for his recovery.

Note that the elders have not come to give absolution or "hear a confession." They have come to support the individual in his spiritual recovery. In doing so, they will anoint him with oil and pray that God will remove the discipline visited upon him. There is absolutely nothing in this passage that supports the Roman Catholic practice of confession.

The Roman Catholic Church has also used this passage to support the teaching of extreme unction, but it's clear that the sick person James speaks about is anointed with a view toward making a full recovery, while the Roman Catholic practice is to anoint the sick person because he is dying.

When taken in context, then, the exhortation to "confess your sins to each other" has nothing to do with the Roman Catholic practice of confessing one's sins to a priest in order to receive absolution.

The Biblical Confession

The confession of sins as advocated by the Roman Catholic Church runs contrary to what Scripture teaches. When we have sinned against another person, then we must seek the forgiveness of that person—not because the person has power to absolve sin (only God can do that), but because seeking forgiveness brings reconciliation where enmity once existed. Nowhere in the Bible do we see God instructing his people to confess their sins to another person in order to receive absolution. The Roman Catholic sacrament of penance, then, must be rejected on the grounds that it lacks authority from God's Word.

QUESTIONS AND ANSWERS

Q. **Didn't Jesus give the Roman Catholic Church authority for the sacrament of penance, or confession, as it is commonly known?**

The Roman Catholic Church cites these words of Jesus as their proof text: "If you forgive anyone his sins, they are forgiven, if you do not forgive them, they are not forgiven" (John 20:23). Yet Jesus entrusted to the apostles not the sacrament of penance but the authority to go into the world proclaiming the forgiveness of sins in his name. In other words, he entrusted them with the good news of redemption in Christ. Those who embrace Christ are forgiven; those who do not obey the gospel remain condemned.

Q. **Should not all our mortal sins be confessed to a priest?**

Absolutely not. First, the Bible teaches that we must confess our sins to God because he is the one whom we have sinned against, and it is his forgiveness we must seek (1 John 1:7-9). There is nothing in the Scriptures to support the idea of a Roman Catholic priest acting on God's behalf in this matter. Second, when we sin against a fellow believer we must seek his forgiveness. Once forgiveness has been granted, the matter is not to go any further. Jesus specifically stated this was to be the case (Matthew 18:15-18). Yet the Roman Catholic Church violates this clear teaching with the sacrament of penance.

Q. **How did people have their sins absolved before the Catholic Church came into existence?**

One example will be sufficient here. King David of Israel committed adultery, then caused the death of the woman's husband and several innocent people in his attempt to cover up his sin. When he repented, he confessed his sin to God, and God forgave him (Psalm 32, 51). David did not turn to a priest to confess his sin.

Q. To whom should we confess our sins?

Every sin we commit is committed against God, and he is the one whose forgiveness we must seek. If we sin against a brother or sister in Christ, then we must seek their forgiveness also, in order to bring about reconciliation. The Roman Catholic practice of confession is not supported in Scripture.

Q. Did not James say we are to confess our sins to each other?

The Roman Catholic Church believes it has an ally in James 5:16, which says, "Confess your sins to each other and pray for each other so that you may be healed." But the context shows that the sick person is seeking prayer for healing. It's possible he is being disciplined by the Lord for his unfaithfulness. In calling for the elders, he is acknowledging that he has sought absolution from the Lord and asking that these spiritual leaders pray for his recovery. There is nothing in this passage that lends support for the Roman Catholic practice of confessing one's sins to a priest.

12
Mary the Mother of Jesus

. . . .

When Mary was told that she would miraculously conceive and give birth to Israel's Messiah, the Savior of the world, she responded, "May it be to me as you have said" (Luke 1:38). Hers was a simple and trusting faith—one worthy of imitation. She, a young virgin girl engaged to be married, would give birth to the world's Savior! This was astonishing news beyond human comprehension. Mary's faith becomes all the more amazing when we consider that she had no reference point for guidance, direction, counsel, or comfort. There was not another virgin who had miraculously conceived to whom she could turn. Nothing like this had ever happened before. Yet Mary believed what she had been told by the angel Gabriel. She didn't doubt his announcement. Her faith is a role model for all.

While Mary was a woman of great faith, when we examine what

the Bible actually says about her, we come to see that there is nothing Mary had done to gain God's favor. The Bible is silent about why she was chosen. And if we look back through the history of God's people, we have to acknowledge that God chooses people however he wants. For example, God chose Abraham to be the father of a nation. He chose the tribe of Judah to be the tribe from which the Savior would come. And he chose the household of David to be the royal family. From the descendants of David, Mary was chosen to be the mother of Israel's Messiah. God's choices are based on his sovereignty alone. And Mary was chosen not because she was the best or was morally superior; she was chosen because God can choose whomsoever he desires. There was nothing about Mary that compelled God to choose her.

Scripture reveals very little about Mary. Many of the Catholic Church's dogmas about Mary are man-made and find no support in Scripture. What's more, they have distorted not only our understanding of Mary, but the whole doctrine of redemption. These teachings do absolutely nothing to compliment Mary, who was a great woman of faith. When I was a Catholic, the Mary I knew was a person who had been reinvented by Roman Catholic dogma.

Let's examine the key Roman Catholic teachings about Mary and compare them to Scripture.

Perpetual Virginity?

The perpetual virginity of Mary is a major Marian doctrine. While Scripture clearly teaches the virgin birth of Jesus, it never suggests the perpetual virginity of Mary as taught by the Roman Catholic Church. In fact, it contradicts it. When we examine Scripture, its message is compelling: Mary did not remain a virgin after she gave birth to Jesus. But first let us hear what the Roman Catholic Church teaches on this subject:

Q. 5 Did Christ have brothers and sisters?

No. The marriage between Joseph and Mary was always completely virginal. Following Jewish usage, the brethren of Christ mentioned in the gospels were merely his cousins or other distant relatives.

Q. 6 How do we know that Mary remained always a virgin? We are certain of it because God, speaking to us through the inspired Scriptures and through His infallible Church tells us it is true.[1]

These are clear, unambiguous statements that leave no room for anyone to misunderstand exactly where the Roman Catholic Church stands. But is the Church in harmony with the teaching of the Bible?

The Testimony of Scripture

According to Matthew

Joseph and Mary were engaged to be married. When Joseph found out Mary was pregnant, he planned to divorce her quietly. His plans were interrupted by an angel, who told him that the child Mary was carrying was from the Holy Spirit. Matthew tells us that "when Joseph woke up, he did what the angel of the Lord had commanded him and took Mary home as his wife. But he had no union with her until she gave birth to a son. And he gave him the name Jesus" (Matthew 1:24-25).

Matthew is careful to point out that Joseph could not have been the father of Jesus. Matthew's words make it clear that while Joseph and Mary lived together as husband and wife during her pregnancy, they had no sexual relations until after Jesus was born. Matthew later mentions Jesus' brothers and sisters (Matthew 12:46-47; 13:53-57).

The key word in Matthew 1:25, the word "until," determines its meaning. We find it helpful to see a similar usage in Matthew 2:15. When King Herod wanted to kill the child Jesus, Mary and Joseph were told to flee to Egypt with Jesus. There, "he stayed until the death of Herod." The meaning Matthew wishes to convey is that Joseph and Mary remained in Egypt *until* Herod died—then they returned home. Similarly, Matthew stated that Joseph had no sexual relations with Mary "*until* she gave birth to a son." This tells us that after Jesus' birth, Joseph and Mary had a normal sexual relationship like any other married couple.

The point needs to be made that there was nothing unholy about Mary and Joseph having sex. How could there be? Marriage was designed by God, with sex as one of its blessings. It must be remembered that Joseph and Mary were engaged to be married. Like any engaged couple, they may have discussed, among other matters, having children. Such a discussion would not have been unholy. Sex within the bounds of marriage has the endorsement of God. The notion of marriage without sex is the opposite of what the Scriptures teach: "Marriage should be honored by all, and the marriage bed kept pure, for God will judge the adulterer and all the sexually immoral" (Hebrews 13:4).

The apostle Paul was very outspoken about the place of sex in marriage and the mutual obligation of both husband and wife to fulfill the sexual desires of their partner:

> The husband should fulfill his marital duty to his wife, and likewise the wife to her husband. The wife's body does not belong to her alone but also to her husband. In the same way, the husband's body does not belong to him alone but also to his wife. Do not deprive each other except by mutual consent and for a time, so that you may devote yourselves to prayer. Then come together again

so that Satan will not tempt you because of your lack of self-control (1 Corinthians 7:3-5).

Joseph and Mary, like any other married couple, would have engaged in sexual intercourse. Not to have had sex within marriage would have been contrary to God's design.

According to Mark

Mark, the writer of the Gospel that bears his name, does not endorse the Roman Catholic teaching that Mary remained a virgin all her life.

Marks tells of an occasion when Jesus was teaching at a house and a crowd had gathered to hear him. When Jesus' family heard about what was happening, "they went to take charge of him, for they said, 'He is out of his mind'" (Mark 3:21).

When Jesus had finished teaching, the crowd told him, "'Your mother and brothers are outside looking for you.' 'Who are my mother and brothers?' he asked. Then he looked at those seated in a circle around him and said, 'Here are my mother and brothers! Whoever does God's will is my brother and sister and mother'" (Mark 3:31-34). If the perpetual virginity of Mary was true, Jesus had the perfect opportunity to set the record straight by telling the people around him that he didn't have any brothers or sisters, and that he was an only child. But he didn't!

Even the people of Nazareth, who saw Jesus grow up, knew he had brothers and sisters. When they reacted to Jesus' teaching with amazement and unbelief, they asked, "Where did this man get these things?... What's this wisdom that has been given him, that he even does miracles! Isn't this the carpenter? Isn't this Mary's son and the brother of James, Joseph, Judas, and Simon? Aren't his sisters here with us?" (Mark 6:1-3). Certainly these people were in the best position to know whether Jesus had siblings. So why not accept their testimony?

According to Luke

Luke, the beloved physician, also stated some important words, on this subject. The opening paragraph of Luke's Gospel tells how thoroughly he researched Jesus' life before writing his Gospel (Luke 1:1-4). Many eyewitnesses were available to Luke, who could interview them to verify facts. Mary would have been the most obvious source for Luke's account of Jesus' birth. Based on his careful research, Luke set forth the virgin birth as a fact (Luke 1:26-38). The evidence must have been compelling for Luke, who was a doctor, to believe it.

At the same time, Luke had no reservations about stating that Mary had other children (Luke 8:19-21). When Luke wrote the book of Acts, he again affirmed that Mary had other children. He tells of a time when the apostles had gathered, and "they all joined together constantly in prayer, along with the women and Mary the mother of Jesus, and with his brothers" (Acts 1:14). Luke, who was a careful historian, believed in the virgin conception of Christ yet denied Mary's perpetual virginity.

According to John

John's testimony is important because he spent considerable time with the Lord and would have been in the company of Mary on many occasions. His close association with Jesus gave him firsthand knowledge of the Lord's family. In fact, John was the disciple to whom Jesus entrusted the care of Mary.

John made it clear that Mary did not remain a virgin after Jesus' birth. When John testifies about Jesus' first miracle, when he changed some water into wine, John records that Jesus "went down to Capernaum with his mother and brothers and his disciples" (John 2:12).

Later, in John 7, John mentions the Lord's brothers three times in one short paragraph: "When the Jewish Feast of Tabernacles was near, Jesus' brothers said to him.... For even his own brothers did not believe in him.... However, after his brothers had left for the Feast, he went also, not publicly, but in secret" (John 7:2-3,5,10). This tells us Mary was the mother of several children.

According to Paul

The great apostle Paul (who wrote over half of the New Testament) never taught the perpetual virginity of Mary. Quite the contrary, for Paul talked about meeting James, the brother of Jesus: "Then after three years, I went up to Jerusalem to get acquainted with Peter and stayed with him fifteen days. I saw none of the other apostles—only James, the Lord's brother." Paul then added, "I assure you before God that what I am writing you is no lie" (Galatians 1:18-20).

Elsewhere, in defense of his right to be financially supported by the church for his work, Paul wrote, "This is my defense to those who sit in judgment on me. Don't we have the right to food and drink? Don't we have the right to take a believing wife along with us, as do the other apostles and the Lord's brothers and Cephas?" (1 Corinthians 9:3-5). Paul's reference to "the Lord's brothers" makes the perpetual virginity of Mary an impossibility.

The Meaning of Words

The Catholic Perspective

At this point one might ask, "With so much evidence that Mary was not a perpetual virgin, why does the Roman Catholic Church still hold to its teaching?" We must remember that the Roman Catholic Church is not dependent upon the Scriptures alone for its teachings; it also draws from Tradition. The Church insists that the doctrine of Mary's the perpetual virginity has always been accepted as true and that any reference to the Lord's brothers and sisters is a reference to his cousins. But what does Scripture tell us?

The Biblical Answer

How are we to know the meaning of a word? One key way is by the context in which it appears. For example, Peter referred to the thousands of Jews who had come to Jerusalem for the Feast of Pentecost as "brothers" (Acts 2:29). When Paul defended himself against hostile Jews, he referred to them in a similar fashion— as "brothers" (Acts 22:1). In both cases the context determines how the word "brothers" is to be understood: It is a reference to common ancestry—that is, their common descent from the same father, Abraham.

Let me cite another example. When the angel Gabriel announced to Mary that she was to be the mother of the Messiah, the angel also said, "Elizabeth your relative [cousin] is going to have a child in her old age, and she who was said to be barren is in her sixth month" (Luke 1:36). How do we know that Elizabeth was not Mary's actual sister, but her cousin or relative? The context in which the statement is made leaves no doubt that Elizabeth is not Mary's sister, but Mary's cousin.

When reference is made to the brothers and sisters of Jesus, how do we know whether the reference is to their common ancestry, or to cousins or relatives? We determine what is correct by taking statements in context. The passages we reviewed from Matthew, Mark, Luke, John, and Paul do not support the perpetual virginity of Mary. All these writers made it clear that Mary had other children from her union with Joseph.

The matter of Jesus' siblings is important because it determines, among other things, our attitude toward the Bible as our only authority. The Roman Catholic Church cannot defend its doctrine of Mary's perpetual virginity from the Bible. It must go outside the Word of God, and as a result, it ends up with a doctrine that contradicts what God's Word teaches. If the doctrine of the perpetual virginity of Mary had originated with God, we would find corroborating evidence in the Scriptures. But no such evidence exists. When, then, did the Catholic Church introduce this doctrine?

Especially revealing is the origin of the doctrine of Mary's perpetual virginity, which is a relatively recent development in the Church's history.

IMMACULATE CONCEPTION?

On December 8, 1854, Pope Pius IX issued the following decree:

> We, by the authority of Jesus Christ, our Lord, of the Blessed Apostles, Peter and Paul, and by our Own, declare, pronounce, and define that the doctrine which holds that the Blessed Virgin Mary, at the first instant of her conception, by a singular privilege and grace of the omnipotent God, in consideration of the merits of Jesus Christ, the Savior of mankind was preserved free from all stain of original sin, and has been revealed by God, and therefore is to be firmly and constantly believed by all the faithful.[2]

This papal decree collides with the belief of several popes who had repudiated the doctrine. Aniceto Sparagna, a former Roman Catholic priest, has documented the opposition of many church fathers and some early popes to this doctrine. Included are St. Bernard, St. Augustine, St. Peter Lombard, St. Albert the Great, St. Thomas Aquinas, and St. Antonius. Sparagna also documents statements by several popes that either directly or indirectly show that they never believed in the Immaculate Conception. For example:

Pope Leo I (440): "The Lord Jesus Christ alone among the sons of men was born immaculate" (Sermon 24 in *Nativ. Dom.*).

Pope Gelasius (492): "It belongs alone to the Immaculate Lamb to have no sin at all" (*Gelassii Papae Dicta*, vol. 4, col. 1241, Paris, 1671).

Pope Innocent III (1216): "She [Eve] was produced without sin, but she brought forth in sin; she [Mary] was produced in sin, but she brought forth without sin" (*De Festo Assump.*, sermon 2).[3]

The Catholic Claim

What evidence from Scripture can the Roman Catholic Church produce to support that Mary was sinless? In the papal decree of 1854, two scriptures were cited. One was Genesis 3:15, which says, "I will put enmity between you and the woman, and between your offspring and hers; he will crush your head, and you will strike his heel." This is not a reference to Mary, though there are pictures and statues that portray her as crushing the head of the serpent. Genesis 3:15 is a prophecy about Jesus, who descended from a woman, and whose atoning death and resurrection defeated Satan. Does this interpretation find support from other sections of God's Word? Yes, it does. The apostle John says, "The reason the Son of God appeared was to destroy the devil's work" (1 John 3:8). Furthermore, we are told that Jesus came to earth so that "by this death he might destroy him who had the power of death—that is, the devil" (Hebrews 2:14). Through his death and resurrection, Jesus defeated and crushed the head of the serpent. So there is nothing in Genesis 3:15 that supports the idea Mary was without sin.

The second Scripture cited in the papal decree is Luke 1:28, which speaks of Mary as being "highly favored." This expression has no reference whatsoever to Mary's supposed sinlessness. The fact she was chosen by a sovereign act of God shows she was highly favored. God was under no obligation to choose her; his choice was not because she was better than other women of her time or that she had been preserved free from the stain of original sin. His sovereign choice was a gracious act, and in that respect, Mary is indeed "highly favored" or "full of grace." Because of her unique privilege of becoming the mother of Jesus, "all generations will call me [Mary] blessed" (Luke 1:48). Let's not make the mistake of thinking that God is giving Mary a title, "blessed," to attach to her name. That she was blessed speaks merely of the privilege God conveyed on her.

The Scriptural Reply

The Testimony About Jesus

Scripture makes it very clear that Jesus alone was without sin. Hebrews 4:15 says that Jesus was "tempted in every way, just as we are—yet was without sin." Everyone else who has ever lived— including Mary—is a sinner. Paul wrote, "There is no one righteous, not even one" (Romans 3:10). And "all have sinned and fall short of the glory of God" (Romans 3:23). John wrote, "If we claim we have not sinned, we make him [God] out to be a liar, and his Word has no place in our lives" (1 John 1:10).

The Testimony of Mary

The testimony of Mary harmonizes with the teaching of Scripture. If we could ask her, "Do you believe you are sinless?" she would dismiss such a thought as a contradiction of God's Word. Why do I say that? Because of Mary's own words.

First, when Mary visited her cousin Elizabeth and was greeted as the mother of the Lord, Mary responded by saying, "My soul glorifies the Lord and my spirit rejoices in God my Savior" (Luke

1:46-47). Notice that Mary called Jesus "my Savior." Now, who needs a Savior? Sinners do! Mary was in the best position to know whether she was a sinner, and she said she was.

Second, Mary's actions after Jesus' birth show that she believed herself to be a sinner. After the birth the time of her purification arrived, and she went to the temple and offered the sacrifices commanded in the law of Moses. This offering of the sacrifices made Mary ceremonially clean and also identified her as a sinner, a fact she did not deny. More specifically, Moses wrote, "These are the regulations for the woman who gives birth to a boy or a girl. If she cannot afford a lamb, she is to bring two doves or two young pigeons, one for a burnt offering and the other for a sin offering" (Leviticus 12:7-8; cf. Luke 2:22-24). Mary complied with the law of Moses and offered as in offering because she was a sinner.

I realize that Catholics mean well when they say they want to honor Mary. But in reality, they dishonor her by attributing to her a sinless life. Mary herself declared her need of a Savior and offered a sacrifice that was necessary for sinners to offer.

THE ASSUMPTION OF MARY?

The Catholic Teaching

On November 1, 1950, Pope Pius XII made an *ex cathedra* pronouncement declaring the Assumption of Mary to be an infallible doctrine of the Catholic Church:

> By the authority of our Lord Jesus Christ, of the Blessed Apostles Peter and Paul, and by our own authority, we pronounce, declare, and define it to be a dogma divinely revealed: that the Immaculate Mother of God, Mary ever virgin, on the completion of her earthly life, was assumed to heavenly glory both in body and soul. Wherefore if

anyone presume (which God forbid) willfully to deny or
call into doubt what has been defined by us, let him know
that he has fallen away entirely from the divine and Catholic faith.[4]

That is a strong statement! This doctrine is said to be of divine
origin, with severe consequences for those who reject it. Given the
gravity of those words, we would expect a generous supply of evidence to be forthcoming for this doctrine, but the Assumption lacks
any basis in the Scriptures.

The Biblical Response

Before Jesus ascended to heaven, he promised the apostles that
he would send the Holy Spirit to guide them, teach them, and recall
for them all that he had taught them during his life: "The Counselor, the Holy Spirit, whom the Father will send in my name, will
teach you all things and will remind you of everything I have said to
you" (John 14:26). "When he, the Spirit of truth, comes, he will
guide you into all truth" (16:13). Since all truth was made known
to the apostles, we would expect to find in their writings some
references to the Assumption of Mary. Paul assured the Christian
believers that he had made known to them everything that God
had to say, yet he never mentioned the Assumption. "You know,"
Paul said, "that I have not hesitated to preach anything that would
be helpful to you.... For I have not hesitated to proclaim to you
the whole will of God" (Acts 20:20,27). Paul shared "the whole will
of God" and yet never mentioned the Assumption. Peter said that
"his divine power has given us everything we need for life and godliness" (2 Peter 1:3), yet never said a word about the Assumption,
even though we have been given "everything we need."

On the day of Pentecost, Peter proclaimed the good news that
Jesus had risen in victory from the grave and had ascended to the

Father's right hand in heaven: "Seeing what was ahead, he [the prophet David] spoke of the resurrection of the Christ, that he was not abandoned to the grave, nor did his body see decay. God has raised this Jesus to life, and we are all witnesses of the fact" (Acts 2:31-32; cf. Psalm 16:9-10). Jesus' resurrection and ascension had been foretold by the prophets. But unlike Christ's body, our bodies will undergo decay when we die. Our resurrection is a future event, and the victory of the risen Christ guarantees our resurrection.

Paul wrote that Jesus is the "firstfruits" of those who will rise from the dead. "Firstfruits" is an agricultural expression that speaks of a coming harvest. It's like the buds appearing on the trees in spring, announcing the coming of summer. "For as in Adam all die, so in Christ all will be made alive. But each in his own turn: Christ, the firstfruits; then, when he comes, those who belong to him" (1 Corinthians 15:22-23). This is plain language—the resurrection of the dead, without exception, will not occur until the Lord returns. The words of the apostle Paul leave no room for the Roman Catholic doctrine of the Assumption of Mary.

What's more, Paul said to the Roman believers, "We know that the whole creation has been groaning as in the pains of childbirth right up to the present time. Not only so, but we ourselves, who have the firstfruits of the Spirit, groan inwardly as we wait eagerly for our adoption as sons, the redemption of our bodies" (Romans 8:22-23). The earth suffers the consequences of sin in that it was cursed by God (Genesis 3:17-19). And each of us awaits redemption—in our case, the redemption of our body. Like every other person who has died, Mary also awaits the coming of the Lord, who will raise us all to life and bring us to our eternal home in heaven. That's all in the future. Yet Pope Pius IX stated, "[Mary] by an entirely unique privilege completely overcame sin by her Immaculate Conception, and as a result she was not subject to the law of remaining in the corruption of the grave, and she did not have to wait until the end of time for the redemption of her body."[5]

The apostle John, who was entrusted with the care of Mary by the Lord himself, wrote five books in the New Testament. From his writing it is clear that Mary's death was no different from anyone else's. He said, "Dear friends, now we are children of God, and what we will be has not yet been made known. But we know that when he appears, we shall be like him, for we shall see him as he is. Everyone who has this hope in him purifies himself, just as he is pure" (1 John 3:2-3). In other words, the resurrected body we receive is a *future* hope. The great truth about Mary—that a virgin would conceive— was foretold by the prophets, and its fulfillment is recorded in the Scriptures. Yet nothing in the Word of God mentions, directly or indirectly, the Assumption of Mary. In fact, there is no mention of what happened when she died. Like all who have died, she too awaits the general resurrection at the last day.

INTERCESSION BY MARY

Father John Walsh, S.J., in setting forth the Roman Catholic doctrine of the Assumption, sees the intercession of Mary as the next logical step. He both asks and answers the following question:

> **Q.** Now that she is in heaven, does the Blessed Mother pay any attention to men on earth?
>
> **A.** Since her son died for all men, Mary is keenly interested in the welfare of every man and woman on earth. She regards us all as her children and continually prays for us.[6]

There are a number of pontifical statements that have taught that Mary is the source of grace and blessings and that she intercedes for people as a mediator:

> Leo XIII: When Mary offered herself completely to God together with her Son in the temple, she was already sharing with him the painful atonement on behalf of the human race... (at the foot of the cross) she was co-worker with Christ in his expiation for mankind and she offered up her Son to the divine justice with him in her heart.

> Pius XI: Mary, by giving us Christ the redeemer, and by rearing him, and by offering him at the foot of the cross as Victim for our sins, by such intimate association with Christ, and by her own most singular grace, became and is affectionately known as Reparatrix.

> Benedict XV: Thus she [Mary] suffered and all but died along with her Son suffering and dying—thus for the salvation of men she abdicated the rights of a mother towards her son, and insofar as it was hers to do, she immolated the Son to placate God's justice, so that she herself may justly be said to have redeemed together with Christ the human race.

> Pius IX: With her Son, the Only-begotten, she is the most powerful Mediatrix and Conciliatrix of the whole world.[7]

The doctrine of Mary as intercessor runs into difficulty in two areas. First, the doctrine of the Assumption of Mary has been shown to be without foundation. Mary has yet to be resurrected, so she cannot intercede for those who petition her. Second, nowhere in Scripture do we find that prayer can be addressed to anyone other than God.

In addition, the Bible teaches that it is Christ who makes inter-cession for us. Christ is our Helper Intercessor:

> Because he himself suffered when he was tempted, he is able to help those who are being tempted (Hebrews 2:18).

> We do not have a high priest who is unable to sympa-thize with our weaknesses, but we have one who has been tempted in every way, just as we are—yet was without sin. Let us then approach the throne of grace with confidence, so that we may receive mercy and find grace to help us in our time of need (Hebrews 4:15-16).

> He is able to save completely those who come to God through him, because he always lives to intercede for them (Hebrews 7:25).

These scriptures tell us Jesus is able to meet all our needs. When we pray, we do not petition a reluctant God, but a loving Father whose Son has identified himself with our trials and tribulations. As our High Priest, Jesus is sympathetic to us and intercedes for us. Because he has complete power, full understanding, and the will-ingness to come to our aid, there is no need for the intercession of Mary or the saints (who, by the way, are all still awaiting the resur-rection at the last day, so they can do nothing for us).

Christ Alone Is Intercessor

Jesus extends an invitation to all people who struggle and are in need: "Come to me," he says, "all you who are weary and burdened, and I will give you rest. Take my yoke upon you and learn from me, for I am gentle and humble in heart, and you will find rest for your souls. For my yoke is easy and my burden is light" (Matthew 11:28-30). There is not a need in our life that he will not meet, no problem he will not solve, no crisis too big for him to handle, and no person too sinful for him to help. Jesus issues his invitation to the hurting people of this world, and he bids them come to him, not to Mary.

Also, when Jesus was asked by his disciples to teach them to pray, he taught them the Lord's prayer, not the Rosary (Luke 11:1-4). In this prayer, God is the One to whom all prayer is directed and the One who is able to meet all of our needs. Jesus never told people to pray to Mary or to any of the worthy men and women of the past, such as Abraham, Moses, David, Esther, or Sarah. Prayer is a sacrifice; it is an act of worship that we offer to God. The Bible says, "Through Jesus, therefore, let us continually offer to God a sacrifice of praise—the fruit of lips that confess his name" (Hebrews 13:15). To pray to Mary or the saints is to engage in offering a sacrifice to someone other than God—it is to engage in worship of someone other than God.

For a person to pray to Mary is to violate the truth that there is but "one mediator between God and men, the man Christ Jesus" (1 Timothy 2:5). Mary cannot mediate for us or intercede for us; neither can any of the departed saints.

The Roman Catholic Church is quick to point to the wedding feast in Cana in order to justify the practice of praying to Mary (John 2:1-11). But a simple examination of the event and its context does not support the Catholic claim. At the wedding, Mary told Jesus that the host had run out of wine. Did this information startle him? Had she told him something he didn't know? Certainly not! He is God the Son and knows all things. Then why did she tell him? She knew who Jesus was and that he was able to meet the need of the hour. Therefore, Mary told the servants to carry out whatever Jesus instructed. They did, and he turned the water into wine.

There is nothing in this story that indicates that it is legitimate to pray to Mary. To reach that conclusion we must ignore what the story actually tells us and give it a meaning other than that intended by John when he recorded the incident.

God Alone Can Meet Our Needs

Finally, why would we need Mary to intercede for us when we have the following promises from the Lord?

> Ask and it will be given to you; seek and you will find; knock and the door will be opened to you. For everyone who asks receives; he who seeks finds; and to him who knocks, the door will be opened. Which of you, if his son asks for bread, will give him a stone? Or if he asks for a fish, will give him a snake? If you, then, though you are evil, know how to give good gifts to your children, how much more will your Father in heaven give good gifts to those who ask him! (Matthew 7:7-11).

> I will do whatever you ask in my name, so that the Son may bring glory to the Father. You may ask me for anything in my name, and I will do it (John 14:13-14).

> Dear friends, if our hearts do not condemn us, we have confidence before God and receive from him anything we ask, because we obey his commands and do what pleases him (1 John 3:21-22).

> This is the confidence we have in approaching God: that if we ask anything according to his will, he hears us. And if we know that he hears us—whatever we ask—we know that we have what we asked of him (1 John 5:14-15).

> My God will meet all your needs according to his glorious riches in Christ Jesus (Philippians 4:19).

> ...the Spirit helps us in our weakness. We do not know

what we ought to pray for, but the Spirit himself intercedes for us with groans that words cannot express. And
he who searches our hearts knows the mind of the Spirit,
because the Spirit intercedes for the saints in accordance
with God's will (Romans 8:26-27).

QUESTIONS AND ANSWERS

Q. **Was Mary a virgin when Jesus was conceived?**

Yes. The prophet Isaiah foretold that Jesus the Messiah would be born of a virgin (Isaiah 7:14). It is the clear testimony of the New Testament that Mary was a virgin when she conceived.

Q. **Did Mary remain a virgin throughout her life?**

No. Matthew, who wrote about Mary conceiving by the Holy Spirit while a virgin, also wrote that Mary did not remain a virgin all her life. Her husband, Joseph, he says, had no sexual intercourse with her until after the birth of Jesus. Matthew lists by name Jesus' brothers and also refers to his sisters.

Q. **Was Mary sinless?**

The Roman Catholic Church teaches that Mary was sinless. But Mary herself, by her own admission, acknowledged that Jesus was her Savior—and only sinners need a Savior. God's Word tells us there is no one sinless, not one (Romans 3:10). And the apostle John said that anyone claiming to be without sin makes God out to be a liar (1 John 1:10). Such statements would not have been made if the apostles believed Mary was sinless.

Q. **Were Mary's body and soul assumed into heaven when she died?**

The doctrine of the Assumption of Mary was declared to be infallible in 1950, yet not a hint of such a doctrine can be found in the Bible. This doctrine was unknown to the apostles and early church, and it conflicts with what the Bible has to say about the fact the resurrection of the dead has not yet taken place.

Q. Can Mary make intercession for those who petition her?

Absolutely not. The Bible instructs us to make our petitions only to God and assures us that Jesus, our High Priest, is always interceding for us. The Holy Spirit also intercedes for us. In addition, there is only "one mediator between God and men" (1 Timothy 2:5), which is Jesus.

Q. What is admirable about Mary?

I am greatly impressed by Mary's response to the news that God had chosen her to give birth to Jesus. She didn't argue or make excuses, but in faith said, "I am the Lord's servant.... May it be to me as you have said" (Luke 1:38). The doing of God's will was more important to her than the personal trauma she would experience, including the trauma of witnessing Jesus' death. Unfortunately, the Roman Catholic Church has distorted the Mary we read about in the Bible and has done much damage to this great servant of the Lord.

13
Apparitions, Signs, and Wonders

. . . .

Mary's alleged apparitions at Guadalupe, Lourdes, Fatima, and Medjugorje, along with the miracles and cures associated with these places, have made them places of pilgrimage and contributed to the growing devotion to Mary among Catholics. Popes Pius X, Pius XII, and John Paul II have endorsed the apparitions as authentic.

On December 9, 1531, Juan Diego, an Indian living in Mexico and a recent convert to Catholicism, claimed to have seen a vision of Mary. He notified a bishop, who was skeptical until Diego claimed he had seen a second apparition. The evidence that convinced him was this:

Three days later during the second encounter with the apparition, Diego asked for a sign that would convince the bishop of his story's authenticity. The woman instructed him to fill his cloak…with roses, which were blooming unnaturally in December, and take them to the bishop. When the seer unrolled his cloak before the bishop, a permanent image of the Virgin Mary was imprinted on his cloak. The bishop accepted this as a genuine sign of the Virgin's presence to the people of Mexico. This tradition is the basis for popular devotion to the one known as Our Lady of Guadalupe.[1]

In 1858 a 14-year-old girl name Bernadette claimed to have seen apparitions of Mary. Over a period of months Bernadette encountered many apparitions, but the identity of the lady was not made known until March 25. In her own words Bernadette recalls that day:

After having poured out my heart to her I took up my Rosary. While I was praying, the thought of asking her name came before my mind with such persistence that I could think of nothing else…. Then she joined her hands and raised them to her breast…. She looked up to heaven…then slowly opened her hands and leaning forward towards me, she said to me in a voice vibrating with emotion: "I am the Immaculate Conception."[2]

Only four years earlier, in 1854, Pope Pius IX had declared that the Immaculate Conception "was revealed by God." In 1917 the three children of Fatima—Lucia, Jacinta, and Francisco—made world headlines when they claimed that they had seen apparitions of Mary. Lucia recalls the incident:

Then Our Lady spoke to us:
Lady: "Do not be afraid. I do you no harm."
Lucia: "Where are you from?"

Lady: "I am from heaven."

Lucia: "What do you want of me?"

Lady: "I have come to ask you to come here for six months in succession, on the thirteenth day, at this same hour. Later on I will tell you who I am and what I want."

After a few moments, Our Lady spoke again: "Pray the Rosary every day, in order to obtain peace for the world, and the end of the war."

Then she began to rise serenely, going up towards the east, until she disappeared in the immensity of space.[3]

It is not an article of faith for Catholics to believe in Lourdes, Fatima, and Guadalupe. However, credibility has been given to Fatima by Pope John Paul II, who attributed his escape from an assassin's bullet on May 13, 1981 to Our Lady of Fatima.

In 1981, apparitions of "Our Lady" were reported in the town of Medjugorje, Yugoslavia. Here she identified herself as the "Queen of Peace." As is customary when apparitions occur, the local bishop was notified. The investigation conducted by Bishop Zanic is most interesting, and a copy of Kenneth Samples's interview with him is found in Samples's book, *The Cult of the Virgin*. Samples wrote,

> Bishop Zanic told me that he found serious discrepancies among the visionaries' testimonies. He affirmed that he caught them in clear fabrications, and that the alleged healings and miracles were either fraudulent or grossly exaggerated. He also stated that the local Franciscans had been guilty of disobedience and, in some cases, unethical practice. His conclusion is that the apparitions in Medjugorje are a fraud perpetuated by the local Franciscans, with whom he has been feuding. According to Zanic, the apparitions must be denounced as invalid, or they will ultimately bring scandal and disgrace upon the church.[4]

Yet Bishop Zanic's outspoken criticism from the beginning did nothing to stem the tide of pilgrims pouring into Medjugorje in the hope of witnessing an apparition, obtaining a cure, or receiving spiritual help. Millions of Catholics have made the pilgrimage.

The message at Medjugorje is similar to messages received at Lourdes and Fatima:

> During one of the apparitions at Medjugorje, the lady requested that the full fifteen decades of the rosary be said every day. On June 25, 1985, the fourth anniversary of the apparitions, the following message was given: "Dear children, I ask you to ask everyone to pray the rosary. With the rosary you will overcome all the troubles which Satan is trying to inflict on the Catholic Church." Six weeks later a similar message was given: "Dear children, today I call you to pray against Satan in a special way. Satan wants to work more now that you know he is active. Dear children, put on your armor against Satan; with rosaries in your hands you will conquer."[5]

A Biblical Response to Apparitions

Counterfeit products are a major problem for manufacturers such as Nike, Puma, and Samsonite. Some of the counterfeit products are so well made that most buyers accept them as the genuine article. Only a trained eye can detect the difference between a counterfeit and a genuine article.

Throughout the history of the church, the counterfeit has existed alongside the genuine. This is particularly true in the area of apparitions, signs, and wonders. It's easy for people to fall victim to anything that has the appearance of the supernatural. This is especially true with regard to the alleged apparitions of Mary at Guadalupe, Lourdes, Fatima, and Medjugorje. The millions who visit these places want to believe that Mary appeared there.

How do we explain these apparitions? I am fully persuaded that they are not from God because the repeated message of "Our Lady" flatly contradicts the inspired Word of God. I take the warnings of the apostle Paul seriously: "I am afraid that just as Eve was deceived by the serpent's cunning, your minds may somehow be led astray from your sincere and pure devotion to Christ....for Satan himself masquerades as an angel of light" (2 Corinthians 11:3,14). Not for a moment do I doubt that those who claim to have seen apparitions believe they saw them. But I don't believe that what they saw was the Mary we read about in the Bible. If they saw the same Mary, her message would be in harmony with the truth contained in the Bible. Her message would not contradict the words of Jesus or the teachings of John, Paul, and Peter.

WHAT ABOUT THE MIRACLES, CURES, HEALINGS?

That extraordinary things have happened at these places is undeniable. But does that prove that everything taking place was ordained of God? Most certainly not! There is no shortage of warnings in the Bible about extraordinary things happening that are not from God but are in fact from the devil. You might think, *Surely nothing supernatural could come from the devil, such as healings, cures, miracles?* It is not only possible, but it actually happens. For example, here is a warning from the Old Testament:

> If a prophet, or one who foretells by dreams, appears among you and announces to you a miraculous sign or wonder, and if the sign or wonder of which he has spoken takes place, and he says, "Let us follow other gods" (gods you have not known) "and let us worship them," you must not listen to the words of that prophet or dreamer. The LORD your God is testing you to find out whether you love him with all your heart and with all your soul. It is the LORD your God you must follow, and him you must

> revere. Keep his commands and obey him; serve and hold
> fast to him (Deuteronomy 13:1-4).

God was warning his people of the possibility that a miracle, a sign, or wonder claiming to be from God might in fact bring a message contrary to the revealed will of God. Sure enough, the message brought via the apparitions contradicts God's Word. Nowhere in the Bible are we instructed to pray the rosary to Mary, to seek her intercession, or to accept her as our Blessed Mother. Such focus on Mary is unbiblical. We are to pray to God and to seek his intercession—he alone is our Father and our Savior.

Jesus gave clear warnings to his people about the evil work done by false prophets. Are we to believe their message simply because they have displayed supernatural power? Certainly not. "False Christs and false prophets," Jesus said, "will appear and perform great signs and miracles to deceive even the elect—if that were possible" (Matthew 24:24).

The apostle Paul warned the new converts in Thessalonica (who had been converted to Christ from a background steeped in idolatry), to be alert to counterfeit miracles, impressive though they be. He said such miracles were not from God but were demonic in origin:

> The coming of the lawless one will be in accordance
> with the work of Satan displayed in all kinds of counter-
> feit miracles, signs, and wonders, and in every sort of evil
> that deceives those who are perishing. They perish because
> they refused to love the truth and so be saved. For this
> reason God sends them a powerful delusion so that they
> will believe the lie and so that all will be condemned who
> have not believed the truth but have delighted in wicked-
> ness (2 Thessalonians 2:9-12).

In the book of Revelation the apostle John depicts the church as victorious yet facing persecution. One of the enemies of the church comes in the form of false doctrines that are from the devil and his fallen angels. It is significant that John said these false doctrines are accompanied by miracles: "He [the second beast] performed great and miraculous signs, even causing fire to come down from heaven to earth in full view of men" (Revelation 13:13). And in his first epistle, John warned, "Dear friends, do not believe every spirit, but test the spirits to see whether they are from God, because many false prophets have gone out into the world" (1 John 4:1).

The miracles, cures, and healings that have taken place at Lourdes, Fatima, and other locations bear no resemblance to the miracles we read about in the Bible. The Catholic Church has a committee that investigates all the miraculous events that occur at these places of pilgrimage. It can take years for the committee to reach a verdict. The reason for the delay is the very thorough investigation conducted into each claim. That is quite different from what we read about in the Bible. When Jesus worked a miracle, there was no need for a team of medical experts to make an investigation, deliberate for years, and then give a verdict. For example, when Jesus healed the man who was born blind, everyone knew that a miracle had taken place, even Jesus' enemies (John 9). And when Jesus raised Lazarus from the dead, those who were planning to kill Jesus said, "Here is this man performing many miraculous signs" (John 11:47). Again, there was no need for deliberation by a medical team. Lepers didn't need to be examined to see if they had been healed, and the paralytic didn't need medical experts to confirm that he had been healed. Everybody could see what had happened; there was no doubt about Jesus' miracles.

The same is true about the miracles performed by the apostles. No one had any doubt that a miracle had occurred. A man crippled from birth became the recipient of God's miraculous healing power through the ministry of the apostle Peter (Acts 3:2-8). No one called for a team of medical experts to confirm what was obvious— a crippled man had been healed. The following day, the religious authorities interrogated Peter and asked him, "By what power or what name did you do this?" (Acts 4:7). Peter told them it was by the name of the Lord Jesus Christ that this miracle had occurred, and the religious authorities continued, "Everybody living in Jerusalem knows they have done an outstanding miracle, and we cannot deny it" (Acts 4:16). The miracle was genuine. It was instant. It could be verified. Blind people did not merely receive partial sight. Lame people did not have to use crutches. No one was healed and then later had a relapse. All who saw the miracles were compelled to acknowledge them. In response to Jesus' miracles, some declared, "We have never seen anything like this!" (Mark 2:12).

The Apparition and the Message

All religious cults claim to speak on behalf of God, and many claim authentication based on visions or the presence of signs and wonders performed among them. But miracles alone are not sufficient. The message from the one who is performing the miracles must be in accord with God's revealed will. As far back as the days of Moses, God warned his people about deception. "'How can we know when a message has not been spoken by the LORD?' they asked. The Lord replied, 'If what a prophet proclaims in the name of the LORD does not take place or come true, that is a message the LORD has not spoken. That prophet has spoken presumptuously'" (Deuteronomy 18:21-22).

A false prophet can foretell future events and perform signs and wonders which defy explanation, and yet proclaim a message that contradicts God's truth. That is why we should be concerned about apparitions that tell us to pray the rosary to the Blessed Virgin Mary, do penance, and have devotion to her. None of those instructions are found in Scripture. Paul would not have hesitated to condemn such messages as false and not coming from God. He warned us to be wary of any message that distracts from God's truth. For example, he said,

> Even if we or an angel from heaven should preach a gospel other than the one we preached to you, let him be eternally condemned! As we have already said, so now I say again: If anybody is preaching to you a gospel other than what you accepted, let him be eternally condemned! (Galatians 1:8-9).

Satan is alive and well and actively working signs and wonders in the world today. He is deceptive and cunning. He promotes error by mixing it with some truth, thereby providing a degree of disguise. The message of the apparitions to pray to Mary sounds good, even appealing, but it serves only to disguise the evil that is concealed in the message. For example, the second apparition of Fatima said that the world would be converted through reciting the rosary and devotion to the "Immaculate Heart of Mary." We know that God's desire is the conversion of the world, yet Satan has mixed the truth of God's desire into a message that promotes devotion to Mary—a practice that is unbiblical.

So where does all this leave us? Only when we compare a message or a miracle with that which is found in God's Word will we know whether something is true or false. And when we compare the messages of Lourdes, Fatima, and other places with the Bible, we can see that they are false and demonic in origin.

QUESTIONS AND ANSWERS

Q. **Why should we not believe that Mary has appeared at Lourdes, Fatima, etc.?**

The apostle John warns us that many false spirits have gone out into the world, and we are to test them to see if they are true (1 John 4:1). These alleged apparitions of Mary must be rejected because of the unbiblical messages that accompany them.

Q. **Is it not true that God wants all people to believe in him and that is why Mary has appeared to people with messages?**

That God wants people to believe in him is revealed in the Bible. And throughout history, God has communicated with his people. However, the Bible says that his means of communication "in these last days" is through his Son, the Lord Jesus Christ (Hebrews 1:1-2). In part this is done through the ministry of the Holy Spirit. Also, God's entire revelation is now contained in the inspired Word of God. According to Jude 3, "the faith [has been] once for all entrusted to the saints." There is no need for further messages or revelations.

Q. **Should we be cautious about accepting apparitions of Mary?**

Every cult has an element of truth contained in its message. And that is what makes them so dangerous. On the surface the apparitions of Mary seem to offer a familiar message, but upon closer examination the real danger is discovered. For Mary to call people back to God sounds good, but when we look closer we see that the apparitions serve to confirm Roman Catholic devotion to Mary, which is unbibilical. Unfortunately, there is enough truth in these apparitions to deceive the unwary.

Q. How can you account for the cures and healings that have taken place in connection with the apparitions?

There has never been a shortage of signs and wonders to deceive people. The Bible teaches that Satan is a master deceiver who works miracles. Likewise, some cults provide signs, wonders, healings, and cures while at the same time proclaiming a message contrary to the revealed will of God. Such activities are clearly from Satan. The important question to ask is, Does the message conform to the teachings of Scripture?

Q. How can we determine whether something is true?

Moses warned Israel that if someone gives a sign or wonder that comes to pass yet the accompanying message *conflicts* with the revealed will of God, then the message cannot be from God, no matter how spectacular the sign or wonder. If we are to believe the sign or wonder is from God, then the message must be in harmony with the will of God. The messages from Lourdes, Fatima, and other places contradict God's Word.

14

Making Sacred
Images

. . . .

Those of us who grew up in the Roman Catholic Church are accustomed to sacred images; they are part of our Catholic faith. In our churches and homes we have statues of the crucifixion, the Blessed Virgin Mary, the Sacred Heart of Jesus, the Little Child of Prague, Saint Joseph the carpenter, the Holy Family, and Saint Christopher carrying the infant Jesus. At home I counted among my treasures a luminous statue of Mary that had been obtained at Lourdes. I would hold it up to the light for a few moments, then turn off the light, and the Blessed Virgin would glow in her blue gown. This captured my imagination.

At church there was an endless supply of holy pictures depicting events in the life of Jesus. In some he pointed to his sacred heart, in others the colors of the rainbow streamed from his heart. There were pictures of angels being present at a child's first Holy Communion, and always pictures of Mary "the refuge of sinners."

Places were provided for a person to kneel in prayer before a specific saint to ask that saint's intercession or favor. I can still recall the array of penny candles burning before the statues of the saints whose intercession I sought and to whom I had great devotion. And I was a frequent visitor to the shrine of Saint Jude, "the patron saint of hopeless cases."

As I grew up, my understanding of God was fashioned by what I saw in all this sacred imagery. And the place of sacred images within the Roman Catholic faith is clearly stated in the Catechism:

> Sacred images in our churches and homes are intended to awaken and nourish our faith in the mystery of Christ. Through the icon of Christ and his works of salvation it is he whom we adore. Through sacred images of the holy Mother of God, of the angels and of the saints, we venerate the person represented. [1192]

But what does the Bible have to say about the making of sacred images and venerating the persons they represent?

THE COMMAND AGAINST SACRED IMAGES

The Ten Commandments were given at Mount Sinai after God had delivered the people of Israel from bondage in Egypt. Israel's deliverance is one of the great miracles recorded in the Bible. Israel had maintained their belief in the one true God during the four centuries they had been living among pagan people who believed in a multiplicity of gods. The ten plagues God sent upon Egypt were in response to Pharaoh's refusal to let Israel go and were designed to "bring judgment on all the gods of Egypt" (Exodus 12:12). The Egyptians had gods for everything. And when Israel's God sent the plagues, he exposed the Egyptian gods as utterly useless. They couldn't defend or deliver the people who worshiped them. It's against this background that we need to hear the commandment prohibiting the making of sacred images.

The Ten Commandments are recorded in Exodus chapter 20. The second one says, "You shall not make for yourself an idol in the form of anything in heaven above or on the earth beneath or in the waters below. You shall not bow down to them or worship them; for I, the LORD your God, am a jealous God" (verses 4-5). What God prohibits is stated plainly, yet the very thing God prohibited— the making of sacred images—is encouraged by the Roman Catholic Church today. The Roman Catholic Church ignores the second of the Ten Commandments by numbering the commandments in an odd way. If you compare the commandments in the Bible with those in the Catechism, you will see that the first commandment as recorded in both the Bible and the Catechism is identical. However, the second commandment, which forbids the making of sacred images, is omitted from the Catechism.

How then does the Roman Catholic Church still have ten commandments in the Catechism if one is omitted? It numbers the commandments so that the third commandment in the Bible becomes number two in the Catechism, the fourth becomes number three, the fifth becomes number four, and so on. When the Church comes to the tenth commandment (which forbids coveting), two commandments are created from it: ninth, do not covet your neighbor's wife, and tenth, do not covet your neighbor's goods. By making two commandments out of the tenth commandment and omitting the one forbidding the making of sacred images, the Catholic Church is able to have ten commandments. Is that the right way to treat the commandments?

WHY GOD IS OPPOSED TO SACRED IMAGES

God has not been slow to express his opposition to the use of sacred images. He has prohibited images because they cannot convey who God is. No image of Jesus, no matter how magnificent it is, can capture the nature of the Lord. And all the well-meaning attempts only incur his displeasure. After God delivered Israel from bondage in Egypt he said to the Israelites, "You saw no form of any kind the day the LORD spoke to you at Horeb out of the fire. Therefore watch yourselves very carefully, so that you do not become corrupt and make for yourselves an idol, an image of any shape, whether formed like a man or a woman" (Deuteronomy 4:15-16). Could God have said it any plainer?

Suppose you show a statue of the crucifixion to someone who has no knowledge of the Christian faith. What would he understand about Jesus? What conclusions would he draw? The message conveyed by the image is of a defeated dead person who was unable to save himself. This Jesus is dead. Yet we know that such a conclusion is incomplete. The most gifted artist cannot capture in stone, wood, or paint what took place when the Son of God offered himself as the perfect sacrifice for our sins. And it should not be attempted. The true image of Christ includes his eternal deity, incarnation, atoning death, victorious resurrection, and glorious ascension to heaven where he now reigns as King. No image can capture the fullness of the Lord; for that reason, God prohibits the making of any sacred images.

God's displeasure at being represented in the form of a sacred image marks the darker moments in Israel's history. After the Israelites left Egypt on their way to the Promised Land God summoned Moses to Mount Sinai, where he gave Moses the Ten Commandments. Moses was gone for a long time, and the people began to grow impatient and complain. "When the people saw that Moses was so long in coming down from the mountain, they gathered around Aaron and said, 'Come, make us gods who will go before us'" (Exodus 32:1). Aaron gathered some gold from the people and "made it into an idol cast in the shape of a calf, fashioning it with a tool. Then they said, 'These are your gods, O Israel, who brought you up out of Egypt'" (verse 4).

What was God's response to this? "Go down," God says to Moses, "because your people, whom you brought up out of Egypt, have become corrupt. They have been quick to turn away from what I commanded them and have made themselves an idol cast in the shape of a calf. They have bowed down to it and sacrificed to it and have said, 'These are your gods, O Israel, who brought you up out of Egypt'" (verses 7-8).

What had the people done? They had made an image that was meant to represent God. They were not trying to create a new god, but rather, to represent in an image the God who had set them free. They were not worshiping a pagan god from Egypt, but God their deliverer. And the fact that they had reduced God to a sacred image, no matter how well-intentioned they may have been, incurred God's wrath. To worship God through the medium of a sacred image is to engage in idolatry. I know that sounds harsh, but it is not my opinion; it is what God has said.

Have you ever wondered why God did not preserve for us the manger in which Jesus lay as a baby, some of the furniture Jesus made as a carpenter, the cross upon which Jesus was crucified, or the grave where he was buried? It's because sinful man has the capacity to take such things and turn them into objects of veneration. An incident occurred in Israel's history which might prove enlightening. On their way to the Promised Land, the Israelites complained and murmured against God and his servant Moses. God punished them by sending poisonous snakes among the people. But in his mercy he also provided a cure for those bitten by the snakes. He instructed Moses to make a bronze snake and mount it on a pole. All who looked upon the bronze snake were healed. The power for healing was not in the object itself, but in God. (Jesus referred to this event to show that we need to look to him upon the cross for our spiritual healing—John 3:14-15.)

Centuries later, Israel began venerating and burning incense before the bronze serpent. In a reformation, King Hezekiah "removed the high places, smashed the sacred stones.... He broke into pieces the bronze snake Moses had made, for up to that time the Israelites had been burning incense to it" (2 Kings 18:4). The Israelites may have thought they were honoring God by what they were doing, but it was never God's intention for this bronze serpent to become an object of veneration. When it did, God was offended.

When I was growing up, in our home we had a "relic of the true cross" that occupied a place of honor beside a picture of the Sacred Heart. We were led to believe this splinter of wood had touched the actual cross on which Jesus was crucified. This relic did nothing to help us live a holy life or enlighten our understanding of what Jesus achieved through his death upon the cross. But its place of honor in the home was irrevocable.

SACRED IMAGES AND DEPARTURE FROM GOD

The Bible reveals to us that whenever God's people began making sacred images, it was a clear sign that they had departed from God; their practice never drew them close to God. Without exception it had the opposite effect. Note the prophet Jeremiah's scathing denunciation of the Israelites for incorporating sacred images into their religious practice:

> The customs of the peoples are worthless; they cut a tree out of the forest, and a craftsman shapes it with his chisel. They adorn it with silver and gold; they fasten it with hammer and nails so it will not totter. Like a scarecrow in a melon patch, their idols cannot speak; they must be carried because they cannot walk. Do not fear them; they can do no harm nor can they do any good.... What the craftsman and goldsmith have made is then dressed in blue and purple—all made by skilled workers.

> But the LORD is the true God; he is the living God, the
> eternal King (Jeremiah 10:3-5,9-10).

I do not intend to be insulting when I say this, but do not the words of Jeremiah fit the Roman Catholic practice of making sacred images, decorating them, and carrying them around in religious processions? I think the similarity is incontrovertible. Israel had adopted gods and given them a place of honor, but in doing so they had demonstrated that they had departed from God. Though offended, God pleaded with Israel to return to him, reminding them of the uselessness of their idols and of his own faithfulness. We read one such beautiful pleading in the book of Isaiah:

> Bel bows down, Nebo stoops low; their idols are borne by beasts of burden. The images that are carried about are burdensome, a burden for the weary. They stoop and bow down together; unable to rescue the burden, they themselves go off into captivity. Listen to me, O house of Jacob, all you who remain of the house of Israel, you whom I have upheld since you were conceived, and have carried since your birth. Even to your old age and gray hairs I am he, I am he who will sustain you. I have made you and I will carry you; I will sustain you and I will rescue you. To whom will you compare me or count me equal? To whom will you liken me that we may be compared? Some pour out gold from their bags and weigh out silver on the scales; they hire a goldsmith to make it into a god, and they bow down and worship it. They lift it to their shoulders and carry it; they set it up in its place, and there it stands. From that spot it cannot move. Though one cries out to it, it does not answer; it cannot save him from his troubles (Isaiah 46:1-7).

In that pleading the Israelites, who are carrying their idols, hear God say that he has carried them since birth. And he will continue to carry them even when they get old and their strength is gone and their hair turns gray. In essence, God was saying, "Instead of carrying your heavy statues, turn back to me, and I will once again carry you!"

One author captures the sentiments expressed by God in this short piece.

FOOTPRINTS

One night a man had a dream: He was walking along a beach with the Lord. Across the sky flashed scenes from his life. In each scene he noticed two sets of footprints in the sand: one belonging to him, and the other to the Lord.

When the last scene of his life flashed before him, he looked back at the footprints in the sand. He noticed that many times along the path of his life there was only one set of footprints. He also noticed that it happened at the very lowest and saddest times in his life.

This really bothered him, so he questioned the Lord about it. "Lord, you said that once I decided to follow you, you would walk with me all the way. But I have noticed that during the most troublesome times in my life, there is only one set of footprints. I don't understand why when I needed you most you would leave me."

The Lord replied, "My precious child, I love you and I would never leave you. During your times of trial and suffering, when you see only one set of footprints, it was then that I carried you."

Once again, there is a sinful tendency in man to attempt to make God in his own image, to bring God down to man's own size, to control, to tame God. Images help to do that. But when we create images, we end up with a reductionist god—a false god.

A STRIKING SIMILARITY

I have visited Hindu temples in India. They are elaborate places of worship with multicolored idols everywhere. I've watched people pray before these images. Some people bring fruits to the temple priest, who will place the fruit on a plate, light a fire on it, hold it up as an offering to the idol, and then return the sacrificed fruit to the worshipers. I've also seen processions in the streets in which images and statues are carried. The sincerity of these worshipers is beyond question, but their worship is contrary to God's will.

Once again I want to emphasize that it is not my intention to be offensive to any Roman Catholic, but the practices I see in Hindu temples and the religious processions in which Hindu worshipers carry their sacred images are not any different than what I once engaged in as a Catholic. I knelt before statues, put flowers before them, lit candles before them, petitioned them, kissed them, and followed them in processions. I was sincere in what I was doing and was not aware that I was doing anything wrong. But sacred images have no place among the people of God. When Paul wrote to the people in the church at Thessalonica, he recalled their conversion by saying, "You turned to God from idols to serve the living and true God" (1 Thessalonians 1:9). Not for a moment was Paul suggesting that they get rid of their pagan idols only to have them replaced with images of Jesus and his mother Mary.

> All idolatry, whether ancient or modern, primitive or sophisticated, is inexcusable, whether the images are metal or mental, material objects of worship or unworthy concepts in the mind. For idolatry is the attempt either to localize God, confining him within limits which we impose, where he is the Creator of the universe; or to domesticate God, making him dependent on us, taming and taping him, whereas he is the Sustainer of human life; or to alienate God, blaming him for his distance and his silence, whereas he is the Ruler of nations, and not far from any of us; to dethrone God, demoting him to some image of our own contrivance or craft, whereas he is our Father from whom we derive our being. In brief, all idolatry tries to minimize the gulf between the

Creator and his creatures, in order to bring him under our control. More than that, it actually reverses the respective position of God and us, so that, instead of our humble acknowledging that God has created us and rules us, we presume to imagine that we can create and rule God. There is no logic to idolatry; it is perverse, topsy-turvy expression of our human rebellion against God.[1]

WOULD THE APOSTLES HAVE APPROVED?

What would the apostles and prophets who spoke so vehe-mently about the violation of the second commandment say about the sacred images in the Roman Catholic Church? What would they say if they saw flowers placed before sacred images, candles lit before them, people kissing them and kneeling before them in prayer? Would they give their approval? Certainly not. And any claim that these practices are part of some sacred tradition that was passed on from them to the church would be utterly rejected. Can you imagine the prophet Jeremiah, whose ministry denounced the making of idols, kneeling before an image of Jesus or Mary and praying? Can you imagine the prophet Isaiah carrying a sacred image in a reli-gious procession in light of what he wrote in Isaiah 46? And do you think the apostle Paul would feel comfortable seeing an image or a statue of himself in a church?

The notion of giving veneration to sacred images of prophets and apostles contradicts the commands of Scripture. The apostle John, upon receiving the revelations recorded in the last book of the New Testament, "fell down to worship at the feet of the angel who had been showing them to me. But he said to me, 'Do not do it! I am a fellow servant with you and with your brothers the prophets and of all who keep the words of this book. Worship God!'" (Revelation 22:8-9). Veneration is reserved exclusively for God. If John was told not to bow before an angel, what does that say about bowing before images of Mary and the saints?

Honoring the Bible's Command

Some Catholics have told me that images help them when they pray. I tell them two things: First, prayer should be offered only to God, not to Mary or the saints; and second, this "helpful practice" of using images is a clear violation of what God has said in his Word. Those converted to the Lord must have nothing to do with sacred images, for they are a clear violation of the second commandment and go against the repeated teachings and warnings in Scripture.

When I was a Catholic, I did not know God was opposed to sacred images until I read the Bible. Today I have no regrets about having abandoned the use of images. I would say to every Catholic, in the words of the apostle John, "Keep yourselves from idols" (1 John 5:21).

I have endeavored to make a clear and honest presentation of what the Bible has to say about images and statues. It is beyond question that this practice offends God and violates his revealed will. Yet as we have seen, the Roman Catholic Church encourages the use of images and statues. With that in mind, I offer two statements below—one from the Catechism, and the other from the Bible. Which will you choose to follow?

> Sacred images in our churches and homes are intended to awaken and nourish our faith in the mystery of Christ. Through the icon of Christ and his works of salvation it is he whom we adore. Through sacred images of the holy Mother of God, of the angels and of the saints, we venerate the person represented. [1192]

> You shall not make for yourself an idol in the form of anything in heaven above or on earth beneath (Exodus 20:4).

QUESTIONS AND ANSWERS

Q. **What is idolatry?**

Idolatry is the giving of worship, adoration, or devotion to any-thing other than God. In the history of Israel, this manifested itself in the making of sacred images.

Q. **Does God forbid the making of sacred images?**

Absolutely. The second commandment forbids the making of any graven image, and there are no exceptions to God's command.

Q. **Why is God so opposed to the making of sacred images?**

Images can be treated as though they are sacred, or they can become objects of veneration. Any reverence or veneration given to an image rightfully belongs exclusively to God. Sacred images lead people away from God; hence God's fierce opposition to them.

Q. **Are not images useful for reminding us of the one to whom we are praying?**

First, we find no support in the Bible for praying to anyone other than God. Second, no matter what line of reasoning is used to justify the practice, the making of sacred images is forbidden by God.

Q. **Is it wrong for Roman Catholics to have statues?**

How could this practice be right when God repeatedly condemns images and statues? Would the prophets and apostles endorse the practice of making statues and venerating them? Absolutely not. The Roman Catholic practice is wrong and an offense to God.

15

God's Provision
for Divorce

. . . .

Marriage is a sacred institution created by God. It is the coming together of a man and woman in a special relationship, and God's desire is that it be for life. The Bible does not give any rules that must be followed in order for a marriage to be valid, so there is plenty of room for variation in how our marriages are carried out.

The Roman Catholic Church, however, has its own rules about what constitutes a valid marriage. In Canon 1086 we read, "A marriage between two persons, one of whom has been baptized in the Catholic Church or received into it and has not defected from it by a formal act and the other of whom is not baptized, is invalid." Of course, there is absolutely no justification for such a law. It is man-made; no such restriction is found in the Bible. The Catholic Church also has some rules about divorce that cannot be supported scripturally.

ADDRESSING THE PROBLEM

The subject of divorce can generate a lot of heat from God-fearing people on both sides of the issue. The Roman Catholic Church opposes divorce and finds its support in the prophet Malachi, through whom God said, "I hate divorce" (Malachi 2:16). For them, that settles the case. And if further proof is needed, the words of Jesus provide additional weight: "Therefore what God has joined together, let man not separate" (Matthew 19:6). With these two verses of Scripture the Roman Catholic Church feels secure in its position—no divorce, ever!

It's true that God hates divorce, and it's true that we should make every effort to keep a marriage together. However, every marriage is not bliss, and some people are tied to intolerable and unfaithful partners. The scars left on those caught in the middle—namely, the children—are all too obvious. A woman married to a man whose affairs with other women are public knowledge (and who might even be living openly with another woman) will be told by the Roman Catholic Church that she is joined to that man for life. *Indissoluble* is the word she frequently hears when she pours out her pain. Contemplation of divorce is out of the question if she is to enjoy the blessings of her Church. The obedient Catholic woman will fight on courageously day after day, trying to resist the strong desires that can only be fulfilled by the husband she has lost to another woman. The dilemma is all too familiar.

Catholics listen to the Church's teaching on divorce believing that it echoes the voice of God on the matter. Over the years I have found that Catholics are often shocked to discover that God does in fact allow divorce under certain circumstances. "So why doesn't the Catholic Church allow divorce?" they ask. The answer is simple: The Roman Catholic Church does not accept the Bible as its only source of authority. As a result, God is not honored by those who prohibit what he is prepared to allow. Those who forbid divorce are not holding to a higher moral standard. In actuality, they are teaching an error in God's name.

God *has* made provision for divorce, but this provision should never be taken up without much prayerful consideration. Before we look at his provision, let's consider some essential background information.

Almost 1,500 years before Jesus came to earth, God made known through Moses that divorce was permitted in certain circumstances (Deuteronomy 24:1-4). Divorce did in fact occur, and there were times when it was allowed. Even godly people found themselves in situations that permitted divorce. Do you remember how Joseph reacted to the news that Mary, his fiancée, was pregnant? Joseph knew that he was not the father of the child, and therefore was determined to divorce Mary. Not until after Joseph was told that the child Mary was carrying was conceived by the Holy Spirit did Joseph change his mind (Matthew 1:18-21). When Joseph thought about divorcing Mary, he was not going outside the bounds of God's will but was availing himself of a provision God ordained. Catholics need to know that to avail themselves of something that God allows is not sinful. No one has the right to prohibit what God allows.

JESUS ON DIVORCE

Unfortunately, many people through the ages have abused God's concession, and it is against that background that Jesus addressed divorce in Matthew 19. Some Pharisees came to test Jesus and asked, "Is it lawful for a man to divorce his wife for any and every reason?" (verse 3). "Haven't you read," he replied, "that at the beginning the Creator 'made them male and female...for this reason a man will leave his father and mother and be united to his wife, and the two

will become one flesh'? So they are no longer two, but one. Therefore what God has joined together, let man not separate" (Matthew
19:4-6).

Jesus made it clear that a man cannot divorce his wife "for any
and every reason." To support his answer, Jesus went back to creation and cited God's expectations for marriage: Marriage is a union
in which God joins a couple for life. No one has the right to undo
what God has joined together; that is the rule. But God has made
one exception to the rule—divorce can be granted when one of the
partners has committed adultery. In practical terms it works like
this: John and Mary are married Christians, and John becomes
unfaithful and commits adultery. According to Jesus, Mary has the
right to divorce John and dissolve their marriage because of his
unfaithfulness. She is also free to enter a second marriage, if she so
desires. Divorce for any other reason is forbidden by Jesus. Should
John and Mary divorce on grounds other than adultery and either
or both of them remarry, they do so without God's approval (Matthew 5:31-32).

PAUL ON DIVORCE

While Jesus discussed divorce in relation to believers, Paul dealt
with divorce between a believer and an unbeliever. Paul was well
aware that the spread of the Christian faith led to a difficult dilemma
for many in the early church. Some who became Christians had
partners who remained unbelievers, and so the new Christians
wondered about the status of their marriage. Paul assured them
that a marriage is still valid even when one person is a believer and
the other is not, and that the believing partner must not put away
the unbelieving one simply because he or she is an unbeliever. The
believer is to stay married (1 Corinthians 7:12-14).

However, what is to be done when an unbelieving partner deserts his believing partner? What should the believer do in such a circumstance? Speaking by the Spirit of God (1 Corinthians 7:40), the apostle Paul said, "If the unbeliever leaves, let him do so. A believing man or woman is not bound in such circumstances; God has called us to live in peace" (1 Corinthians 7:15). What was Paul saying here? He was teaching that desertion by an unbelieving partner leaves the believer free to seek a divorce and remarry.

THE ROMAN CATHOLIC CHURCH ON DIVORCE

There is nothing ambiguous about the Roman Catholic Church's teaching on divorce: It is not permitted under any circumstance. While annulments are granted, they are not equated with divorce. An annulment is given when it can be established that the essential ingredients for a marriage never existed. The fact that the marriage has lasted for years and has heard the patter of several pairs of tiny feet does not prevent Rome from granting an annulment, which frees the couple to remarry.

The Roman Catholic Church has put itself into conflict with what Jesus, Moses, and Paul taught about divorce. What's more, the Catholic Church has not always been the staunch opponent of divorce that she presently portrays herself to be. Her track record shows a different picture, one that most Catholics do not know. In the book *Vicars of Christ*, Peter de Rosa cites a number of interesting cases in which the Catholic Church granted a divorce. For example:

> Two Jews, Isaac and Rebecca, married and divorced. Rebecca became a Catholic, while Isaac married a Catholic named Antonia in a civil ceremony. Next, Isaac wanted to become a Catholic in order to regularize his union with Antonia in the eyes of her church. On 23 May 1894, Leo XIII, stern opponent of divorce, simply divorced

Isaac and Rebecca. This astounding case was, wisely, kept under wraps for forty years.[1]

Peter de Rosa also relates how Gerard G. Marsh, an unbaptized divorcé, wished to marry a Catholic and expressed the desire to become a Catholic. His case was sent to Rome by Bishop Carroll to see if Marsh's first marriage could be annulled. Peter de Rosa comments on what happened:

> The new 1917 code said plainly that in his case these were no longer grounds for annulment. The Holy Office, ignoring the reasoning in the bishop's plea, changed it to a petition to the Pope to dissolve the marriage in favor of the faith.
>
> On 6 November 1924, Pius XI gave Marsh a divorce. There was no mention in the rescript that it depended on Marsh becoming a Catholic. To the canonists' astonishment, the Pope had simply broken up the first marriage. A valid, binding, naturally indissoluble marriage had simple been severed by the say-so of Pius XI.[2]

The activities of the Holy Office in dissolving marriages extend not to just potential converts but to people who have no Christian affiliation.

> No Pope had ever divorced two complete unbelievers. In 1957 it happened. On 12 March in that year Pius XII dissolved the marriage of two Muhammadans. The girl, having divorced civilly, took custody of the child. Her husband went to France, where he married in a register office, his bride being a Catholic. He was a prospective convert. The Holy Office, under the direction of Cardinal Ottaviani, recommended the Petrine Privilege—it took less time than the Pauline Privilege. Pius XII dissolved

that marriage as he was later to dissolve five others that involved no Christian party.[3]

Pope Paul VI is known primarily for having given to the Catholic Church *Humanae Vitae*. However, he was not as staunch a conservative as his position on birth control would lead us to believe. He too engaged in dissolving a valid marriage:

> Paul VI took time off from writing *Humanae Vitae* to grant a divorce to two Jews from Chicago on 7 February 1964. The husband, having divorced his wife, had married a Catholic. He had no wish to convert; he was quite honest about that. He simply wanted to put his new wife's mind at rest. Archbishop Meyer backed his petition to regularize his union. The early church would have said that any marriage between a Catholic and Jew was a crime and sacrilege; as to a second marriage.... But Paul VI was moved to pity. He showed the Catholic girl the compassion he felt unable in conscience to extend to millions who were suffering from the ban on contraceptives. That, in granting a divorce, he was contradicting a hundred pontiffs did not worry him. If Pius XII said it was all right, it was all right by him. Once more, he selected carefully the Popes whom he agreed with.[4]

One final example from de Rosa will be sufficient to show the inconsistency of Roman Catholic teaching on marriage and divorce and the incompatibility of their position with their own history, not to mention with the inspired Word of God.

> A famous American case involved Consuela Vanderbilt, who wed Charles Spencer, Duke of Marlborough, in 1916. After 10 years of marriage, blessed by two children, she asked Rome to annul her union on the grounds that her mother had pressurized her into it. The public was

astonished to hear of Pius XI annulling a marriage entered
into by two Protestants before a Protestant Bishop. Man-
ning, Episcopal Bishop of New York, called Rome's decision an "amazing and incredible" attack upon "the sacred-
ness and permanence of marriage."[5]

Still more alarming is the number of annulments granted by the
Roman Catholic Church in the United States.

The statistics are interesting. In 1968 there were in the
U.S. a total of 338 annulments. In 1992 there were no less
than 59,030, that is one hundred and seventy-five times as
many. Another interesting figure is that the total number
of annulments in the Catholic Church worldwide in 1992
was 76,286, which means that no less than 75% of all
annulments were in the U.S., that is from a little over 5%
of the world's Catholic population. Moreover, not only do
one in two Catholic marriages here in the States end up
with a divorce, but one in five is officially annulled, 90% of
the demands for annulment being successful.[6]

During 1984 and 1986–1994, U.S. Second Instance tribunals ratified 342,218 ordinary process decrees of nullity,
retired and ruled for nullity in 13,303, and decided against
nullity in 1,412. Second Instance tribunals in the rest of
the world, despite adjudicating 250,000 fewer cases, ruled
against nullity in 5,890 cases. Putting this another way, an
American ordinary process annulment has four chances
in a thousand of being overturned at Second Instance, as
opposed to 56 chances in a thousand for ordinary process
annulments granted elsewhere.[7]

THE MIND OF GOD

With the facts before us, we can see what happens when the
Scriptures are abandoned as the only source of authority. The

Catholic Church has made two major errors. First, it does not allow divorce even when one of the partners has become unfaithful. Yet Jesus said that unfaithfulness is grounds for a divorce. Second, the Church's own history exposes its inconsistency, for it has granted divorces and dissolved marriages while lamely trying to maintain that marriage is indissoluble.

God desires that every marriage be for life and would encourage even adulterous partners to repent of their behavior, seek forgiveness from their partner, and reaffirm their marriage vows. That is the ideal that God desires. However, God has also thrown a lifeline to those whose marriages have failed irredeemably. Divorce is available to them on God's terms. The sanctity of marriage is not lost when God-fearing people exercise the option made available to them by a loving God. To teach this is to proclaim the mind of God.

QUESTIONS AND ANSWERS

Q. **Is it wrong to divorce when the Bible says, "What God has joined together, let man not separate"?**

Reading what God has to say about marriage leaves us in no doubt that he wants couples to honor their marriage vows all the days of their lives. In marriage, God takes two people, male and female (yes, we need to stress the gender aspect these days), and joins them together as husband and wife. Therefore, to dissolve a marriage for any reason other than adulterous unfaithfulness is always wrong.

Q. **Has God made any provision for divorce?**

The Roman Catholic Church denies that God has made such a provision, but that is to deny what the Bible so clearly states. In the days of Moses, in order to regulate a chaotic situation, God permitted divorce. Jesus said, "Moses permitted you to divorce your wives because your hearts were hard.... I tell you that anyone who divorces his wife, except for marital unfaithfulness, and marries another woman commits adultery" (Matthew 19:8-9). Denying this provison for divorce is to deny what God allows.

Q. **Why did the apostle Paul allow divorce in specific circumstances?**

There are some who claim Paul was merely giving his own opinion and not reflecting the will of God. However, Paul clearly stated his words in "the Spirit of God" (1 Corinthians 7:40). What he said carries the authority of God. When Paul spoke about divorce, he addressed a situation Jesus did not address—the marriage of a believer to an unbeliever. Paul said, "If the unbeliever leaves, let him do so. A believing man or woman is not bound in such circumstances; God has called us to live in peace" (1 Corinthians 7:15). If an unbeliever deserts a marriage, the believer is free to divorce and remarry.

Q. **Is an annulment the same as a divorce?**

The Roman Catholic Church maintains that annulment is not the same as divorce. An annulment says there never was a marriage in the first place. In other words, the marriage should never have even occurred. An annulment can be granted for a number of reasons: If a person was forced to marry against his will, if he entered marriage with the intention of never honoring the marriage, or if a person has serious mental or psychological problems.

Q. **Is not the Roman Catholic Church displaying faithfulness to God by prohibiting divorce?**

The Roman Catholic Church does not honor God by denying divorce when God has clearly made a provision for it. If God is prepared to allow divorce in specific circumstances, then the Catholic Church should follow his instructions. This is not a call to allow divorce for any reason and let the institution of marriage be destroyed. Every effort must be made to keep marriages together, but denying what God allows is wrong.

Q. **Why does God hate divorce?**

God said, "I hate divorce" (Malachi 2:16). Divorce breaks a covenant that two pepole have entered into. It violates a sacred vow and breaks what God has joined together. Divorce introduces pain to both parties and has a terrible effect on many children, who become victims. And when divorce becomes rampant, it has a negative effect on society in general.

A grave injustice is done when the words of Malachi are read as if they are all God had to say on divorce. God has graciously made provision to allow divorce in the event of marital unfaithfulness. Denying divorce is to deny what God allows.

16

Thinking Jesus Was
in Their Company

. . . .

very year, Joseph and Mary went to Jerusalem for the Feast
of the Passover. One particular year, when Jesus was 12
years old, he stayed behind in Jerusalem after the feast was
over. His parents journeyed home "thinking he was in their company" (Luke 2:44). Later they realized Jesus was not with them, and
he could not be found among their relatives and friends. So they
returned to Jerusalem and, after searching for three days, found
him in the temple sitting among the teachers, listening to them and
asking them questions (Luke 2:45-47).

This account illustrates for us how people can assume that Jesus
is in their company when in fact he is not. They are quite certain
that he is, but when they begin to look around, they realize he is
nowhere to be found.

Many people are making the journey through life thinking that

Jesus is with them, yet he isn't. Why do they assume this? For Catholics, it's usually because they have received the sacrament of baptism, have been confirmed, are in the right Church, go to Mass and confession, and are devoted to the Blessed Virgin. They are good people who don't harm anyone and try to live a religious life. But is Jesus with them?

The problem arises for Catholics because they have not been following Jesus. They have not heeded his voice or followed his directions as given in God's Word. The course of action taken by Joseph and Mary needs to be taken by all of us. We must return to Jerusalem, go back to the beginning of the Christian faith, and discard the traditions that people have accumulated over the centuries—traditions that are fatal and that prevent the glorious gospel of God's free grace from being seen. We need to start the journey all over again.

I have been fortunate to have visited a number of places where the apostle Paul first brought the gospel of Jesus Christ and established congregations of God's people: Athens, Thessalonica, Philippi, Corinth, and Ephesus. What encourages me is knowing that the same gospel Paul preached in those cities to introduce people to Christ as Savior can still be preached today and get the same results. How could it do otherwise?

Jesus spoke about the spreading of the gospel in the parable of the sower. He said, "The seed is the word of God" (Luke 8:11). A seed will produce only after its own kind: apple seeds produce apples, orange seeds produce oranges, and so on. The seed of the Word of God can produce only one fruit—the saving gospel. Peter, in his first epistle, picked up on the theme of sowing seed and said, "You have been born again, not of perishable seed, but of imperishable, through the living and enduring word of God" (1 Peter 1:23). He continued by quoting from the prophet Isaiah: "The grass withers and the flowers fall, but the word of the Lord stands forever" (verses 24-25).

We live in a world where change is occurring all the time, and that's the norm. But in the spiritual realm we need to hold on to the truth that never changes. The Bible tells us that "Jesus Christ is the same yesterday and today and forever" (Hebrews 13:8). He never changes. His message never changes. He received it from his Father and said, "Your word is truth" (John 17:17). And it is that "very word of truth" that will be our judge on the day of judgment. Jesus said,

> As for the person who hears my words but does not keep them...that very word which I spoke will condemn him at the last day. For I did not speak of my own accord, but the Father who sent me commanded me what to say and how to say it. I know that his command leads to eternal life. So whatever I say is just what the Father has told me to say (John 12:48-50).

This is what I love about these words from Jesus: 1) I can read his words, 2) his words are what the Father gave him to say, 3) his words contain the message of eternal life, and 4) it will not be synods, councils, encyclicals, papal bulls, or the Magisterium that will judge us, but the very words of Jesus. The obedient have nothing to fear.

Stepping outside one's religious culture is never easy. I certainly didn't find it so. But the people of God have always been a people of faith who trust in God for guidance. Look at Abraham: "By faith Abraham, when called to go to a place he would later receive as his inheritance, obeyed and went, even though he did not know where he was going" (Hebrews 11:8). Did you notice Abraham went out "not knowing where he was going"? God told him to go and he went, and God went with him. And God will go with you when you respond to what he has commanded.

Faith enables us to launch out in obedience to the commands of Jesus, just as Peter did. Jesus said to Peter, " 'Put out into deep water, and let down the nets for a catch.' [Peter] replied 'Master, we've worked hard all night and haven't caught anything. But because you say so, I will let down the nets.' When they had done so, they caught such a large number of fish that their nets began to break" (Luke 5:4-6). Faith doesn't argue with God; faith responds in obedience and is blessed accordingly.

Listen to the words of Jesus as he bids us all to follow him: "I am the light of the world. Whoever follows me will never walk in darkness, but will have the light of life" (John 8:12). The world is in spiritual darkness, and Jesus is the light that leads us from that darkness. Though Jesus came to build his church, he never told anyone to follow the church. Rather, he repeatedly told us to follow him. Many Catholics are following Church rules thinking that they are following Jesus, but they are not.

And again, Jesus said, "My sheep listen to my voice: I know them, and they follow me. I give them eternal life, and they shall never perish; no one will snatch them out of my hand" (John 10:27-28). Who are you listening to, and who are you following? If you listen to Jesus and follow him, you will never be lost.

All who are obedient to Jesus have the blessed assurance that he is in their company. His name is Immanuel—God with us.